W9-BKO-974

YANKS IN THE RAF

ALSO BY DAVID ALAN JOHNSON

Decided on the Battlefield

YANKS IN THE RAF

THE STORY OF MAVERICK PILOTS AND
AMERICAN VOLUNTEERS WHO JOINED
BRITAIN'S FIGHT IN WWII

DAVID ALAN JOHNSON

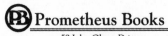 Prometheus Books

59 John Glenn Drive
Amherst, New York 14228

Published 2015 by Prometheus Books

Prometheus Books recognizes the following registered trademarks, trademarks, and service marks mentioned within the text: Plexiglas®, National Museum of the United States Air Force®

Every attempt has been made to trace accurate ownership of copyrighted material in this book. Errors and omissions will be corrected in subsequent editions, provided that notification is sent to the publisher.

Cover design by Jacqueline Nasso Cooke
Cover image: Pilots of 71 Squadron, the first all-American unit in RAF history, in front of a Hurricane Mark II in 1941. Andy Mamedoff, fifth from left, beside Eugene Tobin, sixth from left.

Inquiries should be addressed to
Prometheus Books
59 John Glenn Drive
Amherst, New York 14228
VOICE: 716–691–0133
FAX: 716–691–0137
WWW.PROMETHEUSBOOKS.COM

19 18 17 16 15   5 4 3 2 1

Library of Congress Cataloging-in-Publication Data

Printed in the United States of America

To Laura: Thanks for everything.

CONTENTS

FROM BELLIGERENT ALLIES TO THE SPECIAL RELATIONSHIP

It seems strange that Britain and the United States were once the friend-liest of enemies, but the two countries were antagonists, not allies, for over one hundred years after the American colonies won their independence. After the War of Independence ended in 1783, the two countries fought each other again in 1812 and very nearly went to war in 1861 during the American Civil War. In the half century between the Civil War and the First World War, Britain and the United States did their best to ignore each other. Both the Grand Alliance and the Special Relationship are fairly recent developments.

During the years between the two world wars, and in the early part of the Second World War, Britain and the United States did not have very much use for each other. The British tended to regard the United States as a former colony that had overextended itself, a gangling adolescent of a country that was muscle-bound and brainless and should not be trusted too far. Prime Minister Neville Chamberlain famously declared that the Americans should not be counted upon for anything except talk.

American notions of the British were just as uncomplimentary. Most images of Britain were based upon incidents from American history when the two countries were at war with each other: Bunker Hill, the Boston Tea Party, and the burning of Washington, DC, in 1814. Britain was the traditional enemy of the United States, its ancient foe.

Relations between the two countries were so strained and difficult in 1940 that American volunteers for Britain's Royal Air Force had to sneak across the Canadian border to reach England—it was against the law, actually a violation of the US Neutrality Acts, for an American citizen to join the armed forces of a "belligerent nation," including Britain.

Americans thought they had been taken advantage of—played for suckers—during the First World War by the devious British. Britain had never repaid its war debt of several billion dollars, the thinking went, and should not be trusted. The United States had no intention of helping the British ever again—and that included allowing American volunteers to join the British air force.

Within a few years, over two million Americans would be stationed in the British Isles as part of the buildup for D-Day, and the United States and Britain had formed two-thirds of what Winston Churchill called the Grand Alliance (the Soviet Union was the third ally). After the war, this alliance would evolve into the Special Relationship.

Since the Second World War, the Special Relationship has been strengthened by a good many items and events, including increased military cooperation and trade ties between Britain and the United States over the years, along with films, television programs, and cheap flights across the Atlantic. But it began with the volunteers who secretly made their way to England in 1939 and 1940. The Eagle Squadrons received most of the publicity—as glamour-boy fighter pilots—but Americans were scattered throughout the RAF. These volunteers brought the first taste of American egalitarianism, materialism, and Yankee get-up-and-go to the British Isles.

Appendix B is a listing of the pilots who served with the three Eagle Squadrons. An alarming percentage of these volunteers were killed on active service with the Royal Air Force, including Red Tobin, Shorty Keough, and Andy Mamedoff, the original three members of the first Eagle Squadron. These Americans may have gone to England looking for romance and adventure, but instead found the reality of war.

Appendix A gives the equivalent ranks of the USAAF and the RAF. The Eagle Squadron pilots probably wished they had this appendix in 1942, when they transferred from the British to the American forces. Most of the Eagles had no idea of American rank; it is hoped that this appendix will help the reader to avoid this problem.

The GIs in their multitudes began pushing life in Britain from a class-bound society toward meritocracy between 1942 and 1945—the British were quick to notice that American officers were men and women who were the best at their jobs, not the eldest sons from families that had the best political connections. (Although by 1942, many British officers were also being chosen on the basis of merit—there was simply a need for more officers than the old system could supply.)

But the Eagle Squadrons and their fellow Yank volunteers got to England first and began the transition before the GIs arrived. The change in attitude of the two countries toward each other, from friendly enemies to special allies, first began with the Yanks in the RAF.

★★★ CHAPTER ONE ★★★

NONE OF AMERICA'S BUSINESS

Mike Kolendorski had a dramatic announcement for his family: he was going to England to join the Royal Air Force. It was a decision he had made by himself, without consulting any of his relatives. The reaction he received was predictable, considering the mood of Americans toward England in the spring of 1940.

His family told Mike that he was crazy—the war was England's worry, not his. As an American, he had no quarrel with the Germans. And as a Californian, he did not owe the British one damn thing. California was not at war with Germany and had never, not even in 1776, been a British colony. He would be much better off, he was told, if he stayed home and got a good job.

Besides, it looked as though the British had already lost the war. The British Army had just been chased out of France—what was left of it had been evacuated from Dunkirk, wherever the hell *that* was—and it looked like Hitler was going to invade England any day. Before the summer was over, the German army would probably be in London.

This was a popular point of view among Americans in the spring and summer of 1940, when Britain faced Germany and its vaunted Luftwaffe all alone. Even the American ambassador in London, Joseph P. Kennedy (father of future president John F. Kennedy), was telling anyone who would listen that the British were not only losing the war, but that they had no chance of winning it.

Many American reporters in Britain shared Kennedy's opinion that "chances now seem[ed] less than even that the British Isles [could] hold out" for six months "against intensive bombing followed by an attempted invasion."[1] It was hard to understand why anybody would want to volunteer to join the air force of a country that was going to lose. Besides, the war was none of America's business.

The reasons for wanting to join the Royal Air Force were hard to express, even for a young Polish-American who knew all the answers. Hardly any of the American volunteers, in the RAF or any other branches of the British armed services, could explain their motives very clearly. This was partly because they were young and inarticulate, partly because their reasons were difficult to put into words, and partly because they did not really know the reasons themselves.

Mike Kolendorski did have concrete reasons for wanting to leave home and join the RAF. He and his family still had close ties with Poland, and they spoke Polish at home. Going into the British air force was the best way he knew to fight the enemy who had overrun his family's homeland. He had very strong feelings about this—so strong, in fact, that they would prove to be his undoing.

But most did not have such clear-cut motives. Some joined out of idealism; they had read Ernest Hemingway's *For Whom the Bell Tolls* and wanted to fight the Nazis like Hemingway's hero fought the Fascists in Spain. Others had the feeling that the United States would be in the war sooner or later and that their experiences in the RAF might prove useful later on in the US forces. Some were just restless and looking for a bit of excitement; one volunteer said that it was like running away to join the circus.

One American who volunteered to join the Royal Air Force, James A. Goodson, was just mad as hell at the Germans. He had been aboard the British ocean liner *Athenia* when it was torpedoed by a U-boat on the day that war was declared in September 1939. The idea of joining up occurred to him when he landed in Scotland with some other survivors. In Glasgow he happened to pass a recruiting station and asked one of the men on duty, "Can I join your RAF?" (He actually did not join until he recrossed the Atlantic and made his way to Canada to join the RCAF— Royal Canadian Air Force.)[2]

American author Mary Lee Settle volunteered for the Women's Auxiliary Air Force (WAAF) of the RAF. She is not exactly sure why she joined. She puts it down to being romantic.

Another volunteer who went through Canada to join the RAF explained that he was twenty years old at the time, not going anywhere in particular, and brainless. He had heard that the British were looking for pilots to fight the Germans. Because he was young and stupid and interested in airplanes, he thought he might as well give it a try and join the RAF. In other words, it was a form of temporary insanity.

As an afterthought, he mentioned that all of his relatives tended to agree with him. They thought he was a goddamn screwball; it was bad enough to be drafted into the American army, but to *volunteer*—and with the *British* air force, at that—was something they just could not get over.

The idea to recruit American pilots for foreign forces first occurred to Colonel Charles Sweeny, a wealthy American businessman with family connections in London. His original intention was to send his recruits to France and *l'Armée de l'Air*, the French air force. This plan was modeled on the precedent of the Lafayette Escadrille, a group of Americans who volunteered to fly for France in the First World War.

Thirty-two of Sweeny's *l'Armée de l'Air* volunteers reached France in early 1940. But when France surrendered in June of that year, the Americans found themselves trapped by the advancing German forces. Four of them were killed; nine others were taken prisoner. Six of the group managed to escape to England, and five of these found their way into the Royal Air Force.

The young volunteers may have been vague about their reasons for joining, and sometimes did not seem to have any reason at all, but Britain's Royal Air Force had one solid reason for accepting the Americans— they were desperate for pilots.

Pilots of 601 (County of London) Squadron sprint toward their Hurricanes sometime during the summer of 1940. Number 601 was called the "millionaire's squadron." It was made up mainly of wealthy young men of social standing, including Chicago-born Billy Fiske. (Courtesy of the National Museum of the United States Air Force®.)

After the British army had been evacuated from Dunkirk in June 1940, the Luftwaffe began operating from airfields in northern France. With the Germans just across the channel from the beaches of southern

England, the British Air Ministry had a dire need for trained pilots. Prime Minister Winston Churchill had already referred to the upcoming air battle as the "Battle of Britain." It was certain that RAF Fighter Command would be needing as many trained pilots as it could get.

American volunteers were not the only source for pilots—Fighter Command was scouring flyers from everyplace available. The Royal Navy transferred seventy-five of its pilots to the RAF, many of whom were only partially—and very hurriedly—trained to fly fighter planes. A few army pilots who flew unarmed reconnaissance planes were also pressed into service as fighter pilots.

Even more welcome were the combat-seasoned pilots from countries that were now occupied by the Germans: Belgians, French, Czechs, and Poles. There were very few of them, however—only twelve French pilots managed to escape to England, and just twenty-nine Belgians got away—and these pilots also had their drawbacks. Many were not used to advanced fighters like the Spitfire and the Hurricane. Most had flown planes with fixed landing gear. After giving an expert display of loops, rolls, and dives, they would sometimes wreck their planes when they forgot to put their wheels down before landing.

Language was another problem. The Polish pilots, for instance, were among the best and most determined in RAF Fighter Command, but they did not speak a word of English. They would address their squadron leader as *mon commandant* and the flight lieutenant as *mon capitaine*. They would have to learn the rudiments of Standard English, at least, before they could become operational. They would also have to learn basic flight jargon, such as "angels," "vector," "bogie," and "bandit." Without the ability to communicate with ground controllers, the Poles would be as good as useless, for all their experience and determination.

In an attempt to minimize the language barrier, Fighter Command asked permission to accept American volunteers. The Yanks might not have the combat techniques of the Poles, the French, or the Czechs, but at least they spoke a language that was roughly similar to English. They could be vectored toward an incoming enemy bomber formation by ground control and usually could be understood when they spoke.

And so, with the approval of the Air Ministry, American citizens were recruited to join the RAF. Advertisements were even placed in American newspapers. This notice appeared in the *New York Herald Tribune*:

> *LONDON* July 15 [1940]: The Royal Air Force is in the market for American flyers as well as American airplanes. Experienced airmen, preferably those with at least 250 flying hours, would be welcomed by the RAF.

The article went on to advise candidates that to join the RAF they would be required to travel to Canada at their own expense and would also have to pass the physical examination. "For such volunteers," the notice went on, "there will be no question about signing or swearing an oath of allegiance to the British crown."[3]

When George VI waived the oath of allegiance in June, it was an open admission of the historical prejudices between the two countries. The Air Ministry feared that the oath would frighten away any potential American volunteers, since no American would swear loyalty to the great-great-great-grandson of George III.

Occasionally, however, the oath did become a point of controversy. An RAF group captain, apparently not aware that the requirement had been waived, announced to eight incoming Americans that His Majesty would accept them as pilots as soon as they had sworn allegiance to him. It was a tense few minutes until the group captain was taken aside and corrected by another officer. Maybe it was because of what had been promised in the newspaper notice, or maybe it was because of George III and the Boston Tea Party and Bunker Hill—whatever it was, all eight of the American volunteers were ready to go home instead of taking the oath.

But the oath of allegiance was only one obstacle. A far greater problem was the three Neutrality Acts that had been passed by Congress in the 1930s.

The United States was a neutral country in the summer of 1940 and was determined to stay that way. One of the three Neutrality Acts made it a criminal offence to join the armed forces of a "belligerent nation"—including Britain. It was against the law for an American citizen to join the RAF. Anyone caught trying faced the prospect of stiff punishment: ten years in prison, a $20,000 fine, and loss of US citizenship.

Six potential volunteers found out about the Neutrality Acts the hard way. They had spoken with Colonel Sweeny and, in late 1940, headed for the Canadian border to join the RAF. Just before their train crossed the border and made its first stop inside Canada, the six young fellows were met by agents of the Federal Bureau of Investigation. The FBI men gave them a choice: either go back home or go to prison. It was not a hard decision—the six went back home. But they did try again. On the second attempt they made it to Canada without any interference and, finally, over to England.[4]

When James A. Goodson joined the RCAF, he was warned that he would probably lose his US citizenship because of the US Neutrality Acts. He understood that all other US citizens received the same warning from the RCAF and RAF.[5]

The warning did not deter young Mr. Goodson. He also made the trip from the United States to Canada to England, where he flew Spitfires with 133 (Eagle) Squadron. Pilot Officer Goodson transferred to the US 4th Fighter Group in 1942, when the Eagle Squadrons (there were three of them by this time) were absorbed into the US Eighth Air Force. The Americans were very glad to receive such an experienced fighter pilot into their command. P/O Goodson was commissioned as a lieutenant (the equivalent US rank to P/O), and all warnings concerning loss of US citizenship were conveniently forgotten.[6]

The Neutrality Acts did not prevent other young Americans from joining the RAF, either. Colonel Sweeny was responsible for recruiting many of the volunteers. Some made their own way to England. They either went to Canada and joined the Royal Canadian Air Force, or they booked passage to England as "reporters" or under other false covers. A Wall Street banker told the customs official in Boston that he was going to Canada "for some shooting."[7]

The official records of the Royal Air Force list only seven Americans as having served with RAF Fighter Command in the summer of 1940.[8] But there were many, many more than this. Because it was against the law to join, any number of Americans would not divulge their true nationality when signing their enlistment papers. Nobody knows exactly how many pilots, "officially" listed as Canadians or as Commonwealth citizens, were actually American. Especially suspect are those with Anglo-Saxon names like Johnson, Little, or Mitchell. Air Ministry records list them as Canadian, which is no proof that they really were. Many of them were "American Canadians."

One such American pilot in Fighter Command is mentioned by Pilot Officer Donald Stones of 79 Squadron. P/O Stones recalled a Flight Lieutenant Jimmy Davis, "an American who had been commissioned in the RAF before the war." According to Stones, Jimmy Davis was shot down and killed on the same day that King George visited Biggin Hill, 79 Squadron's base, to award decorations. Davis was to have received the Distinguished Flying Cross on that occasion. The king asked about the remaining DFC on the table and was told about the expatriate American. Stones thought the King was "quite moved."[9]

As it turned out, Stones had his names confused, although his facts were correct. The American pilot he remembered was named Davies, not Davis. (No one named Jimmy Davis is listed in any official records as belonging to any RAF fighter squadron during the Battle of Britain.) Jimmy Davies certainly was an American; he was born in Bernardsville, New Jersey, in 1913. He came to Britain in the early 1930s and was commissioned in the RAF in 1936. He is credited with shooting down one of the first German airplanes of the war—a Dornier Do 17 on November 21, 1939, which he shared with a British flight-sergeant named Brown.[10]

By the time Flight Lieutenant Davies was shot down and killed on June

25, 1940, he was officially credited with six enemy-aircraft destroyed. That would make him the first American "ace" of the Second World War.

FORMER BERNARDSVILLE MAN WINS ENGLISH FLYING HONOR

Acting Flight Lieutenant J. W. E. Davies, 27, a native of Bernardsville, N. J., was awarded the distinguished flying cross early this week. Davies joined the Royal Air Force in 1936.

The citation said Davies had shown "ability as a leader of his squadron on many offensive patrols."

"On one occasion," it said, "while he was attacking a German Messerschmidt 109, he himself was attacked by six Heinkel 111's.

"Davies at once turned on the Heinkels, destroying one and badly damaging a second before being compelled to break off the engagement owing to a shortage of ammunition:

"The following day, while leading a section of his squadron, he sighted and attacked a large formation of Heinkel 111's and shot down one in flames."

Lieutenant Davies was born October 29, 1913, the son of David A. and Catherine Davies, of Bernards Township, who lived in the vicinity of Liberty Corner. Davies' full name is James William Elfas Davies. His nearest known relative is reported to be Mrs. A. H. Davies of 338 Rutledge avenue, East Orange, who still owns the family property in Bernards Township.

Grandfather Davies was an employee some years ago on both the Bensel estate and Wendover Farm here and later moved to Morristown where he took employment on the Gillespie estate.

Prize Awards at Local July 4 Celebration

Cash and trophy awards totalling nearly awarded as follows:

Best Decorated Store — $15 gold trophy.
Best Decorated Residence — $15 cash pri.
Best Marching Musical Unit — $15 gold t
Best Decorated Float — $15 cash prize.
Best Marching Legion Unit — $15 gold tr
Best Marching Firemen's Unit — $15 gold
Best Marching Legion or Firemen Auxiliar:
Best Marching Fraternal or Patriotic Unit
Best Novelty in Parade — $5.00 Cash Pri:
Best Boy Scout Troop Demonstration — $
Best Decorated Bicycles — (3 prizes)
Special Baton Twirling Contest — $10 gol trophies.

Airplane and Golf Driving Contests — Ca A $25.00 cash bonus will be awarded best tion if accompanied by own music.

This story about Jimmy Davies appeared in the *Bernardsville News*, Bernardsville, New Jersey's local newspaper, on June 27, 1940. By the time readers in Bernardsville saw this article, Jimmy Davies was dead. He had been killed in combat on June 25, two weeks and one day before the Battle of Britain officially began. Jimmy Davies was already an ace, having destroyed six enemy aircraft by June 8 and had earned the Distinguished Flying Cross. (Reprinted with permission from the *Bernardsville News*/the New Jersey Hills Media Group.)

Nobody really knows how many "secret Americans" served in the Royal Air Force in the summer of 1940, or how many Canadians were actually "American Canadians," and there are few clues. The only traces that remain of their true nationality are nicknames, buried in the war records—"Tex," or "America," or "Uncle Sam."

One American who made no secret of his citizenship was Billy Fiske. Chicago-born, William Mead Lindsley Fiske III was the son of an international banker and attended Cambridge University. After leaving Cambridge, he enjoyed a life of wealth and leisure, became a champion toboggan sledder, and entered society when he married the former wife of the Earl of Warwick. Fiske settled in England, where he did weekend flying during the 1930s. With his influential friends and family connections, he had no trouble at all getting into the RAF Auxiliary in 1940.

In July, Pilot Officer Fiske was posted to 601 Squadron. Auxiliary squadrons, including 601, were made up mainly of wealthy young men of social standing. In prewar days, pilots were selected for the Auxiliaries because of their school, their club, and their social connections rather than for their talent for flying. These units have been referred to as associations of snobbery and class prejudice.

Number 601, nicknamed "the millionaire's squadron," was no exception. "They wore red linings in their tunics and mink linings in their overcoats," according to Mrs. Fiske. "They were arrogant and looked terrific, and probably the other squadrons hated their guts."[11]

Billy Fiske was highly thought of by the other members of his squadron. His commander, F/Lt. Archibald Hope called Fiske "the best pilot I've ever known . . . natural as a fighter pilot. He was also terribly nice and extraordinarily modest. He fitted into the squadron very well."[12]

During the Battle of Britain, 601 Squadron was based at Tangmere. The Tangmere wing was responsible for the defense of southern England against the German bomber fleets. In July and August, the Germans did their best to destroy Fighter Command and its airfields in preparation for the pending invasion of England. Operational fighter squadrons, including 601, saw combat nearly every day.

On August 13, during one of his first operational sorties, Pilot Officer Fiske shot down a Junkers Ju 88 twin-engine bomber. Three days later, while Tangmere was under attack, Fiske's Hurricane was jumped while he was returning to base. Fisk crash-landed his shot-up fighter on the aerodrome's grass landing field.

An ambulance crew lifted Fiske out of the Hurricane's cockpit. Flight Lieutenant Hope saw him lying on the grass next to the fighter plane; Fiske was burned on the face and hands, but did not seem seriously injured. Hope told Fiske that he would be all right, since he seemed to be suffering from only a few minor burns.

When the squadron adjutant visited Fiske in hospital that night, what he saw seemed to confirm Hope's optimism: "Billy was sitting up in bed, perky as hell." But, Hope recalls, "The next thing we heard, he was dead. Died of shock."[13] He died on August 17, the day after he had been shot down.

Pilot Officer Fiske's obituary in the *Times* (London) of August 19 ran for thirty-nine lines—unusually long for such a junior officer. The standard obituary for officers ran seven or eight lines; senior officers sometimes received fifteen or twenty lines of print. Fiske was given so much space partly because he was married to the former Countess of Warwick and partly because he was an American—a major concern of the British press was to show Americans that their fellow countrymen were already in the war. It was part of a subtle—and sometimes not so subtle—propaganda campaign to arouse American sympathy and enlist American support for Britain.

Billy Fiske is usually described as "the first American serving as an officer in the RAF to lose his life in action against the enemy in this war."[14] He was certainly the first "official" American to be killed, but it is likely that some of the US citizens listed as Canadians lost their lives even earlier. Jimmy Davies of 79 Squadron, for instance, was killed on June 25, nearly two months before Billy Fiske.

Fiske is buried in the churchyard of Boxgrove Priory Church in West Sussex, not far from Tangmere. He is also commemorated by a memorial plaque in the crypt of St. Paul's Cathedral in London—which cynics cited as yet another propaganda attempt to sway neutral Americans to Britain's side. The plaque is dedicated to WML Fiske: "An American citizen who died that England might live."

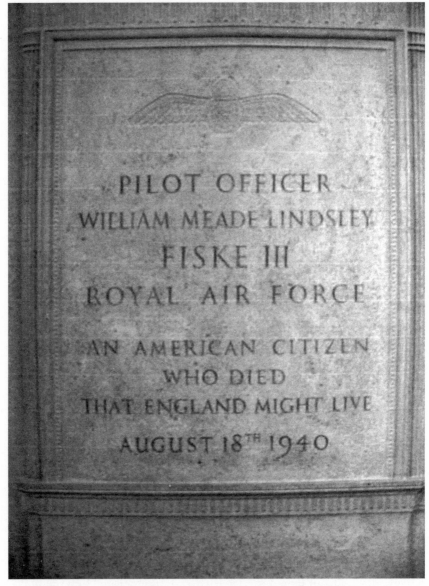

Pilot Officer Billy Fiske's memorial plaque in St. Paul's Cathedral. Cynics said that the plaque was an attempt to sway neutral America to Britain's side. (Photo by the author.)

A somewhat more everyday American—he described himself as "a farm boy" from St. Charles, Minnesota—was Arthur Donahue. Donahue went to Canada to join the RAF after Dunkirk. He arrived in England on August 4, 1940, and was assigned to 64 Squadron, which flew Spitfires out of Kenley Aerodrome, south of London.[15]

On his first sortie, Donahue damaged a Messerschmitt Bf 109—after first making sure that it was not really a Spitfire or a Hurricane—and had his own Spitfire damaged by a German cannon shell. The 20 mm shell severed several control cables and blew out the battery connection that operated his gunsight. When he brought his Spitfire back to Kenley, it needed a new fuselage.

On August 8, Donahue's flight was on patrol over the Channel when the six Spitfires were jumped by a "gruppe" of about twenty-seven Messerschmitts. In the resulting free-for-all, Donahue (nicknamed "America" by his squadron mates) shot at several Bf 109s, "just firing whenever I saw something with black crosses in front of me." He locked onto the tail of one, fired a good burst into it, and was credited with a "probable" when he returned to base.[16]

Four days later, he attacked a flight of three Bf 109s by himself and got shot down for his pains. Cannon shells proved his undoing for the second time, putting a hole in his Spitfire's fuel tank and setting the plane on fire. Donahue was able to bail out, but not before being severely burned by the exploding fuel tank. He came down in an oat field; fortunately, he landed close by a detachment of soldiers who were able to call an ambulance. Donahue spent the next seven weeks in hospital.

Three of the Americans signed by Charles Sweeny for l'Armée de l'Air managed to leave France on the very last ship for England. After France gave up the fight and signed an armistice with Germany on June 22, these three Yanks—Andy Mamedoff, Eugene Q. "Red" Tobin, and Vernon C. "Shorty" Keough—joined the RAF and wound up in 609 (West Riding) Squadron.[17]

Red Tobin and Andy Mamedoff originally had signed up as pilots in

Finland's air force after Russian troops invaded Finland in November 1939. Neither one of them had any experience with fighter planes or military flying—Tobin claimed 200 hours in light civilian aircraft, and Mamedoff had done some barnstorming (flying demonstrations, often at county fairs). But the prospect of being fighter pilots sounded exciting, and the promised pay of $100 per month also helped to persuade them. The fact that Andy Mamedoff's family had been driven out of Russia by the Communists, the same people who had invaded Finland, was added incentive for him.

But the Russo-Finnish war ended in the winter of 1940, when Finland was forced to surrender. At that stage, Tobin and Mamedoff had not yet left California. They were still determined to be fighter pilots, though. Since the French air force looked as good to them as the Finnish, they signed up with *l'Armée* and set off for France.

Between California and France, they met up with four-foot-ten-inch Vernon "Shorty" Keough, from Brooklyn, New York. Shorty had been a parachute jumper in the 1930s, making hundreds of jumps at air shows and county fairs. He probably would have been the shortest pilot in the French air force, but the war did not last long enough for him to find out.

Although the Americans arrived before France surrendered, they did not get the chance to do any fighting. Which was probably just as well, considering the antiquated state of the French air force—*l'Armée* did not have any fighter that could hold its own with the Bf 109. France formally surrendered on June 22, the same day that Tobin, Keough, and Mamedoff reached the French port of Saint-Jean-de-Luz after managing to evade the advancing Wehrmacht. Two days later, they landed in England aboard the steamer *Baron Nairn*.

They went to the US embassy in London for assistance and were nearly deported. The embassy staff was not overjoyed to see three US citizens trying to enter the armed services of a foreign government and tried to have them sent back to the United States. Ambassador Joseph P. Kennedy was a staunch isolationist, if not outright anti-British. The three

Americans had already violated the Neutrality Acts by joining the French air force. Kennedy was determined that they would not join the RAF.

But Tobin, Keough, and Mamedoff got around Ambassador Kennedy with the help of a sympathetic member of Parliament. The MP got them into the RAF, and the Air Ministry sent them off to a training school in Cheshire where they were taught to fly Spitfires. From the training units, the three were sent as replacements to 609 Squadron based at Warmwell in Dorset. Warmwell was one of Fighter Command's front-line bases against the Luftwaffe.

The three new Pilot Officers fit in very nicely with their new squadron and seemed to be well liked. None of the British flyers had ever seen a real, live Yank before. Now there were three of them, right in the officers' mess.

Everyone seemed amused by their transatlantic squadron mates. Lanky Red Tobin, with his wisecracks and easygoing manner, was thought to be "typically American." Because he was from California, which every movie-loving Brit knew was somewhere in the Wild West, Red was compared to a film cowboy—one pilot said that he might have stepped right out of a western.

Andy Mamedoff, stocky and mustachioed, was known for his over-fondness of gambling—he would make a bet with anybody on just about anything. And Shorty Keough, at four-feet-ten-inches, was known for being short. A squadron mate said that Shorty was "the smallest man I ever saw, barring circus freaks."[18] Keough needed two cushions in the cockpit—one to sit on, the other for the small of his back. With the help of his pillows, he was able to fly a Spitfire, although "all you could see of him was the top of his head and a couple of eyes peering over the edge of the cockpit."

During his career as a parachute jumper, Shorty had survived 486 jumps. Whenever anybody asked him why he was so short, he would reply that he used to be of normal height until he became a jumper—the impact of all those landings pushed his legs right up inside his body. You ask a stupid question, you get a stupid answer.

Soon after the Americans joined 609 Squadron, Warmwell was visited by Air Commodore Prince George, the Duke of Kent. The Yanks had only just arrived in the country and had never met a Duke before. "Say," Shorty wanted to know, "what do we call this guy—Dook?" He was told that "sir" would do very nicely, which must have put his mind at ease. Shorty's stories about his varied and colorful career, told in fluent Brooklynese, kept the "Dook" spellbound.

The squadron seemed to accept the Yank replacements without any sign of condescension, which is surprising. Number 609 was an Auxiliary squadron. Auxiliary pilots usually regarded members of the Volunteer Reserve—and all three Americans were with the Volunteer Reserve—as being of inferior social rank, if not absolutely subhuman.

The standard Auxiliary joke about VR pilots was: "A regular RAF officer was an officer trying to be a gentleman; an Auxiliary was a gentleman trying to be an officer, and a Volunteer Reservist was neither, trying to be both." There was no joke about American VRs. Or, at least, none were ever repeated outside the officers' mess.

There was no snobbishness at all shown toward the three Yanks. "They were typical Americans," said one of their fellow squadron members, "amusing, democratic, always ready with some devastating wisecrack—frequently at the expense of authority—and altogether excellent company. Our three Yanks became quite an outstanding feature of the Squadron."[19]

According to the findings of an opinion poll that was taken during the war, the British tended to look upon the "typical American" with a detached familiarity, albeit with the recognition of a few certain defects of character, most of which stemmed from the Declaration of Independence in 1776. The men of 609 Squadron were even willing to overlook this last flaw.

Tobin, Keough, and Mamedoff were "affectionately . . . regarded as considerably larger than life," and one RAF history referred to them as the "amazing trio."[20] In addition to a great deal of curiosity, some admiration, and maybe just a tinge of condescension, they were also regarded with a touch of awe. The awe was certainly misplaced, since it was based largely upon inflated flight histories—Red Tobin, for instance, increased his flying time from 200 hours to 5,000 hours.[21]

Great things were also expected from the three Yanks in gunnery. Each Spitfire had eight .303 machine guns, and from Hollywood cowboy and gangster films, everybody knew that Americans were "good with guns." The squadron commander did not share this enthusiasm, however. Squadron Leader Horace "George" Darley was not about to let the three "new boys" go up against the Luftwaffe until he was satisfied that they could look after themselves. The Yanks might have been keen, courageous, and all that, but these qualities were no substitutes for solid training.

When they joined the squadron, Darley assigned the three Americans to noncombat duties. Mostly, they flew ferrying jobs—delivering a Spitfire to another base and being flown back in a twin-seat Miles Magister trainer—until they knew everything there was to know about Spitfires. Tobin, Keough, and Mamedoff were not wild about this arrangement. Nearly every day they heard the other pilots talking about their encounters with enemy bombers and fighters, while all they were allowed to do was run errands.

On August 16, the three of them were finally pronounced "operational." This was the third day of Reichsmarschall Hermann Göring's *Adlerangriff* (Eagle Attack), the Luftwaffe's concerted effort to destroy the Royal Air Force, including its radar network and all of its communications facilities.

When the "scramble" order came over the telephone on the 16th, Pilot Officers Tobin, Keough, and Mamedoff ran for their Spitfires along with the other pilots of 609 Squadron. Red Tobin shouted "Saddle her up! I'm ridin'!" to his four-man ground crew—that was one thing about these Yanks, they certainly had a style all their own.

As junior men in the squadron, the Americans would be "Ass-End Charlie" in their three-man formations—weaving and turning to protect the tail of the section leader and their wingman. The only trouble was that there was no one to protect *him* and warn him if Messerschmitts were attacking *his* tail. Naturally, Ass-End Charlie did not enjoy a very long life expectancy.

At 18,000 feet, Red got the word—"OK, Charlie. Weave." He began snaking behind the leader and his wingman, who kept flying straight and level. Over his headset, he heard someone call: "Many, many bandits, three o'clock." He looked off to his right and could see the enemy planes, more than fifty of them. Another call said that there were more bandits at twelve o'clock, straight overhead, but Tobin could not find these. This put a scare into him; squadron veterans said that it was the ones you couldn't see that got you.

Tobin's leader went into a sharp dive, followed by his wingman. Tobin dove after them but could not see if they were diving on a target or trying to evade enemy fighters. After they pushed over, he lost sight of them. The only other plane in sight was a twin-engine Messerschmitt Bf 110, which was turning to evade him.

He closed to within firing distance of the Bf 110 but could see from his string of tracer bullets that his shots were wide. He pulled back on his stick to correct his aim. But he pulled too hard; G-forces drained the blood from his brain and he nearly blacked out. The Bf 110 was gone by the time he recovered, and he found himself all alone in the sky— not another plane to be seen, where there had been dozens only a few minutes before. With his flight leader nowhere in sight and his ammunition supply nearly gone, Tobin decided that it was time to head back to Warmwell.

When he landed, Tobin found out that all the effort had been wasted. The Luftwaffe's bombing raid had not been stopped, or even hindered. Middle Wallop (nicknamed "Center Punch" by the Americans) had been bombed for the second time that month. The airfield was still open, but just barely: the runway was cratered by bombs; some hangers and workshops had been destroyed and others were very badly damaged; and the aerodrome was dotted by unexploded bombs that threatened to go off at any time.

Warmwell, which was one of Middle Wallop's satellite airfields, had not been touched, but this was not because of 609 Squadron's efforts—the Luftwaffe had simply ignored the small field. But the Germans had tried, and succeeded, in their attacks against RAF stations all along the south coast. Ventnor radar station, on the Isle of Wight, had been knocked out. Tangmere Airfield had also been bombed, and fourteen of its planes had been destroyed on the ground (this was the day that Billy Fiske was shot down). Other airfields and vital communications stations had also been attacked and badly damaged.

All in all, it had been a highly frustrating day, both for Red Tobin and RAF Fighter Command. Tobin had burned eighty gallons of gasoline and fired two-thousand rounds of .303 ammunition, and he had not accomplished one damn thing. He had not come all the way from California for this.

★ ★ ★

Tobin, Keough and Mamedoff were not the only non-British members of 609 Squadron. Two Polish pilots were also attached to the squadron, as well as a Canadian.

The two Poles, Flying Officers Tadeusz Nowierski and Piotr Osta-szewski, had escaped to England after their country had been overrun by the Wehrmacht in 1939. Like the other Poles who flew with Fighter Command—there were three all-Polish fighter squadrons—they displayed a hatred for the Germans that astonished both the British and Americans. These Poles had seen what the Germans had done to Poland and fought with total abandon, not caring for tactics or even their own lives. They had no homes to return to and nothing to lose.

But although 609's Poles were more intense than the three Americans, the Yanks got more publicity. In fact, the three American volunteers probably received more publicity than everyone else at Warmwell combined.

The British have a curiosity about their American cousins that sometimes gets the better of them. Tobin, Keough, and Mamedoff received so much attention from the press and the other news media that a good many people became indignant. Some of their squadron mates, along with a lot of other members of the Royal Air Force, resented all this fuss. Twenty years after the Battle of Britain ended, the author of 609 Squadron's history still felt bitter about all the media coverage given to the three Americans.

But all the publicity was not entirely due to curiosity. The subject of the "Yanks in the RAF" was also a tailor-made propaganda device by which to influence the stubbornly neutral United States. The British news media was using the topic to make Americans aware that their own countrymen were already fighting the Germans in spite of the Neutrality Acts.

Most of the Americans in the British forces—serving in Bomber Command or in the navy—received little publicity or none at all. The fighter pilots, however, captured the romantic fancy of the press and public, although not even all Yank fighter pilots got their names in the paper. Most were still masquerading as Canadians and hiding from US authorities. (Technically, they were fugitives from justice.)

There were also Americans who flew in bombers, either as pilots or as members of the crew. They received a good deal less publicity than the "glamour boys" of Fighter Command. One Yank in Bomber Command, who had a few ideas of his own, was Robert S. Raymond of Kansas City, Missouri. His family was one of the pillars of Kansas City society and owned the Raymond Furniture Company. But when the war broke out in September 1939, Robert Raymond decided to join the American Volunteer Ambulance Corp—more shades of Ernest Hemingway—and set out for the fighting in Europe. He claimed that he had no romantic illusions about war, but admitted that he would be taking a financial loss by going to France to drive an ambulance.

In some ways, Raymond's story was not all that different from those of Red Tobin, Shorty Keough, and Andy Mamedoff. He arrived in France in late May, evaded the advancing German forces for the next few weeks, escaped across the border to Spain, and sailed to England from Gibraltar. In London, Raymond experienced a couple of air raids, did some sightseeing, and tried to visit Colonel Charles Sweeny. He had heard something about an all-American unit called the Eagle Squadron that Sweeny was trying to form. He never did get to meet Sweeny, but this really did not matter—Raymond had already changed his mind about joining Sweeny's organization.

Raymond had been warned against joining the Eagle Squadron by a friend who had served in the International Brigade during the Spanish Civil War. They always threw the foreigners in first, Raymond was told, so stick with the home troops. Raymond took the advice and wanted nothing to do with the Eagle Squadron.

Raymond applied to the Air Ministry in November 1940. After being tested "for everything from flat feet to vision, hearing, lungs, teeth, et cetera, and examined as to family history, algebra, geography, whether [he] could ride a horse . . ." he was accepted into the Royal Air Force.[22]

After training as a bomber pilot in Britain and in Canada, Raymond was pronounced "operational" in June 1942 and began to fly minor missions. His first fully operational tour began in October 1942, as second pilot in a four-engine Lancaster of 44 Squadron. His sorties over enemy territory included Milan, Genoa, Düsseldorf, and Nuremberg.

Robert Raymond was not the only American who served with the British bombers. William T. Kent of New York, where his father owned a nightclub, went to Canada to join the Royal Canadian Air Force. After washing out as a pilot, he applied for air-gunnery school and soon became a tail gunner in a Halifax bomber. Among the twenty-nine missions he flew were Emden, Hamburg, Berlin, and Cologne. After his tour of duty in RAF Bomber Command, he transferred to the US Army Air Force and was sent to the States as a gunnery instructor.

The British military experience of other American volunteers was eventually put to use by the United States. They were scattered throughout the bomber force, employed as navigators, air gunners, bomb aimers, and second pilots. These men helped their country in spite of its laws, although they had to become fugitives from justice in order to do so.

Among the many members of Bomber Command's "Yank Auxiliary" was Harris Goldberg of Brookline, Massachusetts. Goldberg flew 273 hours as a gunner in Wellington bombers and later transferred to the US Army Air Force. "Tex" Holland also flew in Wellingtons as a pilot. F/ Lt. Joseph McCarthy was a member of 617 Squadron, the famous "Dam Buster" squadron, which flew highly secret and very dangerous operations. McCarthy came from Brooklyn, New York. He joined the RAF in 1941 and elected to remain with the British forces after the United States entered the war.

★ ★ ★

While Robert Raymond was serving with the "home troops," his fellow countrymen in Fighter Command were learning the lessons of aerial combat, usually the hard way. Andy Mamedoff's first action came on August 24, which 609 Squadron's historian called the Luftwaffe's most aggressive and destructive day during the entire Battle of Britain. On the 24th, the German air force launched another series of massive attacks against airfields throughout southern England.

It was not a very auspicious beginning for Mamedoff. As a result of his first encounter with a Messerschmitt, his Spitfire was a complete write-off. One of the enemy pilot's 20 mm shells gutted the Spitfire. According to the damage report the shell "entered the tail of the aircraft, went straight up the fuselage, through the wireless set, [and] just pierced the armor plating behind the pilot's seat." Luckily, Mamedoff was left with nothing more serious than a badly bruised back.[23]

The Yanks who had come to England to fight were not disappointed.

Nearly every day from August 24 to September 6 the German air fleets turned their full attention to the destruction of Fighter Command and came very close to succeeding. The RAF's fighter units were all that prevented the Wehrmacht from invading England, and the Luftwaffe intended to inflict heavy losses upon the young Spitfire and Hurricane pilots who stood in the way.

On the day following Andy Mamedoff's brush with disaster, squadron mate Red Tobin shot down his first enemy aircraft and had a very close brush with death himself.[24] The airplane that Tobin shot down was a Bf 110. After closing to within machine-gun range, he pressed the firing button and could see his bullets striking all along the twin-engine fighter's fuselage. He watched as it reared up almost vertically, stalled out, and plunged out of sight. A moment after that, he spotted another Bf 110 and went after it. He held his gunsight on the enemy aircraft's engine and pressed the firing button.

The big twin-engine fighter took hits and began to lose altitude. Tobin dove after it. When he reached the same height as the enemy fighter, Tobin yanked back on the stick to pull out of his dive. Once again, he pulled back too abruptly. The results were the same as last time—G-forces made him black out "colder than a clam." His Spitfire spun out of control toward the Channel. When he came to, his fighter had righted itself; he was only 1,000 feet above the water.

Tobin was a bit annoyed with himself—he had finally got his first enemy airplane, but he knew that he should have had two. Still, he realized that he was lucky—he might have ended up dead, crashed in the Channel.

Red's next chance against the Luftwaffe came on September 15, which was the climax of the Battle of Britain. On this day, hundreds of Spitfires and Hurricanes—nearly two hundred over London alone—flew from their bases to intercept about two hundred German bombers and nearly twice that many fighters. Tobin's day began when a fellow pilot shook him awake just after dawn.

Red was annoyed at having his sleep interrupted and demanded to know why he should get up when it was hardly daylight. "I'm not sure, old boy," the pilot replied. "They say there's an invasion on or something." Tobin was more impressed with the calmness of the response than with the news itself.

Number 609 Squadron was assigned to patrol over London at altitudes between 20,000 and 25,000 feet. At about 11:30 a.m., Tobin could see more than a hundred German aircraft approaching from the south—about fifty Bf 109s at 4,000 feet above him, twenty-five twin-engine Dornier bombers below him, and twenty-five or so bombers off in the distance.

Tobin was Ass-End Charlie again, weaving behind the flight leader and his wingman. His three-man section was about to dive on the Dorniers, and he had already heard his leader call, "OK, Charlie, come on in," when he spotted three yellow-nosed Bf 109s boring in from dead astern.

Tobin shouted a warning—"Danger, Red Section! Danger! Danger! Danger! Danger!"—throttled back, and kicked his Spitfire into a 360-degree turn. The three Messerschmitts could not slow down from their dive and overshot him. Tobin fired a burst from his eight .303 Browning machine guns at the last of the planes and saw smoke trail from it. All three enemy fighters then disappeared.

By this time, Red was down to about 8,000 feet. He pulled the stick back and began climbing; at about 10,000 feet, he spotted a lone Dornier Do 215 below him heading for a cloud bank. The lanky redhead pushed his throttle and control stick forward, diving on the Dornier before it could reach safety.

It did not take long for the Spitfire to overtake the bomber. As soon as he was within range, Tobin thumbed the firing button. He could see his bullets hitting the Dornier's port aileron—after a second or two, it was completely perforated with bullet holes. An instant later, the stricken bomber's port engine began trailing a stream of white vapor.

"I followed him down," Tobin recalled, "and saw a Dornier 215 make a crash landing two or three miles from Biggin Hill. Three of the crew got out and sat on the wing."

Pilot Officer Tobin had another enemy aircraft confirmed as destroyed, as well as a Bf 109 damaged. This time he remembered not to pull back on the stick too sharply and did not knock himself out with G-forces. He was learning. So were his fellow Americans Shorty Keough and Andy Mamedoff.

Between the three of them, the Yanks accounted for three enemy aircraft destroyed during the Battle of Britain. This may seem a trifling number when compared with the spectacular scores posited by some of the leading aces on both sides, but most fighter pilots who took part in the Battle were not credited with any confirmed victories at all, not even one German airplane shot down.

Tobin was credited with two German aircraft destroyed. Keough and Mamedoff each received credit for half a victory. Shorty Keogh's half-kill, which he shared with a pilot from another squadron, was also a Dornier 215 and also came on September 15.

★ ★ ★

The Battle of Britain did not end on September 15, although the Air Ministry's designation of it being "the Greatest Day" was not an exaggeration. Aerial combat between the Luftwaffe and Fighter Command continued on throughout September and October—on October 29, for instance, the Luftwaffe lost thirty-one aircraft and the RAF lost eighteen—and the Blitz against London and other British cities went on until May 1941.

But the Luftwaffe's losses on September 15—originally reported as 185 aircraft, but reduced to sixty or fifty-six or fifty by more objective postwar accounts (depending upon which source, German or British, is consulted)—persuaded the German High Command to postpone their planned invasion of England. The invasion, code-named "Operation Sea Lion," was pushed back to September 21. On September 21, it was postponed "indefinitely." Not many people knew it at the time, but Britain was safe from Hitler and his Wehrmacht after September 15.

Four days after taking part in the great air battle, Red Tobin, Shorty Keough, and Andy Mamedoff were posted to Church Fenton, Yorkshire, where the first all-American "Eagle Squadron" was being formed. According to RAF records, Tobin, Keough, and Mamedoff were the original Eagles, the first members of 71 (Eagle) Squadron. Their squadronmates in 609 were sorry to lose the wisecracking Yanks who'd been with them for only about six weeks. They were leaving "just as they were becoming really good," according to one pilot. The squadron would be losing three pilots and were also being deprived of a source of constant amusement.[25]

During their time with 609 Squadron, the three had picked up quite a few tricks of the fighter pilot's trade—the fine points of tactics and deflection shooting; the value of conserving ammunition. They would do their best to pass these vital skills along to the rookie members of the Eagle Squadron. If the new batch of volunteers hoped to survive their first encounters with the Luftwaffe, they would need all the coaching and instruction they could get.

★ ★ ★

Nobody really knows how many Americans served with Fighter Command during the Battle of Britain (or, for that matter, with Bomber Command). The Neutrality Acts prevented most of them from declaring their true nationality. But there were at least twelve—enough pilots to man an entire squadron. (There were probably many times more than twelve, but any sort of estimate would be nothing but guesswork.) By September 1942, when the Eagle Squadrons were absorbed into the US Army Air Force, more than one thousand Americans were serving in the RAF. Nobody can be absolutely sure how many enemy aircraft the Americans shot down either, but the count comes to at least 21 ½—almost two full Luftwaffe squadrons.

Clearly the Yanks were skilled pilots, yet in the eyes of the Air Ministry and Winston Churchill's government, the real advantage of having them in the RAF was their propaganda value. As many British pilots noted, with a good deal of resentment and jealousy, the Yanks certainly did get a lot of publicity. From the government's way of looking at the situation, all the Yank publicity might help to make American opinion more pro-British.

It was difficult to make the most of the situation because the American volunteers were scattered throughout Fighter Command, serving in several squadrons. (The seven "official" Americans, that is.) If there could be an entire squadron of Americans in the Royal Air Force, it would be an even greater source of publicity. The American public could then be shown that their fellow countrymen were taking part in the war as a body, not just as a few adventurous (cynics would say "scatterbrained") individuals.

The Air Ministry could also use some favorable publicity for its own purposes—getting the RAF into the newsreels never hurt. The additional volunteer replacements would also be welcome since its fighter squadrons had been decimated by the Luftwaffe. The Air Ministry decided to adopt Colonel Charles Sweeny's idea of forming a squadron made up entirely of Americans. A British officer would have to command the all-American squadron, of course. The Yanks could not be trusted *that* far; somebody responsible would have to keep an eye on them.

And so, a unique chapter in Anglo-American history was about to begin. One British observer called the Eagle Squadron a "unique institution." Notably, the same phrase has also been used to describe both marriage and slavery.[26]

★★★ CHAPTER TWO ★★★

HISTORICAL PREJUDICES

T he idea of an all-American fighter squadron in the Royal Air Force was met with a surprising amount of opposition from both sides of the Atlantic.

One reason that the senior officers at the Air Ministry accepted the idea of the Eagle Squadron was because Fighter Command had lost so many pilots in the Battle of Britain. In just two weeks of fighting during late August, 231 fighter pilots had either been killed or put out of the fight—almost one-quarter of Fighter Command's total complement, enough to man almost twenty-nine squadrons. The Luftwaffe was killing the RAF's fighter pilots faster than Training Command could replace them. The pilot shortage had become desperate.[1]

American volunteers were one answer to the replacement problem. However, many squadron leaders, wing commanders, and officers in the field were opposed to having an all-American squadron. The Air Ministry saw the Americans in the abstract—they were replacements and would also serve as a useful propaganda tool. But the field commanders would have to deal with them on a daily basis and were not enchanted with the prospect.

This reluctance to have American volunteers was partly based on the deep-rooted, traditional British dislike of *any* foreigners (a trait that is shared by a good many Americans). It was also based on resentment over America's attitude during the First World War: the general sentiment in Britain was that the Yanks had entered the war much too late, had done far too little fighting, and had made too much noise that the war never could have been won without them. Some British feared that they might try the same thing again—send a few volunteers and then claim to have won the war single-handed.

In Britain, the general opinion of Americans—not just of US volunteers—was fairly evenly divided between pro and anti. An opinion poll taken at the end of 1940 disclosed that 27 percent of those interviewed had a favorable opinion of their transatlantic cousins; 26 percent said that they did not like Americans for a number of reasons; and 29 percent were "half and half"—unable to decide whether they liked Americans or not. The other 18 percent had not really thought very much about Americans at all and did not feel anything about them one way or another.[2]

According to another poll, the British thought of Americans as likable, attractive, democratic, freedom-loving, and efficient. That was the good part. On the other hand, they also believed that Americans were impractical, mercenary, conceited, and smug.

But all of Britain was unanimous when it came to US neutrality—everybody was angry and resentful over America's refusal to come to Britain's aid. The British saw American neutrality as nothing short of a retreat from responsibility; the United States was willing to supply Britain with arms and cash so that the British could fight America's battle. Anyone in the British Isles would have agreed whole-heartedly. An RAF airman angrily announced that the Americans could not afford to see Britain lose, but that they would only come into the war for mercenary reasons; they would only fight for what they could get out of it.

In short, the Americans were thought of as being not very reliable in wartime. They acted mainly out of self-interest and should not be counted upon very much. But, like it or not, the United States was the wealthiest nation on earth and would have to be counted upon if Nazi Germany was ever to be defeated.

British civilians were not the only ones who thought of Americans as unreliable. As has already been seen, many RAF officers were against taking US volunteers in spite of the vital need for pilots. Air Vice-Marshal Trafford Leigh-Mallory was quite outspoken in his opposition. Leigh-Mallory commanded 12 Group, which was responsible for defending central England. Number 71 (Eagle) Squadron had been assigned to 12 Group.

Trafford Leigh-Mallory had never been renowned for either his tact or his discretion. He was a plump, stocky career officer, always neatly dressed with a cleanly trimmed moustache. Before the First World War, Leigh-Mallory had taken a degree in history from Cambridge. After leaving Cambridge, he joined the army and, in 1916, became a pilot in the Royal Flying Corps. His manner was usually brutally direct; he said exactly what was on his mind and did not give a damn if anyone was offended by it.

The air vice-marshal stated that he was "very strongly opposed" to having an entire squadron of Americans in the RAF, and he especially objected to having them in his 12 Group. He had experiences with American volunteers in the Royal Flying Corps during the First World War and did not have much use for them. He considered them charming as individuals, but on the whole they were "completely undisciplined." Some of Leigh-Mallory's colleagues shared his opinion, although they were usually not as outspoken about it.[3]

Other opinions were not as personal. "At this stage, America was neutral and England wasn't awfully keen on taking Americans into our armed forces," said a flying officer in 609 Squadron (the same unit as Red

Tobin, Shorty Keough, and Andy Mamedoff). "There were an enormous amount of Germanophiles in America at that time. They would have made hay with the idea that American boys were being subordinated to the dreaded British."[4]

The British have always had the idea that America is absolutely swarming with Germans and Germanophiles. This idea persists even a half century after the Second World War ended. A newspaper editorial in the late 1980s claimed that "American society is built much more on Teutonic lines than Anglo-Saxon," and that most "typically American" concepts, such as Building a Better Mousetrap, seem German in origin.[5]

Eugene "Red" Tobin, Vernon "Shorty" Keough, and Andrew "Andy" Mamedoff flew with 609 (West Riding) Squadron during the Battle of Britain. In September 1940, all three were posted to the new, all-American 71 (Eagle) Squadron. Here, Shorty Keough models the squadron's shoulder patch. All three were killed on active service with the RAF. (Photo courtesy of the National Museum of the United States Air Force®.)

Prime Minister Winston Churchill knew that it would take a lot more than a few American volunteers to swing the United States toward direct involvement in the war. Yet he believed that the Eagle Squadron might help to win at least a few converts in Washington, DC, and he was practical enough to know that a few influential friends in Washington could help sway public opinion, along with the opinion of a few leading senators and congressmen. In other words, a squadron of US volunteers could not hurt the British cause and might just help it. The Air Ministry got its American squadron, despite all objections.

★ ★ ★

There was opposition on the American side as well. Some objections had historical roots, while others stemmed from the official taboos set down by the Neutrality Act. In US history textbooks, for instance, every red-blooded American was taught that Great Britain had been the traditional enemy of the United States since 1776. Even though the two countries had been allies during the First World War, this ill-feeling continued right into 1940.

Some objected to sending *any* help to Britain, including volunteers, because the British were "the damned redcoats" and had always been at odds with the United States—right through the First World War. Others suspected that Churchill's government was trying to drag them into "the British war," and were merely starting off by recruiting volunteers.

Most Americans wanted no part of the war at all. They believed that it was none of their affair; the fighting in Europe did not seem to be a threat to American security and, as far as they were concerned, their best course was to remain neutral. Nearly seven hundred isolationist groups pressured Washington to stay out of the war. America First was the name of the largest of these groups. It was made up of thousands of men and women who were of the very strong opinion that any American support of the British was wrong and thought "that the country should prepare to fight for the United States, not Britain."[6]

Another problem, one of "image," was how the British war effort was perceived in the United States. During the summer of 1940, Americans believed that Britain was losing the war. This bleak picture of Britain's situation had been formed by several events. The evacuation of British children to the United States and Canada did not bolster confidence in Britain's chances. Neither did Winston Churchill's famous speech about fighting in the hills and on the beaches. It sounded like Britain was getting ready to give up, just like France had done. Nobody wanted to back a losing cause.

But isolationism and a large measure of Anglophobia (which is not the same thing as Germanophilia) were the foundation of most objections. In July 1940, during the Battle of Britain, President Franklin D. Roosevelt angered and irritated the Anglophobes and isolationists when he announced that the United States was going to transfer fifty US Navy destroyers to Britain. This action served as the proverbial red flag.

Isolationists were outraged. It made no difference that the fifty destroyers were obsolete (they were of First World War vintage) and of no immediate use to the US Navy. America Firsters insisted that Roosevelt had no right to dispose of American warships, especially not to the British. One demonstrator against FDR's destroyer deal carried a placard that read: "Benedict Arnold Helped England, Too."

Colonel Charles Sweeny ran into similar obstacles when he was organizing the Eagle Squadrons. "For months," Sweeny said, "I was hounded like a criminal. I began to have a friendly feeling for [the notorious gangster] Baby Face Nelson."[7]

Americans did not dislike all foreigners, and a good many American citizens held no real animosity toward the British—at least not openly. They just could not have cared one way or the other about Britain or its people. Alex Cherry, a Wall Street banker who left New York to join the Royal Navy, believed that there would have been a flood of volunteers to join the French forces if France had not been knocked out of the fight so quickly. The general attitude of most Americans was of friendliness toward France, an ally and a sister republic, Cherry thought. When he was growing up, he remembered hearing heroic stories about the Americans who had flown with the Lafayette Escadrille during the First World War. Americans were sympathetic toward France, even though most of them did not speak French.

But the feeling toward Britain was far different. Most of Cherry's friends thought they had nothing in common with the British. Cherry had heard that Americans had served with Britain's Royal Flying Corps in World War One, but did not see anything particularly glamorous about it. He just assumed that the Americans who served with the RFC probably had been born in the British Isles.

Alex Cherry was not the only American who felt nothing in common with Britain. In a September 1940 opinion poll, 64 percent of the Americans questioned said that they opposed helping the British.[8] Some came right out in the open and claimed that they were not neutral. They were completely against helping the British out of another mess as they had done during the First World War.

This attitude was also evident in Washington. Although the Neutrality Acts were used to discourage civilian pilots from joining the Royal Air Force, the government actually encouraged military pilots, trained by the US Army and Navy, to join the American Volunteer Group (AVG) in China. The AVG became more famously known as the Flying Tigers.

The commander of the Flying Tigers, retired US Colonel Claire Lee Chennault (a Chinese Air Force brigadier general), did not want a bunch of crackpots and screwball barnstormers for his Chinese Air Force volunteer group. He wanted experienced military pilots. With the help of Washington, he got what he wanted.

General Chennault was given permission by the US government to recruit his pilots right on army and navy bases. He offered his men one-year contracts with the AVG; at the end of one year, they would be allowed to reenter the US forces without loss of rank. They would also retain their US citizenship. If the United States entered the war, they would be allowed to resign from the AVG at once and return to the US forces. Pilots would be paid $600.00 per month; squadron leaders would get $750.00.

This was a far cry from what the RAF volunteers were offered: $67.00 per month (actually, 16 pounds, 14 shillings, and seven pence), service in the RAF for "the duration," and possible imprisonment in an American jail along with loss of their citizenship.

Behind this line of thought—encouraging trained military pilots to fly for China but making it illegal for civilians to go to England—lay a basic distrust of Britain. This distrust dated from before 1776 and the War of Independence. Americans had no long and belligerent relationship with China. Instead, the Chinese were thought of as noble and oppressed allies, fighting the treacherous Japanese against great odds. The British were remembered as ungrateful allies, who never repaid their debt of millions of dollars from the First World War. And now, the thinking went, they were probably up to some other trick—recruiting volunteers into the RAF would only be the first step toward even deeper American involvement in the war.

Even Franklin D. Roosevelt, who was anything but anti-British or isolationist, did not entirely trust Britain. He warned a diplomat that the British were always sly and foxy and advised that it was prudent to be the same with them. Americans had a deep-rooted suspicion of Britain, a suspicion that stretched from Main Street all the way to the White House.

★ ★ ★

The formation of Number 71 (Eagle) Squadron, which took place in spite of all the opposition, did not get off to a roaring start. This probably should not have come as a very great surprise considering all the suspicions and objections on the part of almost everyone concerned, in both Britain and the United States, when it came to creating the squadron in the first place.

The Eagle Squadron patch, which was first worn by members of 71 Squadron more than a year before Pearl Harbor. The idea of an all-American squadron in the Royal Air Force met with a surprising amount of opposition from both sides of the Atlantic. (Photo by the author.)

When Andy Mamedoff, Shorty Keough, and Red Tobin arrived at Church Fenton, Yorkshire, on September 19, they found out that they *were* the squadron. There was nobody else around. There was no officer in command, no equipment, and no airplanes—just three pilot officers with no orders. (Actually, there was one airplane on the station: a Miles

Magister trainer that could not fly.) So the three men just waited around for someone to show up and assume command. It was not a very happy time for them. The North Sea coast of Yorkshire is not the most cheerful place in the world, even under the best of circumstances. After having flown combat with 609 Squadron, not to mention the anticipation of joining the all-American Eagle Squadron, Church Fenton came as a very gloomy letdown.

Ten days later, on September 29, Squadron Leader Walter Churchill arrived to take over. Distinguished-looking and highly qualified, S/L Churchill had seen his share of combat since the war began. He had been in command of 605 Squadron, which operated out of Croydon Aerodrome, at the height of the Battle of Britain. While he was there, Croydon had been bombed twice. He and the rest of the squadron, basically every man who could fly, went up against the Luftwaffe every day.

Before Dunkirk, and before he took over 605 Squadron, Churchill had flown fighter patrols over France. He had also indoctrinated two all-Polish fighter squadrons into the RAF, a feat that involved showing the surly Poles how to fly the Hawker Hurricane and teaching them English at the same time.

But command of 71 Squadron was an assignment that Churchill was not expecting. The Air Ministry reasoned that if he could transform a bunch of ill-tempered Poles into an efficient fighter unit, he should not have any trouble with a squadron of Yanks. At least he would not have to teach them how to speak English.

The Air Ministry had been indulging in 100-proof wishful thinking, as usual. The Americans were no improvement over the Poles. If anything, they turned out to be a lot more difficult, right down to the language problem.

The Poles might have been unruly and hard to handle, but at least they had discipline—they had learned its value in combat. The Americans would prove themselves to be a mob of ill-disciplined, crackbrained kids. And the language they spoke might have *sounded* like English to the untrained ear, but frequently made no sense at all to anyone who had gone to school in England. The novelist G. K. Chesterton was absolutely correct when he said that Britain and the United States were two nations divided by a common language.

Walter Churchill had not originally been slated as 71 Squadron's commander. The original candidate, Billy Fiske, had been chosen for several reasons. For starters, he was an experienced fighter pilot with an enemy kill to his credit; he had shot down a Ju 88 on August 13. He had flown Hawker Hurricanes in combat, and 71 Squadron was to be equipped with the Hurricane. Fiske was also a university graduate, with a degree from Cambridge. And, last but certainly not least, he was an American.

It would have been a relief to have an American in charge of a squadron of American pilots, particularly an American who had spent so much of his life in England. Fighter Command would not have run any sort of risk when it came to trusting Billy Fiske with command of 71 Squadron. Fiske would have been "bilingual"—British enough to communicate with his RAF superiors, but better able to get along with the Eagle Squadron pilots than a "foreigner" from the regular RAF. For the newly arrived Eagles, Fiske would have been a bridge between home and the still unfamiliar ways of England. This would have been a great help, especially in the squadron's early days.

But Billy Fiske was dead, and Walter Churchill had been given command. Churchill quickly discovered, however, that he was not the squadron's only commander. A former US Navy flyer, William E. G. Taylor, had been appointed "co-commander." The Air Ministry wanted a regular RAF officer to lead 71 Squadron, but also appointed an American as a figurehead commander for the sake of publicity.

William Taylor had a brusque manner and a no-nonsense attitude. He expected to be obeyed and did not give a damn if of his men liked him or not. He had spent several years as a naval aviator in the US Navy. In 1939, Taylor received permission to join the Royal Navy and flew from the aircraft carrier HMS *Glorious* during the Norwegian campaign early in 1940. After a brief stint with the Royal Navy, Taylor transferred to the RAF.

Taylor came to the RAF with the rank of squadron leader and was publicly named the Eagle Squadron's first commander. Reporters, photographers, and newsreel cameramen were invited to the ceremony. During the media event Colonel Charles Sweeny was appointed "honorary commander," and the Colonel's nephew Billy Sweeny was to be Taylor's adjutant.

The publicity campaign certainly had an impact. Squadron Leader Taylor from the United States appeared in newspapers and newsreels all over the country. But when Taylor arrived at Church Fenton, Squadron Leader Churchill had already taken command. A fourth pilot had also arrived: P/O Arthur Donahue, from 64 Squadron.

Taylor was not thrilled with the situation; Churchill wasn't either. Both held the rank of squadron leader. Both had been promised 71 Squadron. And neither was prepared to relinquish command to the other. The four pilots were also not wild about the situation. They were exasperated and discouraged—stuck on the gloomy coast of Yorkshire, with no airplanes and two commanders who did not like each other.[9]

After four weeks of just sitting and complaining and wondering what would happen next, Arthur Donahue got fed up and left the Eagle Squadron. According to the squadron's logbook, he was "unhappy with us due to our complete lack of any airplanes at all."[10] He went back to 64 Squadron, wishing he had never left. Donahue thought the Eagle Squadron was "a motley crew that would never amount to anything."[11]

The situation did not improve very much after Donahue left, not even when the squadron finally received some nominally serviceable airplanes. Instead of improving morale, the newly arrived fighters only lowered it further.

Somebody in the Air Ministry had the bright idea of sending the American volunteers some American-built fighters. But unfortunately, the only American fighters available were four ancient Brewster F2A Buffalos. The stubby, radial-engined Buffalo had been designed for US Navy carrier operations in the 1930s. It looked like a gumdrop with wings, and it flew like one, too. It was slow, sluggish, lightly armed, and without self-sealing fuel tanks. In short, the Buffalo would have been a death trap in a fight with a Messerschmitt.

Before any of his pilots killed themselves, Churchill decided to scuttle the Buffalos. He ordered Tobin, Keough, and Mamedoff to land their aircraft without locking the tailwheel, which effectively destroyed the planes. Churchill discreetly kept his mouth shut about what had happened. All that the Air Ministry knew was that four Brewster Buffalos were sent to 71 Squadron and very quickly became "unserviceable."

The loss of the Buffalos was no loss at all. On November 7, nine Hawker Hurricane Mark Is were delivered to the Eagles by 85 Squadron, led by S/L Peter Townsend (who, many years later, would be romantically linked with Princess Margaret). The Hawker Hurricane is generally considered inferior to its more glamourous cousin, the Spitfire, and most pilots complained if they were assigned to a Hurricane squadron instead of a Spitfire unit. A British writer described the Hurricane as "a halfway house between the old biplanes and the new Spitfires."[12] It could outturn the Spit in a dogfight, but the Hurricane was made of wood and fabric, like the fighters of World War I, and was larger than the Spitfire. Still, the pilots of 71 Squadron were not complaining—the Hurricanes looked absolutely wonderful compared with the decrepit Buffalos, even if they were hand-me-downs. Morale improved immediately. The three veterans from 609 Squadron finally had something decent that would fly.

On the same day that the Hurricanes arrived, eight new pilots also showed up straight from flight school. Among them were Chesley G. "Pete" Peterson, a Mormon from Utah, and Gregory A. "Gus" Daymond, who had been a makeup man in Hollywood. These two would eventually rise to the rank of squadron leader and would command 71 Squadron. They would also become the squadron's top-scoring aces. P/O Mike Kolendorski, the Pole from California who had been told that he was crazy for joining the RAF, was also among the new arrivals.

Number 71 (Eagle) Squadron in February 1941: William Nichols, Ed Bateman, Mike Kolendorski, Bill Taylor, Andy Mamedoff, Eugene "Red" Tobin, Nat Marantz, Luke Allen, Peter Provenzano, Kenneth S. Taylor, Reginald Tongue (a British pilot on temporary assignment with 71 Squadron), Gus Daymond, and Sam Muriello. (Courtesy of the National Museum of the United States Air Force®.)

Pilot Officer Peterson came to 71 Squadron from Church Fenton, though he had initially been earmarked for 609 Squadron—the same unit as Tobin, Keough, and Mamedoff. Apparently, 609 Squadron had been on its way to becoming an all-American unit, or at least a mostly American unit, before Colonel Sweeny's idea for the Eagle Squadron was officially approved.

The eight new pilots brought 71 Squadron up to strength. The four veterans—Keough, Mamedoff, and Tobin from 609 Squadron and Philip "Zeke" Leckrone, a volunteer who had flown with 616 Squadron—would form the nucleus of the new unit. It was hoped that they would give the untried Eagle Squadron a much-needed degree of stability.

Only one of the six "official" American volunteers in Fighter Command did not join the Eagles. P/O J. Kenneth Haviland joined 151 Squadron in September 1940 and took part in the battle over southern England. He elected to stay with his old squadron instead and remained in the RAF throughout the war.

Squadron Leader Churchill had his hands full with his raw but eager Yanks. He did his best to tutor them in the basics of combat flying, which allowed the pilots to become acquainted with the Hurricane's good points (it was highly maneuverable and could absorb a terrific amount of punishment without crashing) and bad points (it was slower than both the Spitfire and the Messerschmitt).

Churchill also tried to teach the Eagle Squadron military procedure, including courtesy and discipline, on the premise that proper ground discipline was the basis for good air discipline. He had a lot more success with teaching them flying, as most of the pilots could not have cared less about self-control and teamwork. Their idea of air combat was based on films like *The Dawn Patrol*—one man in a single-seat fighter plane against the wily Hun. In the films, success in combat was a matter of rugged individualism. Teamwork never entered into air fighting, at least not in their minds, so why bother about it? They would have to learn the hard way.

Toward the end of November 1940, the squadron was transferred to Kirton-in-Lindsey. Kirton is in Lincolnshire, about 40 miles south of Church Fenton—which the Eagles saw as 40 miles closer to the Luftwaffe. Things were definitely beginning to look up. Even though the squadron was still weeks away from being declared operational, it was still considerably better off than it had been a month earlier. And it was certainly better off than when it consisted of just four exasperated pilots, no airplanes, and two "co-commanders" who did not get along.

At Kirton, the Yanks continued to learn the things they would need in combat: formation flying and, even more important, individual tactics. But Squadron Leader Churchill was not able to instill the vital element of discipline. By this time, S/L Bill Taylor had transferred from the Eagles at his own request and had been posted to another assignment. That would at least give the pilots one less distraction in the coming months. They did not need to put up with warring co-commanders in addition to everything else they would have to endure.

Now that 71 Squadron was formed and active, the Air Ministry decided to let the press in on what was happening at Kirton-in-Lindsey. It was time that the Yanks began to make good on their publicity value. If the three Americans of 609 Squadron made headlines in the US, then an entire squadron of Yanks should get at least four times as many headlines.

At Kirton, the Eagles were surrounded by representatives of the press and other news media. A small army of newsreel cameramen, from both London and the United States, arrived at the airfield for pictures and interviews. The press visit, as arranged by the Air Ministry, was a complete success. Stories about the Yanks in the RAF appeared on newsstands from New York to California. *Harper's* and the *Saturday Evening Post* were among the many magazines that ran features on the Eagles.

P/O Byron Kennerly recalls being "attacked" by thirty-one reporters and newsreel men. He also received "fan mail" and requests for autographs long before the squadron became operational. One letter was from an eighteen-year-old girl in the United States who wanted to know "all about England."[13]

The Eagles made the British papers, as well. One London front-page headline announced: "US Squadron Forms to Fight with RAF."[14] The Eagles were even welcomed in Parliament in a speech by Secretary of State for Air Sir Archibald Sinclair.

All the publicity and press coverage irritated pilots of other RAF fighter squadrons. The media exposure was making them angry and not a little jealous, especially since the bloody Eagle Squadron had not even finished training yet. The outbreak of Eagle publicity produced at least one joke, which was told over the radio. It used the theme of the jazz-happy American, and went something like this: "I wanted to join the RAF, but I didn't know how to play the saxophone." Another version went, ". . . but I couldn't speak the language."

In the United States, the Air Ministry's publicity campaign was not having its desired effect. Although Americans were interested in hearing about the Eagles, the fact that a group of their countrymen had formed an entire RAF squadron did not alter public opinion about joining Britain in the war against Nazi Germany. Isolationists suspected something fishy about all the news coverage. They correctly believed it was all part of a propaganda program to promote US intervention.

Only 13 percent of Americans approved of intervention. The vast majority still believed that England was going to be invaded and would lose the war. One more fighter squadron was not going to make very much difference, the country thought, even if it *was* an American squadron. The screwball flyboys would just be taken prisoner by the Germans, along with Winston Churchill and everybody else in Britain.

Fighter Command got its squadron of Americans. But in spite of all the newsreels and photos and press coverage, the United States remained, as one British reporter phrased it, "stubbornly neutral."

★★★ CHAPTER THREE ★★★

A VERY ODD ASSORTMENT

During the buildup for D-Day in 1943 and 1944, nearly two million Americans would be stationed in the British Isles. There would be Yank servicemen in virtually every corner of the country; even the smallest village seemed to have one or two. But in 1940, not many people in Britain had ever encountered a real, live Yank. Everybody had heard about them, but few people had actually encountered one (except in films, and that did not really count). The members of 71 (Eagle) Squadron gave the British their first look at these New World citizens.

The story of the Yanks in the RAF is essentially the story of the relationship between Britain and the United States that existed in 1940 and for a good many years afterward. Each country had an attitude toward the other that can best, or at least most tactfully, be described as "wary." This wariness came out of mutual distrust as well as almost complete ignorance.

Because of language similarities and historical links, many Britons had the idea in the backs of their minds that Americans were actually an eccentric kind of Englishman. Even renowned Anglo-American interpreter Alistair Cooke admitted that he once thought of Americans as Englishmen gone wrong. But when the first Americans arrived in England, this way of thinking quickly changed. A resident of a London suburb remarked that the Americans seemed to have come from another world, not another country. A fellow countryman seconded the motion: "If they'd dropped from Mars we couldn't have been more surprised."[1]

The Eagles shared the base at Kirton with two all-British squadrons: 255 Squadron, which flew two-man Boulton Paul Defiants; and 616 Squadron, which flew Spitfires. The British pilots were absolutely amazed to discover that Americans came from a widespread diversity of backgrounds and nationalities—it seemed to them that there was no such thing as "the American people," just a hodgepodge of ethnic groups and religions.

After meeting the Eagle Squadron pilots for the first time, an officer in 616 Squadron declared that the Americans were "a very odd assortment." The Yank unit included "a Hollywood set designer [actually, a makeup man], a professional parachutist . . . a Mormon from Salt Lake City, and an officer who spoke fluent Polish."[2] (The noted Yanks were Gus Daymond, Shorty Keough, Chesley Peterson, and Mike Kolendorski.)

This "odd assortment" was just the opposite of what anyone would have found in a British squadron or in most British towns. In English country districts, families lived in the same village for generations. A "foreigner" was someone from the next town. Everyone came from the same racial stock and background. Even those from different social classes— and class barriers were wide and deep—were still British.

The idea that people could come from such diverse national and cultural backgrounds as the members of 71 Squadron and still be citizens of the same country was a very foreign concept to the British of the 1940s. They soon discovered that Americans were not "Englishmen gone wrong" but rather a completely different species, not like the British at all.

Some RAF officers at Kirton took one look at this group of independent and disparate souls and predicted that the Eagle Squadron would never make a team. "These Americans differ among themselves as much as they differ from us," said Kirton's station commander. "They're not a unified group in their background, or in their ways of living, or in their thinking."[3] So much for the "typical American."

If the British were amazed by the Americans' mixed background, they were absolutely appalled by their behavior. The members of 71 Squadron seemed to go out of their way to be as loud, ill-mannered, and irritating as possible. They refused to show any discipline or military courtesy, such as saluting, and displayed barnyard table manners in the officers' mess, shouting for "some goddam water" and eating with their hands.

Some observers have pointed out that Americans tend to react in one of two extreme ways when they come to England. They either become "more English than the English," acting as much like their hosts as possible (or, at least, acting the way they *think* their hosts act), or they exaggerate their American mannerisms. Most of the Eagles chose the second course, carrying on like cowboys and behaving like characters in a bad Hollywood western.

The official historian of 71 Squadron seemed proud that one Eagle "could make more noise, day or night, than thirty Englishmen or ten Australians."[4] It was no wonder that the members of 255 and 616 Squadrons thought of the Eagles—and probably all Americans—as loudmouthed adolescents. The RAF pilots just watched in silence. They knew that the Yanks' immaturity would instantly disappear after their first contact with the Luftwaffe.

But the Eagles were not ready to meet the Luftwaffe yet. Some of the pilots had been rushed through training school so quickly that they would be useless to an operational fighter squadron. They knew how to perform takeoffs and landings, but could not do much beyond that. Number 71 Squadron's operations record book noted that the first pilots from the training course had been "pushed through in record time." They were certainly no match for the veteran German fighter pilots, some of whom had been flying combat operations since the Spanish Civil War (1936–1939).

The Eagles continued their training at Kirton right through 1940, learning how to shoot, how to take evasive action, and how to attack an enemy airplane without being spotted, and they were also taught other skills that they would need to survive in combat. Not until the end of January 1941 was 71 Squadron pronounced "operational"—fully trained and qualified to join Fighter Command as a fighting unit.

The first casualties were not long in coming, although they did not come at the hands of the Luftwaffe. The squadron's early deaths were caused by air crashes. In the first instance, Pilot Officers Zeke Leckrone, Edwin "Bud" Orbison, and Shorty Keough were flying a tight "V" formation when Orbison and Leckrone collided in midair. Leckrone was knocked unconscious, either by the impact or by the lack of oxygen. Shorty Keough followed him down, shouting to him over his radio, but Leckrone made no attempt to bail out. Bud Orbison brought his Hurricane back to Kirton with a badly mangled right wing. Pilot Officer Leckrone was buried in a Lincolnshire village churchyard with full military honors. His coffin was draped with both a Union Jack and the Stars and Stripes.

Bud Orbison was killed just over a month after his collision with Leckrone. No one was able to determine what caused him to crash. He probably became disorientated in some low cloud and flew his Hurricane straight into the ground. Six days later, the squadron also lost Shorty Keough. His official epitaph only mentions that he "did not return from a scramble" to protect a coastal convoy. Nobody actually saw Keough crash, but coastwatchers found the wreckage of an aircraft near his Hurricane's last-known position. Among the debris found in the wreckage were the tops of size 5 flying boots. "Nobody but Shorty could wear such small boots," noted the squadron's logbook. [5]

Three deaths in just over a month did nothing to boost morale. The loss of Zeke Leckrone and Shorty Keough had a special impact. If these two veterans, both Battle of Britain survivors, could come to such an end, what chance did anyone else have?

The accidents did not improve the opinion of senior RAF officers concerning the Eagle Squadron, either. The Air Ministry had hoped that Keough and Leckrone would give the upstart squadron some badly needed leadership and maturity. But now both of them were dead, before 71 Squadron was even close to being ready for combat.

The station commander at Kirton-in-Lindsey thought that the Eagle Squadron should be disbanded and given up as a bad idea. The Eagles certainly were not helping the war effort, he protested. There was no point in keeping them on just so that they could kill themselves at the government's expense.

Air Marshal Sir Sholto Douglas, the chief of Fighter Command, was inclined to agree. Unless they showed some improvement, and soon, Douglas recommended that 71 Squadron be dissolved and the pilots sent back to the United States. They were "a wild lot," in his opinion and not worth the RAF's time and effort. He thought that all the publicity had turned the Eagles into "prima donnas."[6]

Douglas did not mean his remarks as compliments. By "prima donnas," he was saying that the Eagles were swellheaded and undisciplined, and that they did not fit into the RAF. But the Eagles, typically, laughed off Douglas's comments. When he heard what Douglas had to say, Pilot Officer Chesley Peterson snapped, "if the Old Man thought we were prima donnas, why, let's be the best prima donnas there are."[7]

But there were some in the RAF who might have taken the Eagles' side and argued that their wild behavior was actually in the very best RAF tradition. The RAF's prewar flyers had also been a mob of colorful individualists who had no use for order and discipline. During the early days of the war, a group captain called one auxiliary squadron the moteliest collection of unmilitary young flyers he had seen in a very long time. So instead of being wild and irresponsible, as Sholto Douglas had charged, it could be said that the Eagles were actually conforming to RAF tradition by being reckless and unconventional.

Squadron Leader Walter Churchill did his best to change Sholto Douglas's opinion. Churchill did not think that the Eagles were beyond redemption and said that they should be given a chance. "He had to take this mob of wild cowboys, bronco-busters most of them, and with infinite patience and tact, weld them into a fighting unit without destroying . . . their individual bravery and initiative," according to the squadron's historian.[8]

The Eagles appreciated Churchill's attitude of tolerance. Gus Daymond had a high opinion of Churchill and his "intelligence, enthusiasm, and outstanding personal leadership," saying that "if the Eagles ever amounted to anything, Churchill played the major role . . ."[9] But Churchill was replaced by Squadron Leader Bill Taylor at the end of January 1941. Taylor was the American who had been Churchill's "cocommander" during the Squadron's first weeks. He had gone to the Air Ministry to complain that the Eagle Squadron was rightly his, since they themselves had promised it to him (which they had). The British sense of fair play prevailed, and the Air Ministry made good its promise, although a few months late. S/L Churchill was promoted to the rank of Wing Commander and posted elsewhere. Bill Taylor finally inherited the Eagles—warts, discipline problems, and all.

A few days after Taylor assumed command, 71 Squadron finally became operational. The Eagles' first operational flight took place on February 5. They were assigned to patrol above a convoy of merchant ships in the North Sea, protecting the freighters from attacks by marauding German bombers.

Bill Taylor turned out to be much more of a disciplinarian than Churchill had been. He had served as an officer in the US Navy and had picked up the Navy's way of enforcing rules and regulations. Among other things, he believed that a commanding officer definitely should not be friendly with the pilots—trying to be everyone's buddy would take away from his authority. But this was only the first step in his new way of running the squadron.

Following Churchill's low-key approach to leadership, Taylor decided that sterner measures were needed to curb the Eagles' unruly manners and lack of discipline. He knew all about 71 Squadron's reputation for being disorderly and "bore down on the lads hard."[10] Pilots had to be at readiness at least thirty minutes before first light, "shaved, buttons shined, uniforms pressed, shoes or boots shined and inside their pant leg . . ."

The free spirits of 71 Squadron did not take kindly to this sudden crackdown. There was no doubt that the newly imposed discipline was making a better and more efficient squadron, but the pilots still did not like it. Another thing that irritated the pilots was Taylor's rule about unbuttoning the top button of their tunics. They read that fighter pilots in the First World War had done this, but Taylor would not allow anyone to unbutton their top button until they shot down their first enemy plane. Whenever anyone disregarded any of the new rules—which was often— Taylor would tell off the offender in loud, ringing tones.

At the root of the discipline problem was the RAF's low standards for accepting American volunteers. "The requirements into what became known as the Clayton Knight Contingents were considered lenient," admitted Leo Nomis, a pilot with 71 Squadron.[11] And most of the incoming pilots exaggerated their actual flying hours, which meant that even these minimal standards were frequently not met. It might have helped if Clayton Knight had been able to increase the number of flying hours for his pilot candidates before turning them over to the RAF.

Standards for an American joining the Royal Air force were a lot less demanding than the requirements for enlisting in the US Army Air Force. The RAF accepted men with 20/40 vision, correctable with goggle lenses, and allowed their pilots to be married. The USAAF insisted that their pilots be unmarried and have 20/20 perfect eyesight. There were many other differences as well.

General Henry H. "Hap" Arnold, chief of the US Army Air Force, told Clayton Knight: "According to the rules I'm working under, if a cadet gets fractious, goes in for low stunt flying, gets drunk even once, or we discover he's married, we've got to wash him out. If I was fighting a war, they're the kind I would want to keep. I wouldn't be surprised if a lot of our washouts look you up."[12] And a lot of US Army Air Force washouts did, in fact, look him up—much to the alarm of senior RAF officers.

Another Eagle Squadron pilot who found the RAF's entry qualifications too lenient, if not almost nonexistent, was William R. Dunn.[13] Originally, Dunn had joined the army—he went to Canada in 1939 and volunteered for the Seaforth Highlanders, a regiment of the Canadian Army. When enlisting, he told the sergeant that he was from Moose Jaw. Dunn had no idea where Moose Jaw was, but it was the first Canadian town that came to mind. The Seaforth Highlanders departed for England a short while after the war began, and Dunn, wearing regimental kilts, went with them.

In the spring of 1940, just after Dunkirk, the Air Ministry invited anyone with 500 or more flying hours to transfer to the RAF. Dunn did not have anywhere near 500 hours—he had more like 160 hours. But, he said, his pen must have slipped when he was filling out the application, "with my 160 looking like a 560." The Air Ministry did not say anything, so Dunn did not say anything, either.

Dunn and his 160 hours were accepted into the Royal Air Force, and Dunn was posted to Service Flying Training School. Because of the urgent need for pilots, SFTS was an "accelerated" course. Pilots were rushed through like quick-lunch hamburgers. In SFTS, Dunn learned Morse code, navigation, and the basics of military flying. It was a very elementary course, not meant for producing fighter pilots. Because of the food shortage in Britain, each student pilot also learned gardening; when the weather was too bad for flying, Dunn worked on his vegetable garden.

In April 1941, Dunn was informed by his flight lieutenant that his SFTS training was over, and he would be posted directly to an operational fighter squadron: 71 Squadron. This came as a rude surprise to Dunn—he only had 56 hours flying time with SFTS, and this was limited to trainers. After SFTS, he was supposed to go on to an Operational

Training Unit, which would qualify him to fly Hawker Hurricanes. But Dunn was told that there was no room for him in any OTU. He was also told not to worry—when he arrived at 71 Squadron, the Eagles would get him checked out on the Hurricane. This, however, was news to S/L Bill Taylor. He told Dunn that 71 Squadron was too busy flying convoy patrols to spend time training new pilots. Taylor arranged a place for Dunn at the Hurricane training unit at Debden.

Pilot Officer Dunn spent a grand total of 7 hours 40 minutes flying Hurricanes at Debden. At the end of this abbreviated training stint, he was pronounced "operational" and sent back to the Eagle Squadron. Dunn was no more enthusiastic about joining 71 Squadron than he had been the first time—only four days before. At this point, his total RAF flying time came to about 64 hours, mostly in trainers. At Debden, he had fired his Hurricane's machine guns exactly twice.

Luckily for Dunn, his flight instructor at Debden telephoned a British member of 71 Squadron to explain the situation. The British pilot, Flight Lieutenant George Brown was asked to take Dunn "under his wing a bit" and show the new boy a few of the things he would need to survive in combat—aerobatics, simulated attacks on bombers, mock dogfights, and the like. F/Lt. Brown did what he was asked and did a very thorough job. Dunn credits Brown's teachings as a prime reason for his having survived the war.

When Bill Dunn arrived at 71 Squadron, he thought the other squadron members were "somewhat cool" toward him. He really did not know why. It could have been because he was a new arrival, he thought, or because he had been an enlisted infantryman "who had crawled from the muddy trenches into their blue heaven." But Dunn had seen a lot more combat with the Seaforth Highlanders than any of the Eagles and had even shot at two Stuka dive bombers that had attacked the Seaforth camp, so he did not feel awed by their presence. One of the few pilots who did strike up a conversation with him was Red Tobin, a veteran of the Battle of Britain. The two had a great deal to talk about.

Before leaving Debden, Dunn's flight instructor had a few words about 71 Squadron. "That's a crazy outfit you're being assigned to," he said. "They all lack proper training." Which could be taken as another example of British understatement. A more tactful term than "crazy" might have been "overeager" or "reckless." The Eagles were certainly both—and slightly crazy, as well.

Most of the American volunteers had not given a great deal of thought about what they would be getting themselves into when they joined the RAF. They were keen on flying but had no idea what it took to be a fighter pilot. They had not reckoned with the training and discipline they would encounter before they saw any combat. And they had not thought about the fact that they would be entering a country at war and would not have all the liberties they had enjoyed in the United States.

On top of these realities, another problem presented itself—boredom. Flying convoy patrols over the North Sea tended to be long and tedious, a far cry from the First World War "knights of the air" stories they had read about or seen in the movies. "Convoy patrols were monotonous," Bill Dunn said, "just boring a hole in the sky over and around the ships for a couple of hours two or three times a day."[14]

Once in a while, the air controller would report a "bogie," an unidentified aircraft, in the area: "Red section. One bogie approaching from the east, six miles. Vector 090, Angels 10, Buster." When the four Hurricanes of Red section reached the interception point, what they usually found was not very exciting—a Coastal Command flying boat or a large flock of birds. Once in a while, though, a bogie turned out to be a German bomber on the prowl.

In the course of one typically boring convoy patrol, P/O Gregory "Gus" Daymond spotted a Dornier Do 17. The Dornier was well beyond machine gun range, but was already beginning its bombing run on the convoy. Daymond pushed the throttle all the way forward and opened fire on the convoy. When he saw the Hurricane, the Dornier pilot broke off his attack and began to dive. He very quickly began to pull away from the single-engine fighter.

Daymond's Hurricane was already at full throttle. The only thing to do now was to apply emergency power boost—to "pull the tit" (so named, according to one wit, "because of its appearance and effect when pulled").[15] Daymond pulled, but the Hurricane did not respond, and the Dornier got away.

When he returned to Kirton, nineteen-year-old Daymond was angry and frustrated. He was even angrier when he found out why his fighter was not able to catch the Dornier. The ground crew explained that the Hurricane's emergency power boost had been wired shut. The crew chief told Daymond that he had taken the Hurricane that was normally flown by Mike Kolendorski. Mike was more than a little enthusiastic when it came to chasing the enemy and would frequently charge about at full boost whether he had a target or not. This placed more than the normal amount of stress on the engine. The ground crew became tired of constantly rebuilding it so they decided to impose their own brand of restraint on Kolendorski's enthusiasm.

Daymond was not satisfied by this explanation and complained to S/L Taylor about the mechanics' actions. But even though he did not shoot down the Dornier, Daymond did have the distinction of firing the Eagles' first shots in anger. The operations record book entry for August 17, 1941, states that P/O Daymond "got the squadron's first burst" at an enemy aircraft.[16]

The squadron got its "first blood"—as noted by the squadron logbook—just under a month later. Unfortunately, the blood belonged to another member of 71 Squadron and was the result of a near-fatal comedy of errors.

Near Calais on May 15, P/O John Flynn was attacked by a Messerschmitt Bf 109. While the German pilot was concentrating on Flynn's Hurricane, Flynn's wingman, P/O James Alexander, managed to get behind the Bf 109 and started shooting. He held the firing button down for a full thirteen seconds, spraying everything in front of him with .303 machine gun bullets. Quite a few of the bullets hit the Messerschmitt; it flew off, trailing smoke. But Flynn's Hurricane also received an ample dose from Alexander's guns. He managed to bring his badly shot-up fighter back to England, landing at Manston on the Channel coast. When the ground crew examined it, they found that the Hurricane had been riddled by .303 bullets.

When word got round to the other squadrons that the crazy Americans had nearly shot down one of their own planes, the reaction was predictably sarcastic. After the big media buildup by the press, radio, and newsreels, the Yanks responded to all the publicity by nearly killing one of their own pilots. The incident did not do anything to raise the stock of the Eagle Squadron in Fighter Command.

Mike Kolendorski in the cockpit of his Hawker Hurricane early in 1941. He was shot down on May 17, 1941, the first Eagle Squadron pilot to be killed on active service with the RAF. (Courtesy of the National Museum of the United States Air Force®.)

Two days later another incident took place. This one involved Mike Kolendorski. Kolendorski was one of the squadron's leading rugged individualists. None of the Eagles had much use for discipline, but Kolendorski was wild even by Eagle Squadron standards. Over France, he would throw empty beer bottles out of his cockpit at any German installations that happened to be near. He burned up so many engines that his ground crew wired shut his Hurricane's emergency boost—as Gus Daymond found out the hard way. Everybody in 71 Squadron predicted that Kolendorski would either be the first to win the Distinguished Flying Cross or the first to get himself killed.

On May 17, during a fighter sweep, the Eagles encountered a formation of Messerschmitt Bf 109s. Two of the Bf 109s broke formation and wandered off on their own. It was obvious "sucker bait," a trap for some overeager RAF pilot to go after them. The RAF flight leader called over the radio for everyone to stay in formation.

The worst possible breach of air discipline, as well as the most stupid thing a pilot could do, was to go off on a lone attack. Breaking formation not only jeopardized the other pilots, but was also a quick way to get killed. Experienced RAF pilots tried to drum the importance of air discipline into the green American volunteers: "You're in for a surprise if you don't look to see what's waiting in the sun"; "It's the man you don't see who shoots you down"; and "Always report your intentions to your squadron leader and wait for his orders."[17]

But the temptation was too great for Mike Kolendorski; he broke formation and charged after the two Messerschmitts. Before he could even get close to them, a second pair of Bf 109s was right behind him, firing their cannon and machine guns. A warning was shouted over the radio, but it was too late. Kolendorski's Hurricane was hit several times. One bullet must have killed him outright. Bill Dunn watched Kolendorski spin into the Channel. On the following day, the Germans broadcast that his body had washed up on the Dutch coast.

By this time, Fighter Command were probably wishing that they had never heard of either Charles Sweeny or Clayton Knight. In the eight months that they been in existence, the Eagle Squadron had accounted for three of their pilots killed, either in flying accidents or other unfortunate circumstances; had lost one of their pilots through lack of air discipline; and had nearly shot down one of their own aircraft. Nobody had any idea what the Eagles were going to do next. But it would be certain to come as a surprise, and probably an unpleasant one.

One of the few bright spots in 71 Squadron was Chesley "Pete" Peterson. Peterson was the first Eagle pilot to be promoted above the rank of pilot officer; he was given the acting rank of flight lieutenant. (In the US Army Air Force, it would have been the same as being promoted from second lieutenant to captain.) "Acting," according to Bill Dunn, means "temporary, on probation, unpaid."[18]

The rest of the squadron probably would have been abandoned if the need for pilots had not been so desperate, with the better pilots being posted off to other squadrons and the others sent back to the United States. In spite of the fact that they had been in the RAF for months, the Yanks were still civilian pilots at heart.

Few of the pilots had any experience with instrument flying, formation flying, or anything in navigation beyond the basic rudiments. In other words, they did not know much beyond what was necessary for flying around California. They also did not seem to care very much about learning, at least not in Fighter Command's view. Sholto Douglas was in complete agreement with General Claire Chennault of the Flying Tigers for refusing to take crazy barnstormer stunt pilots into his American Volunteer Group.

But in spite of all misgivings, 71 Squadron was moved south into 11 Group, the area in England that was closest to the Continent and had the most contact with the Luftwaffe. The Squadron had already been moved south—from Kirton-in-Lindsey to Martlesham Heath on April 9. Mike Kolendorski had flown from Martlesham Heath when he was shot down, and so had John Flynn when his Hurricane had been damaged by squadron mate James Alexander.

On June 22, the squadron moved again. This time they went to North Weald on the northeastern fringes of London. The first reaction to North Weald was that it was not all that impressive. "Rather a disappointing move as regards to buildings and equipment," says the squadron logbook, "but apparently a good station."[19]

Now that they were at a sector airfield in southern England, the Eagles realized that they would be seeing a lot more of the enemy and would be taking part in fighter sweeps over the Continent. The squadron members were excited and wondered what the next few months would be like. Top-ranking officers in Fighter Command and the Air Ministry, including Sir Sholto Douglas, also could not help wondering.

★★★ CHAPTER FOUR ★★★

FAILURES TO COMMUNICATE

About 150 years before the first Yank ever thought of leaving home to join the RAF, French writer and observer Jean de Crèvecoeur spent a good deal of time and effort traveling throughout the United States trying to figure out exactly what an American was. After much travel and even more thought, he divided Americans mainly into two categories: the industrious farmer and the uncivilized frontiersman.

According to Crèvecoeur, the farmer was hard working, sociable, responsible, family orientated, and had a sense of community. But the frontiersman, a fellow Crèvecoeur did not have much use for, was a loner: footloose and antisocial with no respect for law and order.

What Fighter Command wound up with was a squadron of Crèvecoeur's wild frontiersmen. Which should not have come as any great surprise—when restless young men decide to run away from home, they do not run away to become farmers. "They run away," according to one writer, "to become romantic isolates, lone riders who slit their eyes against steely distances and loosen their carbines." In other words, they become fighter pilots.[1]

There were some in 71 Squadron who would have met with Creve-coeur's approval, as well as Fighter Command's. Gus Daymond joined the RAF at age nineteen because of a "sophomoric, but genuine, sense of social consciousness."[2] He had been working as a makeup man in Hollywood, which had a large Jewish community. "People on film sets used to listen to Hitler's speeches between takes. We were immensely concerned and there was an atmosphere of dread and foreboding. Well, I went tearing off to do my stuff."

But many more had motives that were a good deal less idealistic than Gus Daymond's. An Essex woman asked the Eagles why they had come to England, "expecting to hear about the defence of the Mother Country, and all that."[3] Instead, "this one told me he was browned off at his wife, that one was browned off at his girl, a third was in debt." Of course, a lot of this was just a front—most of the young pilots were not used to expressing their feelings and would not have told anyone that they were fighting for the mother country even if it happened to be true. But a lot of the "footloose" explanation had more than a grain of truth in it.

Fighter Command and the Air Ministry saw the situation as worse than it really was. They saw the Eagles as a collection of rugged individualists who could never make a fighting unit, even if they tried. The Eagles were a crew of primitive cowboys who grew up with too much freedom, and they would never be willing or able to learn discipline.

Actually, most of the Yanks had already found out exactly how far they could push their "free and independent" act. They knew that some of their squadron mates had been dismissed from the Eagle Squadron and sent home. Some had left for personal reasons; a few, because they thought they should be getting higher pay; but others had been discharged from the RAF because they had been judged "unsuitable" as fighter pilots— mostly because of lack of discipline. There was no punishment involved;

their service records were simply marked "returned home." After all the trouble they had gone through to reach England, no one wanted to be sent back to the States. Also, they heard about what happened to Mike Kolendorski when he failed to obey orders. They had no desire to be killed, either.

In short, the wild Yanks decided to learn discipline because they knew they had to. On the ground, they could still be cowboys and hell-raisers. But in the air, they realized that their lives depended upon paying attention to their flight leader. There is nothing like the fear of death to make a fellow more conservative. Even Jean de Crèvecoeur would have agreed with that.

★ ★ ★

An RAF squadron consisted of twelve airplanes, but to keep at full strength about eighteen were actually needed. Airplanes were always having things go wrong with them, especially high-performance fighters—overheated engines, bad radios, jammed guns, battle damage. Spares always had to be brought up as replacements.

Normally, three squadrons operated out of an aerodrome, forming a "wing." The North Weald Wing was made up of 71 (Eagle) Squadron, 111 Squadron, and 222 Squadron. Along with the two other squadrons, the Eagles were frequently assigned to escort bombers on raids against targets in northern France. They also took part in fighter sweeps, flying low over enemy territory in an attempt to entice the Luftwaffe to come up and fight.

On June 26, all twelve fighters of 71 Squadron "carried out Bomber Escorts three times during the day," according to the squadron logbook. The last Hurricane returned to North Weald at 11:35 p.m., with no losses due to enemy action. This was typical for the first ten days at North Weald; nothing much happened.

The routine had not changed very much from Kirton-in-Lindsey.

Instead of flying convoy patrols over the North Sea, the Eagles were escorting bombers across the Channel. It seemed that they had only exchanged one dull routine for another. But on July 2, the dull routine ended—courtesy of the Luftwaffe.

A force of twelve bombers was sent to bomb the Lille electric power station; 71 Squadron was one of the fighter units assigned to protect them. Going to Lille meant an encounter with the famous Jagdgeschwader 26, the "Abbeville Boys," who had nine squadrons of Messerschmitt Bf 109s based at several airfields in the area. JG 26, commanded by Adolf Galland, was generally considered the elite of German fighter units. Galland alone had seventy enemy aircraft destroyed to his credit. The Abbeville Boys were not about to let an enemy formation go unchallenged.

Over Lille, the RAF formation quickly found itself under attack by many Bf 109s. It immediately became apparent that this particular sortie was going to be a far cry from flying convoy patrols. The first Eagle Squadron pilot to shoot down an enemy aircraft was Pilot Officer William Dunn, who destroyed a Bf 109 at 12:35 p.m. Five minutes later, Pilot Officer Gus Daymond got the squadron's second Messerschmitt. He shot away the Bf 109's right aileron; the pilot jettisoned the canopy, bailed out, and "just seemed to float out of his machine."[4] The squadron leader, Henry "Paddy" Woodhouse (who had replaced Bill Taylor in June), also accounted for a Bf 109.

Although Bill Dunn got the squadron's first kill, the press and news media reported that it had been Gus Daymond. Bill Dunn was not happy about this error. He thought that politics and favoritism were behind it, and he especially credits the oversight to the squadron's intelligence officer, J. Roland "Robbie" Robinson. Robinson was a member of Parliament, had contact with a good many influential people in London, and would later become Lord Martonmere. Dunn thought that Robinson always chose his friends, his fair-haired clique, for promotions and awards at the expense of everyone else. It was not the last time that Dunn would feel slighted.

At the moment, though, there were other things to worry about. On July 6, the squadron was given another escort assignment. A flight of RAF bombers were going near Lille again, and 71 Squadron had another brush with the Abbeville Boys. Gus Daymond shot down a Bf 109 in the resulting fight. Bill Dunn was credited with a half-kill, sharing a Bf 109 with a Polish pilot from 306 Squadron.

Actual combat came as a nasty shock to some of the Eagles. They realized they would be doing their share of shooting at the Germans, but it somehow never occurred to them that they would be firing live ammunition—real bullets—at the enemy, or that German pilots were living, breathing human beings who could be killed.

One of Gus Daymond's first encounters with the enemy came when 71 Squadron was flying with a Polish squadron. Over his earphones, Daymond heard a "terrific quacking" from the Poles; they had been jumped by a flight of Bf 109s. At first, they called to each other in English. But after a few minutes, they "blew their gaskets and began to garble-garble among themselves in Polish, and we didn't know what the hell was happening."[5]

Daymond looked all over the sky, trying to figure out what was going on. He spotted a Bf 109 going down, with a Pole chasing it and "shooting it into mighty small pieces."[6] The Pole stayed right behind the German all the way down and kept on shooting at the Messerschmitt and "the poor guy inside it." For the first time, it dawned on Daymond that he was in the middle of a real war and that "these guys were really playing for keeps."

Throughout the month of July, an unfriendly rivalry developed between Bill Dunn and Gus Daymond. The contest was to see who could destroy the most enemy airplanes, and the tone was not cordial. The lead changed hands several times—Dunn took a half-plane lead when he shared the Bf 109 with the Polish squadron on July 6. Daymond then shot down a Bf 109, which then gave *him* a half-plane lead. Then Dunn moved ahead again when he destroyed another Bf 109 near Lille. By August 10, Dunn was ahead: three and a half to Daymond's three.

In a publicity photo, Red Tobin and other pilots of 71 Squadron "scramble" for reporters and photographers. The original caption for this photo is: "The Eagle Squadron is ready for action: The American Eagle Squadron is now an operational squadron." Actually, 71 Squadron took a lot longer to become operational than Fighter Command had expected. (Courtesy of the National Museum of the United States Air Force®.)

The magazine *Flight*, in its August 15 edition, mentioned: "In their first month as a front-line squadron of RAF Fighter Command, pilots of the American Eagle Squadron have shot down six German aeroplanes—five fighters and a Do 17 bomber."[7] The article went on to say that "one pilot has bagged two of the fighters." The magazine got its figures wrong and forgot to mention the Bf 109 shot down by S/L Woodhouse, but at least this sort of coverage was an improvement over the glamour-boy publicity that the squadron usually received.

The two veteran pilots from 609 Squadron, Red Tobin and Andy

Mamedoff, were not having the same success as Dunn and Daymond. Since joining the Eagle Squadron, neither had accounted for any enemy aircraft destroyed. Andy Mamedoff could never seem to find the enemy. As 71 Squadron's historian put it, "on the day Andy was flying over the Channel, the big fight was over France; when he went over France, the fight was somewhere over the Channel."[8]

Red Tobin faced the same situation, coming back empty handed after every sortie. At night, in the officers' mess, the always garrulous Red would regale the rest of the pilots with stories about his time with 609 Squadron and in *l'Armee de l'Air*. Some of the things were about the grim summer of the year before, when RAF sector airfields were under almost daily attack by the Luftwaffe. During the attack on Middle Wallop Aerodrome, Red had seen one man with his foot blown off and another with his arms blown off "up to the shoulder blades."[9] Most stories had a dose of humor, even though no one laughed at the time of the incident.

One story that was told over and over was of the time that Red, Andy Mamedoff, and Shorty Keough tried to escape from France by stealing a French airplane. Two Czech pilots came up with that particular idea. The French army was quickly disintegrating, and everybody kept saying that the Germans would be arriving any day. "Just what would happen if we were taken prisoners we didn't know," Tobin said, "but we weren't interested in finding out."[10]

So the two Czechs decided that the best way to get out of France would be to borrow an airplane from *l'Armee*—without asking permission. The plan sounded simple enough: take a plane and fly to England. It seemed like a good idea. But the French sentries did not think much of it. They thought the five pilots were German paratroopers and started shooting. The two Czech pilots were killed. Tobin, Mamedoff, and Keough managed to get away.

The three Americans now had no choice but to join the army of French refugees that were heading toward Spain. At the port of Saint Jean-de-Luz, they were lucky enough to board the steamer *Baron Nairn*, which was bound for England. Their plan to escape the German army worked, but just barely—two hours after *Baron Nairn* sailed, the Germans arrived at Saint Jean-de-Luz. Red's reaction to every predicament was that it was all a huge joke—a million laughs, as he used to say.

Both Red and Andy Mamedoff were frequently questioned about the good points and bad points of the Hurricane and the Spitfire—a subject of more immediate interest, since 71 Squadron was due to have its Hurricanes replaced by the renowned Spitfire "any day." Or at least that was what everybody said. The Eagles also asked the pilots of the two British squadrons at North Weald about the differences between the Spitfire and Hurricane. Both 111 and 222 Squadron had played highly active roles in the Battle of Britain, and the Eagles were more than interested in what they had to say. The only trouble was that they could not always understand what the British pilots were saying. It came as a surprise to learn that British English and American English are two different languages— related to each other, but still different.

"One thing American visitors to Britain are seldom warned about is the 'language problem,'" commented a British authority, who went on to say that even the "most mundane negotiation, the simplest attempt at communication with the natives, can lead to unutterable confusion."[11] A columnist from the *NewYork Herald Tribune* agreed, observing that "English is a vast, beautiful but improbable language that resembles American . . . just enough to throw you off."[12]

Byron Kennerly found this out just after he arrived in England. He remarked to his group captain that a nearby Hurricane looked like a "powerful ship."[13] The group captain took the opportunity to give the ignorant Yank a lesson in English usage. "Kennerly . . . for centuries the British have been seamen," he pointed out. "To us, a ship is still a ship. Most of us wouldn't know what you meant if you called an aircraft a ship."

"I was having a tough time learning the English language," Kennerly admitted. Bob Raymond, the Kansas native who wound up in Bomber Command, found himself in the same predicament. "Cannot understand half of the English talk yet," he wrote in his diary. "It is very much like a foreign language."[14]

On top of everything else, the Yanks found out that the RAF had a language all of its own. It was very colorful and self-consciously vivid. To take another fellow's girl away from him was to "bird-dog" him. To have sex was a "prang." (To crash an airplane was also a "prang.") There were probably hundreds of other useful phrases to be learned, as well.

The Americans picked up the RAF slang with no trouble at all. Maybe it was because it was so lively and not all that dissimilar to American slang. It did not take long before the Yanks were talking about their "kite" (airplane), a pilot who "bought it" (was killed), or a "piece of cake" (anything easy, an enemy kill or a girl). They were soon also saying things like "good show" and "bad show" and using a number of other expressions that they had not picked up in Dallas, Texas or Jersey City.

★ ★ ★

The day finally came, after weeks of talk, for 71 Squadron to trade in their Hurricane Mark IIs for Spitfires. The squadron flew their Hurricanes to Kenley to pick up their Spitfire Mark II-As. (These were actually another squadron's castoffs. That squadron was getting the new Mark V-B.) None of the Eagles had flown a Spitfire before, but that did not cause any worries. It was just a matter of skimming through the pilot's manual, taking a quick look at the cockpit and its controls and dials, and then starting the engine. Watching that first takeoff must have been quite a sight—Spitfires lunging into the air like drunkards, staggering all over the place until the pilots started to feel comfortable. The ground crews must have had quite a snappy little conversation afterwards about the crazy Yanks who could not even fly straight.

A popular topic of conversation—as soon as the Eagles learned to understand what the British pilots were saying—was which fighter was better, the Hurricane or the Spitfire. Everybody had their own opinion.

Wing Commander Robert Stanford-Tuck said that the Spitfire was like "a fine thoroughbred racehorse, while the dear old Hurricane was rather like a heavy workhorse."[15] Both fighters had the same armament—eight .303 machine guns—but had few other features in common.

For attacking formations of bombers, the Hurricane had the advantage. It had better visibility and was much steadier for shooting. The Spitfire was "a slightly higher performance airplane—faster, better rate of climb, and very much more responsive to the controls."[16] In other words, each had its good points and its bad points. Or, as another pilot said, "the Spitfire and the Hurricane complimented each other." The Spitfire's job was to engage enemy fighters, to draw the Messerschmitts away from the Dorniers and Heinkels. When the Bf 109s were out of position, the Hurricanes would then jump the bombers. That was the plan, at least, but things did not always work out that way in real life.

Most German pilots had more respect for the Spitfire than for the Hurricane. The standard wisecrack among Luftwaffe fighter pilots was that the Hurricane was "a nice little plane to shoot down."[17] As far as any direct comparison between the Spitfire and the Messerschmitt was concerned, Wing Commander Stanford-Tuck thought the two planes were "virtual equal performers"; the Spitfire could out-turn the Messerschmitt, but they were "basically comparable."

But among RAF pilots, the Spitfire versus Hurricane controversy went on and on, with no quarter given by either side. The argument was not always confined to the officers' mess.

Shortly before the Battle of Britain began, a practice "air raid" was arranged between a Spitfire squadron and a Hurricane squadron. The Hurricanes were to make a mock bombing run over Kenley Aerodrome; 64 Squadron was to send six Spitfires to intercept the incoming "bombers." It looked like a nice, easy practice drill on paper, but whoever planned the exercise did not reckon with the rivalry between the Spitfire and Hurricane pilots.

The drill began according to plan—the Spitfires patrolled above

Kenley, and the Hurricanes showed up flying in "V" formation. But when the Spitfires dove to attack, the plan quickly fell apart. As soon as the Hurricane pilots saw their adversaries closing in from behind, they turned to meet their attackers—a highly un-bomberlike tactic. For the next several minutes, the two squadrons chased each other for miles in all directions. The strain of the aerial combat quickly wore down the pilots' enthusiasm, and both squadrons landed after several minutes of wild aerobatics.

Nothing much was accomplished by this little drill. Nobody's skills at breaking up bomber formations were improved, and neither side could brag about a clear-cut victory over the other. But at least it gave the pilots something else to argue about.

★ ★ ★

Americans never realized how much the British resented the stubborn neutrality of the United States. Even if they had known, it would not have made any difference. The country was determined to stay out of the fighting, and did not really care how much the British objected.

Pilot Officer Arthur Donahue of 64 Squadron was constantly being asked when the United States was going to enter the war—"When is your country going to give us some help, America?"[18] Donahue would answer, "I don't know. They've sent me, haven't they?" The RAF pilots wondered if this was supposed to help them or if this was part of a sabotage plan to give aid and comfort to the enemy.

By the early part of 1941, most Americans seemed fairly certain that it would only be a matter of time before they were drawn into the war. The majority—71 percent percent—now approved of sending aid to Britain.[19] But the reasons for wanting to come to the assistance of the British were anything but unselfish and altruistic. One Londoner defined the American position of sending aid as, "Supply the British with arms and cash in order that they might fight our battle." This opinion came a lot closer to the truth than many Americans would have cared to admit.

The official legislation that sent aid to Britain was House of Representatives bill number 1776: Lend-Lease (known as Reverse Lend-Lease in Britain). H.R. 1776 was subtitled, "A Bill: Further to Promote the Defense of the United States, and for Other Purposes," which was signed into law on March 11, 1941. In less official language, the intent of Lend-Lease was to lease, lend, or sell war goods—anything from paper clips to fighter planes—"to any country whose defense the President deems vital to the defense of the United States."[20]

Regardless of American motives, Lend-Lease was met with enthusiasm in Britain. After Lend-Lease was announced, the British opinion of Americans improved dramatically. Even those who did not like Americans, and did not care who knew it, admitted that their feelings toward the United States had changed for the better because of Lend-Lease.

However, there was still a great deal of resentment over America's refusal to declare war on Germany. An opinion poll asked "average" Britons when they thought the United States would enter the war. Most of the replies were either pessimistic or sarcastic. People had various opinions on when the Americans would enter the war, ranging from: toward the end, just like in 1917; a month before the end; when they felt like it; and only when it became necessary.

They were right—the United States was not going to come in until necessary. "To the Americans war is a business, not an art," wrote D. W. Brogan in *The American Character*. "They are not interested in moral victories but in victory."[21] If isolationist America could promote victory by providing the hardware of war—by becoming "the great arsenal of democracy," to use Franklin D. Roosevelt's phrase—then that was what the country was going to do.

Americans also recalled the First World War, just as the British did. They saw themselves as having been taken advantage of and swindled and felt that they had nothing to show for their part in the war but a huge, uncollected debt, which the British had run up and then failed to repay. Many Americans were opposed to lending or leasing *anything* to the British until they paid back what they owed from the 1914–1918 war.

Another point, which was being overlooked by both the British and the Americans, was the fact that the United States was not ready to enter the war. Although over sixteen million men had registered for the first peacetime draft in American history, those draftees were a long way from becoming a trained army. And the US Army Air Force had no fighter planes that could hope to compete with the Luftwaffe's Messerschmitt Bf 109s—which the pilots of the Eagle Squadron would eventually find out for themselves.

Lend-Lease, which was passed by Congress in March 1941, helped to simplify Britain's war effort. But the event that really took the pressure off took place three months later, on June 22, when Germany invaded the Soviet Union. Adolf Hitler had the idea of overrunning Russia in a short, dramatic campaign, just as his armies had done in France the year before. Once he had overwhelmed Russia, he could then come back and finish off Britain at his leisure.

If Hitler had not attacked Russia, the Eagles would not have been so impressed by Red Tobin's stories of more than one hundred German aircraft that attacked southern England during the Battle of Britain—they would have been facing the same number of Luftwaffe fighters and bombers themselves in the summer of 1941. But by the spring of 1941, during preparations for the invasion of the Soviet Union, a major part of Germany's air strength had been transferred to Russia.

After Adolf Hitler and Josef Stalin signed their famous nonaggression pact in August 1939, the Russians thought themselves safely out of the war. They had even sold oil to Germany, which had fueled the bombers that attacked London. Now, Russia would feel the main fury of the German military machine and its blitzkrieg tactics, and Britain would be given some much-needed breathing room.

In the eyes of many Britons, the Soviet Union was now Britain's main ally. The Yanks could remain as neutral as they damn well pleased.

The Russian army, under Josef Stalin, would probably have the war won before the Americans got around to waking up. Even after the United States formally entered the war in December 1941, this point of view continued to enjoy an enormous amount of popularity. In April 1942, Secretary of State for Air Sir Archibald Sinclair said in a speech before the House of Commons, "Our two mightiest weapons are the Russian army and the RAF."[22] America's efforts, including Lend-Lease, were considered too small and insignificant to mention.

The word soon spread that Russia was also heavily dependent upon American Lend-Lease, including for the Red Army's supply of Sherman tanks. Still, the myth of the heroic Soviets, who were portrayed as noble and valiant in the face of the German onslaught, was preferred to the notion of the noncommittal Americans. The public was in love with the Soviet Union and everything about it. Frequent radio programs were broadcast about Russian history, and a special broadcast was given in honor of Josef Stalin's birthday. "America's far greater, and far less selfish, contribution to the common war effort was taken for granted," according to a British historian.[23]

To the British, especially of the upper and upper-middle class, the Americans came under criticism no matter what they did. They were still viewed as outsiders, though they were not true foreigners, like the French and the Spanish. The Americans were more like cousins to the British, in other words, which made them more likely to be criticized.

★★★ CHAPTER FIVE ★★★

CONFLICTS AND RIVALRIES

T he spring and summer of 1941 were filled with what some historians like to call "momentous events"—events so dramatic and significant that they pushed everything else off the front page. On May 10, for instance, Deputy Führer Rudolf Hess parachuted into Scotland on his own private peace mission and was imprisoned in the Tower of London for his efforts. Two weeks later, the battleship *Bismarck*, pride of the German fleet, was sunk off the coast of France. On June 22, the Wehrmacht invaded Russia, which would prove to be another turning point in the war. In August, President Franklin D. Roosevelt and Prime Minister Winston Churchill met aboard HMS *Prince of Wales* in Placentia Bay, Newfoundland, and issued a joint statement of war aims that would come to be known as the Atlantic Charter. (This meeting only caused more disappointment for the British, who had hoped that an American declaration of war would come out of the conference.)

To the members of 71 Squadron, these were only stories heard on the radio or read in the newspapers. On May 14, however, something happened that would have a direct impact on them. On that day, before pilot officer James Alexander claimed the squadron's "first blood" by shooting down squadron mate John Flynn, a second Eagle Squadron was formed. "No. 121 (Eagle) Squadron was formed at Kirton Lindsey" was the official entry in the new squadron's logbook.[1] Hardly stirring prose, but certainly to the point.

Because so many Americans had volunteered to join the RAF, another squadron was necessary to make use of them all. This was another of the Air Ministry's ideas; neither Sholto Douglas nor Trafford Leigh-Mallory were asked for their opinion. (Or if they were asked, their opinions were ignored.)

Commanding the brand new 121 Squadron was Squadron Leader Peter Powell, a veteran of the Battle of Britain credited with seven German aircraft destroyed. His two assistants were Flight Lieutenant Hugh Kennard, from 306 Squadron, and F/Lt. Royce "Wilkie" Wilkinson, a Yorkshireman with a thick North Country accent. F/Lt. Wilkinson had spent time in 71 Squadron and was at least somewhat familiar with the Yanks and their habits. Between May 16 and May 26, the new squadron's twelve pilots filtered into Kirton. Two of them, Pilot Officers Moore and Marantz, were transferred from 71 Squadron.

Fighter Command was trying to give the new unit a degree of stability from the very outset of its existence, which accounted for the two pilots from 71 Squadron. F/Lt. Wilkinson, who had presumably grown accustomed to American speech and manners during his tenure with 71 Squadron, was also on hand to add a measure of stability as well as to provide assistance in foreign relations. In addition to his time with 71 Squadron, Wilkinson had also lived in the United States for three years before the war. It was hoped that this experience had allowed him to adjust to the behavioral patterns of the strange transatlantic men.

After the painful breaking-in ordeal of 71 Squadron, Fighter Command's chief, Sir Sholto Douglas, realized that he was going to need all the help he could get with this new bunch of Yanks. He was preparing for the worst, but luckily, the newcomers of 121 Squadron were not cut from the same cloth as the early members of 71 Squadron; they were not impatient hotheads who had no time for discipline or British training methods.

The original members of 71 Squadron had been recruited by Colonel Charles Sweeny. Colonel Sweeny had been looking for barnstormers and fly-by-the-seat-of-your-pants individualists—which is exactly what he and Fighter Command wound up with. The recent arrivals of 121 Squadron had been selected by the Clayton Knight Committee, a much more thorough and selective organization. Clayton Knight screened his candidates a good deal more thoroughly than Sweeny, which led to better candidates for the RAF—more mature and usually better pilots.

On the day after the Second World War began in September 1939, Knight received a telephone call from Ottawa. It was his friend and former colleague Air Vice-Marshal William "Billy" Bishop of the Royal Canadian Air Force. Bishop had shot down seventy-two enemy planes and was Canada's leading air ace of the Great War. He was calling to ask if Knight would recruit and screen American volunteers for the RCAF. Knight liked the idea and agreed.

Knight's recruiting drive did not meet with much success until the spring of 1940 when the Phoney War came to an abrupt end, and German forces invaded France and the Low Countries. When the war became front-page news, pilots began to come forward. Knight posted notices at airfields, placed small advertisements in flight magazines, and generally spread the word that he was looking for volunteers. He and his assistants interviewed civilian pilots in cities all across the United States. By late summer, he went to Canada with three hundred potential volunteers for the RCAF.[2]

By this time, both the Air Ministry and the British embassy in Washington, DC, were having second thoughts about Charles Sweeny and his recruiting methods. While Clayton Knight went out of his way to use discretion in selecting and interviewing candidates, Sweeny seemed to be going out of his way to attract as much attention as possible—giving night-club parties for his recruits, complete with newspaper coverage and press photographers in one instance. Sweeny complained that he had encountered "many obstacles" while recruiting his volunteers. The Neutrality Acts and a hostile American press were two of them, but his main difficulty lay with his own gaudy approach to recruiting.

Sweeny's flashy methods threatened to kill off the Eagle Squadrons before any of his selected pilots could reach England. The FBI had already tried to stop US citizens from volunteering by boarding trains at the US–Canada border and telling any potential RAF candidates that they had two choices: either go home or go to prison. The Air Ministry decided to use Clayton Knight's organization to interview and screen Charles Sweeny's pilot candidates. Instead of joining the RCAF, Knight's pilots would go right into the Royal Air Force, along with Sweeny's.

The Clayton Knight Committee was also looking for proven experience and flying ability but, unlike Sweeny's recruits, their pilots also had to demonstrate maturity and discipline. Clayton Knight's rejection rate was fairly impressive—out of 49,000 applicants, only 6,700 were accepted as volunteers for the RAF, a rejection rate of over 86 percent. The highly strung, hot-headed, and impatient were eliminated. They would not have had the discipline to fly monotonous North Sea patrols or to avoid combat when ordered by their squadron leader.

It must have been disappointing and frustrating for the pilots who were turned down by the Knight Committee, especially after they had heard about the RAF's desperate need for flyers. But it was better to be weeded out by Clayton Knight than by the Luftwaffe. Of Colonel Sweeny's original group of twenty-eight adventurers, only three were left after one year: Chesley Peterson, Charles Bateman, and Gus Daymond. This represents a very permanent rejection rate of over 89 percent; some of the pilots had returned home, but most had been killed.

After the middle of 1941, the pilots of 71 Squadron also appeared to be "less bizarre" than the original group of Eagles, according to the squadron's historian.[3] This was largely because of the Knight Committee's standards, though the stabilizing influence of the early survivors was certainly another factor. The really wild volunteers, like Mike Kolendorski, were dead. Not that the current bunch of pilots were completely domesticated, either. The tensions of combat flying still led to the occasional five-alarm outburst.

One pilot, after he was grounded because of poor eyesight, decided to exorcise his frustration by taking a machine gun and blasting at his reflection in every mirror he could find. Another pilot took a shot at his wing commander. Sometimes a group of pilots would get totally drunk and destroy the officers' mess, or at least do their best. This came under the RAF heading of "picturesque" conduct.[4]

Although the standard of new pilots improved, the aircraft issued to the brand new 121 Squadron were no upgrade from what 71 Squadron had been issued in its early days. The squadron received seventeen Hurricane Mark Is that were "very tired," to put it politely[5]—which most of the squadron members did not. Of the seventeen Hurricanes, only eleven were found to be serviceable. This was the usual practice in RAF Fighter Command. The experienced squadrons got the best planes, and the green units got what was left, which was why the newly arrived Eagle Squadron was awarded somebody else's cast-offs.

By May 31, 121 Squadron consisted of thirteen officers, four sergeant pilots, and one hundred thirty-four ground crew, as well as eleven serviceable Hurricanes. For the next month, the pilots practiced formation flying and aerobatics, training for the inevitable day when they would come into contact with the Luftwaffe. They flew formations, had mock dogfights—did all the things that 71 Squadron had done earlier in the year—but 121 Squadron became operational much more quickly than 71 Squadron had. This was mainly because the Clayton Knight Committee had screened out all the wild individualists before they could get anywhere near a Hawker Hurricane.

A Hawker Hurricane of 71 Squadron. The Hurricane has been referred to as a halfway house between the bi-planes of the First World War and the all-metal monoplanes like the Spitfire. It was made mainly of wood and fabric, like the Sopwith Camel. It could outturn the Spitfire in a dogfight, but the Eagles preferred the Spit. (Courtesy of the National Museum of the United States Air Force®.)

On July 21, 121 Squadron was officially pronounced "operational." The men had worked hard and had gone from newly formed unit to combat-ready fighter squadron in just three months and seven days. It had taken 71 Squadron more than twice as long to accomplish this.

Michael Assheton-Smith (real name Sir Michael Duff), 121 Squadron's intelligence officer, noted with a hint of disapproval that "a number of pilots" went to London to celebrate their Independence Day.[6] On this same July 4, Assheton-Smith also logged the arrival of nineteen Hurricane Mark II-Bs, a notable improvement over their old Hurricane Mark Is. This entry went into the logbook with a great deal more enthusiasm.

Despite the fact that both Eagle Squadrons were made up of American volunteers, the two units did not get along very well. The members of 71 Squadron saw themselves as the senior squadron and looked down their noses at the upstarts of 121 Squadron. The "new boys" of 121 Squadron regarded 71 Squadron as publicity hounds and glamour boys who were mainly interested in getting their pictures in the papers as often as possible. This feeling did not diminish with the passing of time.

The members of 121 Squadron resented 71 Squadron's publicity. The press and the media did mention 121 Squadron when it was formed—"Second American Squadron for the RAF" ran a two-column headline in a London newspaper[7]—but the event was not given anything approaching the publicity deluge given 71 Squadron. The senior squadron protested that it never asked for all the press and newsreel coverage. But they did not discourage it, either.

Number 121 may have been operational, but there were few combat opportunities anywhere near Kirton-in-Lindsey. Sorties consisted of convoy patrols but no shooting. Disappointment in the Luftwaffe's refusal to come up was fairly evident in the squadron's logbook entries. "Twelve pilots went on a sweep today as part of a Wing," one entry states, but concludes with a note of frustration: "All returned safely without firing a shot, and without being molested by e/a [enemy aircraft]."[8] Two of 121 Squadron's pilots intercepted a marauding Junkers Ju 88 on August 8, shot at it, and claimed it as "damaged." Ten days later, S/L Powell claimed a Bf 109 as "probable." Two German airplanes in ten days—not exactly the heart of the battle zone.

But even though 121 Squadron lacked experience, its formation did give Fighter Command another active fighter squadron on its roster. There is no record of Sholto Douglas's reaction to 121 Squadron's early days, which were calm and steady compared with those of its rival Eagle Squadron. It must have come as a relief, though, to realize that *all* Americans were not hotheads, screwballs, and "prima donnas." It also probably came as a very great surprise.

This attitude was not really anti-American. It was simply based upon what most Britons knew, or thought they knew, about the United States. Most people's ideas of Americans came from newspapers, magazines, films, and the radio. (There was no television to complicate the matter still further; that would come later.) From these less-than-scholarly sources, the British population concluded that Americans were a violent, ruthless people, who have no use for discipline and no regard for law and order.

In the British press and American films, Americans always seemed to be shooting each other or making huge sums of money from gambling, bootlegging, or other illegal methods. Some of this mental baggage came from Hollywood gangster films, but some of it was based on solid news. The St. Valentine's Day Massacre of 1929, for instance, made the headlines in London and Manchester as well as in New York and Boston.[9]

There was an anti-American feeling in Britain, especially among the middle and upper-middle classes—the "officer classes" of the RAF. British writer George Orwell observed, "anti-American feeling was a middle-class, and perhaps an upper-class, thing, resulting from imperialist and business jealousy and disguising itself as dislike of the American accent etc."[10] But the image of the average-American-as-hooligan—even if some were well-bred hooligans—was based as much upon news coverage and American films as it was upon preexisting prejudices.

★ ★ ★

Besides the rivalry between the two Eagle Squadrons, there was also an intense rivalry taking place between two of 71 Squadron's best pilots. Between July 2 and August 27, 1941, P/O Bill Dunn had been credited with three and a half enemy aircraft destroyed. His competitor, P/O Gus Daymond, was close behind with three German aircraft shot down. Dunn had also been shot down himself. He bailed out of his Spitfire, parachuted into the Channel, and was picked up by Air-Sea Rescue.

On August 27, 71 Squadron was assigned to escort nine Blenheim bombers over to France. The target, again, was Lille, which meant yet another encounter with the "Abbeville Boys" and their yellow-nosed Bf 109s.

As soon as the formation crossed the enemy coast, dark brown puffs of antiaircraft fire began popping all around it. Enemy fighters were expected at any time, so everyone kept a sharp eye out for them. Dunn spotted three Bf 109s that had been pointed out by an alert squadron mate, but he did not see the one behind him.[11] He found out about them the hard way when tracer bullets started whizzing past him. Dunn shouted a warning to his flight, which immediately broke up into individual combats, and also threw his Spitfire into a violent turn to evade his pursuer. He was lucky—the only damage done had been to his composure.

When he came out of his evasion tactics, Dunn could see fighting all around—yellow-nosed Messerschmitts trying to get through to the bombers; a Spitfire trailing white smoke—but he was not under attack himself. Below him, he caught sight of two Bf 109s that were waiting to finish off any straggling Blenheims. Dunn pushed his stick forward and dove after them.

The German leader saw the Spitfire coming and quickly broke away, but his wingman executed a climbing turn—right in front of Dunn. When he was about 150 yards away from his target, Dunn pressed the firing button. Tracer shots converged on the Messerschmitt from Dunn's eight .303 caliber machine guns, and the enemy fighter staggered under the impact. Dunn was able to close to within 50 yards, near enough that oil from the stricken Bf 109 splattered the Spitfire's windscreen. The German pilot never made any real effort to evade Dunn. His Bf 109 fell away, on fire, and crashed into a French field. Dunn felt a bit sorry for his adversary; he was probably just a green kid, right out of flight school. But—"what the hell, they all count."

Off in the distance, Dunn could see the Blenheims bombing their target—there were still nine of them. While he was keeping an eye on the bombers, another Messerschmitt locked onto his tail. His first warning came in the very nasty form of bullet holes in his port wing and a jagged tear near the tip—the Bf 109, closing in from behind, was firing tracer bullets and cannon shells.

Dunn reacted instantly. He throttled back, changed propeller pitch to fine, opened his flaps, and skidded the Spitfire out of the Messerschmitt's gun path. The Spitfire's speed dropped immediately, and the Bf 109 shot past, skimming not more than ten feet above Dunn's head. He was able to see the black crosses on the German fighter, as well as the unit markings and a red rooster insignia on the side of the cockpit.

Within seconds, the situation had been reversed—the Bf 109 was now in front of the Spitfire's guns. Dunn fired a three- or four-second burst, which was all it took to set the Messerschmitt on fire. It rolled over and veered away, out of control. On the way down, its tail section broke off. Kill number two for the day.

About 500 feet below, Dunn spotted another Bf 109 and dove after it. When he got within range, he fired a short burst and saw smoke trail from the German fighter. He was just about to fire another burst when four Messerschmitts got behind him and began shooting. The first one missed—cannon shells darted past Dunn and curved away. But the second one did not. Dunn heard "explosions and a banging like hail" against the Spitfire's fuselage. A cannon shell blew a hole in his instrument panel; his foot was hit and went numb. His leg and head also hurt, and he began losing consciousness. Through his increasing haze, he could see bits of metal and broken glass on the cockpit floor.

Dunn had been dazed by the impact of the bullets and cannon shells. When he came to, he found himself all alone in the sky. He did not know how badly he had been injured, but his head hurt, and he could see that his right foot was covered with blood. Luckily his Spitfire was still flyable, which meant that he would at least be able to get back home.

Dunn made his way back to England by gently weaving his Spitfire across the Channel. (Weaving allowed a pilot to keep an eye out for enemy fighters on the prowl—flying straight and level for any amount of time was an excellent way for an enemy to sneak up behind you and shoot you full of holes.) On the way across, Dunn was picked up by two Spitfires from another squadron and given an escort. He brought his damaged Spitfire down on the grass landing field at Hawkinge, near Folkestone, Kent, just inland from the Channel coast.

In the Royal Victoria Hospital in Folkestone, Dunn was informed that a cannon shell had blown off the front of his right foot. In addition, two machine-gun bullets had gone through his right calf, and another had hit a glancing blow to his skull, cutting the scalp and leaving an indentation several inches long. One of the doctors told Dunn he was lucky to be alive. Dunn already knew this.

When the cast was taken off his leg about a month later, he saw the damage for the first time. The two machine gun bullets had left "reddish scars," and he could feel the place where one of the bullets nicked his shin bone. His head wound had already healed, leaving a raised scar. The injury to his right foot caused him the most alarm. The cannon shell had blown away three toes and had also shattered bones inside his foot. He still had his big toe and the one next to it, but the second toe was not connected to anything—all the connecting bones having been shot away—and "just flapped loose."

While he was undergoing rehabilitation, Dunn was given a shoe fitted with a metal plate, which gave his foot the support it would need in lieu of its missing toes. It would be several weeks before he became used to it. When he was finally discharged from the hospital, he was given a month's leave. He used the time to return to the United States and visit his family. He would be posted to a training command in Canada when he returned to duty.

Before leaving England, however, Dunn decided to visit his squadron mates at North Weald. He was glad to see most of them, but was saddened to find out that several pilots had been killed while he was in the hospital. He also noticed several new faces around the airfield. When he went to collect his personal belongings, Dunn was annoyed to find that somebody had helped themselves to his socks, underwear, towels, ties, and shirts. What was left over had been dumped into a parachute bag, which had then been thrown into a puddle of water on the hut floor.

Dunn was even more annoyed to find out that Chesley Peterson and Gus Daymond had been awarded the Distinguished Flying Cross— normally awarded to a fighter pilot with five victories—and that Gus Daymond had been officially credited as being the "first American ace." Dunn had collected his fifth victory nearly a month before Gus Daymond. And Peterson did not even have five victories; he only had two. Dunn was the first member of 71 Squadron with five enemy aircraft destroyed (actually five and a half) and never got the DFC. "What about my victories," Dunn wanted to know, "didn't they count?"

He credits this omission to the squadron's intelligence officer, J. Roland "Robbie" Robinson. Robinson had influence at the Air Ministry and had "worked the DFC gongs for his two fair-haired boys." Dunn felt that Robinson was always pushing his friends, his "fair-haired clique," for promotions and decorations at the expense of anyone not in the charmed circle.

Although he never received the DFC, Bill Dunn finally did receive credit for being the first ace in the Eagle Squadrons. In 1968, nearly twenty-seven years after the event, he was given official credit for being the first American ace of the Second World War. Air Marshal Sir Patrick Dunn (no relation to William R. Dunn), along with an officer with the RAF Historical Branch, rechecked Dunn's logbook and RAF files. After careful study, they concluded that William R. Dunn had scored his fifth victory before any other American pilot.

Dunn received a letter from Raymond E. Tolliver, historian of the American Fighter Aces Association, dated March 19, 1968, which confirmed the RAF's findings. In the letter, Tolliver said, "The American Fighter Aces Association is happy to inform you that in a recently completed study in conjunction with the Royal Air Force, victory credits clearly indicate that you are America's first fighter ace of World War II." The letter went on to say that the records of the association, which has the final say on victory claims, "are being changed to reflect his fact."

Dunn was serving as an air strike plans officer at Tan Son Nhut Air Base, Vietnam, when the letter reached him. "I was certainly glad to have the matter settled," he later said, even though it had taken over a quarter of a century.

★ ★ ★

Squadron Leader William Taylor left 71 Squadron and the Royal Air Force in June 1941.[12] He was followed by a succession of British commanding officers, which did not stop the press and news media from referring to 71 Squadron as the "all-American squadron." Publicity is not necessarily based upon fact, especially publicity involving Americans and especially during 1940 and 1941.

Taylor was actually removed from command as the result of a quiet revolt staged by the Eagles themselves in response to his strict discipline. (Surprisingly, the Americans could do something quietly when the need arose.) Taylor had been bearing down hard on the pilots, insisting that they obey all the minor rules and regulations regarding dress code and other small matters. He held to the pet US Navy idea that punctual attention to minor details, such as keeping shoes and buttons polished, would make the squadron a better and more disciplined fighting unit. The squadron members emphatically did not agree.

When pilots asked permission to fly low-level strafing missions over France and the Low Countries, Taylor refused. The reason he gave was that the squadron was not at full strength (recent flying accidents had made several Spitfires unserviceable). This incident prompted some of the pilots to complain about the situation to their former squadron leader, Walter Churchill. Churchill took the complaint to 11 Group headquarters, And headquarters sent a group captain to investigate.

Taking action by way of the chain of command usually takes time, but sometimes produces results. A month after the group captain's visit, S/L Taylor was summoned to appear at 11 Group headquarters. The summons came from the group's new commander, Air Marshal Trafford Leigh-Mallory. The air marshal already had his hands full of the Yanks while he was still in 12 Group; now here they were again.

Leigh-Mallory told Taylor that, between the US Navy and the RAF, he had accumulated too many operational flying hours and that he was too old—at age 36—to command an operational fighter squadron. In other words, Squadron Leader Taylor no longer had a squadron to lead. Leigh-Mallory was never known for being subtle, and this was typical of him—nasty but effective. As a consolation prize, Taylor was offered a training command and a promotion to wing commander. He turned down the training job, as Leigh-Mallory knew he would.

The offer having been made and turned down, Taylor was given two weeks to decide what he wanted to do. But he did not need that much time. Both the US Navy and the Royal Navy had asked him to return, and he was pretty fed up with the RAF and everybody in it by this time. Since the Americans had asked him first, Taylor decided to return to the US Navy. (Trafford Leigh-Mallory's reaction to Taylor's decision is not known, but it was probably a sigh of relief—one less Yank for him to worry about.)

When Taylor returned to 71 Squadron, his entire attitude changed. Knowing that he would be leaving the squadron in two weeks' time, he decided to become "one of the boys." He suddenly became friendly with everybody in the squadron and even joined them in the officers' mess. The pilots quickly came to like the "new" S/L Taylor and decided they wanted him to stay after all. But by that time it was too late; Taylor was soon on his way to join the US Pacific Fleet.

After Taylor's departure, the squadron was taken over by squadron leader Henry de Clifford Anthony Woodhouse, given the nickname "Paddy." He and the Eagles did not hit it off, to put it mildly. For one thing, he was an even sterner taskmaster than Bill Taylor had been. For another thing, he was British. The squadron did not like this stuffy Limey; they considered him to be a typical look-down-your-nose-officer-class

type. They thought they should have another American commander—
that way, if they were going to be harassed, as least it would be in a language they understood.

The men never really liked Woodhouse—he was too much of an
authoritarian to become popular—but he did come to be respected eventually. The pilots realized they were learning a great deal about flying
from him, in spite of themselves. Maneuvers were practiced over and
over again until Woodhouse was satisfied, which meant until they were
performed to perfection.

In August 1941, after two months with 71 Squadron, Woodhouse was
promoted to the rank of wing commander and posted to Tangmere to
take over the famous "Bader Wing." The wing was named after the well-
known but controversial Douglas Bader, who had become an ace in spite
of the fact that he had lost both legs (they had been amputated after a
flying accident in the 1930s). Bader had recently been shot down over the
Continent and captured by the Germans. Woodhouse was sent to replace
him. No one in 71 Squadron was sorry to see him go.

Squadron Leader E. R. Bitmead took command after Woodhouse.
But Bitmead had not fully recovered from an earlier accident and was
not yet fit enough to lead an operational squadron. He left after only
nine days, before the squadron could get to know him. Bitmead was
replaced by Squadron Leader Stanley T. Meares, who had flown with
54 Squadron during the Battle of Britain. Bitmead was just the opposite
of Woodhouse—friendly, affable, and maybe just a little too easygoing.
Meares was also a first-rate leader, and he had the benefit of the discipline
imposed by Taylor and Woodhouse.

The pilots of 71 Squadron had three commanders in three months. If
Trafford Leigh-Mallory, or anyone else in Fighter Command, still wondered about the squadron's steadiness and reliability, at least the Eagles
had an excuse for being undependable. Nobody could be expected to
perform at their best with revolving-door squadron leaders. But with
Meares in command, the Eagles were expected to improve—they had

discipline instilled by past squadron leaders, and now they had a good, and experienced, British commanding officer running things. The one hope was that Meares would last longer than his two predecessors.

★ ★ ★

On August 1, 1941, the rivalry between the two Eagle Squadrons was given something additional—the formation of a third Eagle Squadron.

Most of the pilots of the new unit, designated Number 133 (Eagle) Squadron, had been recruited by the Clayton Knight Committee.[13] These volunteers had been trained in Canada, at bases operated by the RAF. Enough pilots had passed the training course to form a brand new all-American squadron.

Reaction to the new squadron in Fighter Command was mixed. The newly qualified pilots were both needed and welcome. But yet another Eagle Squadron was an idea that was treated with skepticism—the early days of 71 Squadron, with its crazy ways and flying accidents, were still too fresh in everyone's mind. As far as Trafford Leigh-Mallory was concerned, a Yank was a Yank, wherever he was trained, and should not be trusted too far.

The pilots of 133 Squadron had the advantage of starting out with up-to-date fighter planes. Instead of the war-weary hulks that had been supplied to both 71 and 121 Squadron, the new unit was issued Hurricane Mark II-Bs that were in excellent condition. The Mark II-B was a much more modern fighter than anything the other two Eagle squadrons had seen in their early days. It could fly higher than its predecessors, because of its Rolls-Royce Merlin XX engine, and was also armed with twelve .303 machine guns, as opposed to the eight guns of earlier models.

Commanding the new squadron, which was based at Coltishall, Norfolk, was Flight Lieutenant George A. Brown, who had been promoted to the rank of acting squadron leader. F/Lt. Brown had been a flight leader with 71 Squadron and was also the pilot who taught Bill

Dunn how to survive in combat. Because he had been exposed to Americans, their language and their habits and customs, Brown was expected by Fighter Command to know something about these oddball foreigners.

The squadron adjutant, Pilot Officer J. G. Staveley-Dick (also a pipe-smoking lawyer), did not have the benefit of such exposure and seemed to have some very peculiar notions about the Yanks. One of 133 Squadron's pilots said that Staveley-Dick seemed "always to be in a state of amazement at his close association with such odd-ball Americans." To a class-conscious, university-educated English lad, everything about the Yanks—their accents, behaviors, manners, just about anything they said or did—probably struck him as strange, if not absolutely bizarre.

If the British thought Americans were peculiar, the Yanks likely found many Britons, especially the higher-ranking officers, to be almost surreal. Americans tended to think of these lofty gentlemen as formal, coldly polite, standoffish, remote, and just plain freakish. The feeling about being strange was entirely mutual.

Squadron leader Brown's welcoming speech to the new squadron was anything but cheerful and reassuring. He invited the men to have a good look around the room because, "in a year from now, most of you will be dead."[14] It was a startling prophesy. It also turned out to be true.

Early entries in 133 Squadron's operations record book deal almost entirely with practice drills—formation flying, machine-gun practice, and all the other things that new squadrons have to go through before becoming operational. The drills continued throughout September. A few new pilots also joined the squadron—including Acting Flight Lieutenant Andy Mamedoff from 71 Squadron.

Fighter Command wanted to have an American officer with 133 Squadron—an officer above the rank of pilot officer—and Mamedoff was the obvious choice. He was an excellent pilot, he had combat experience, and nobody ever accused him of being standoffish or reserved. Mamedoff's old unit, 71 Squadron, was not wild about losing him, but an order was an order. Mamedoff joined 133 Squadron on September 2.

The rivalry between the Eagle squadrons was beginning to intensify, especially now that there were three of them. The members of 71 Squadron believed they were the best of the three units and resented accusations that they received too much publicity. In 121 Squadron, the pilots thought themselves equal to the "publicity hounds" of 71 Squadron, even if they did not get their pictures in the paper as often. They had become operational in less than half the time of 71 Squadron and did so with fewer than half the casualties and wrecked airplanes.

At Coltishall, 133 Squadron took a somewhat wary view of both of the elder squadrons. They received practically no media coverage at all; in August 1941, because of the fighting against Field Marshal Erwin Rommel's Afrika Korps in Libya, as well as fighting on all other fronts, the story of another Eagle squadron was not considered a very hot news item. Also, the pilots resented the other two Eagle Squadrons looking down their noses at them. And they hated being called the "third Eagles."

All three squadrons would receive increasingly advanced fighters as their flying ability improved (and as Fighter Command's confidence in the Yanks increased). All new squadrons—including 133—started out with Hawker Hurricanes and moved on to the Spitfire: first to the Spitfire Mark II-A and then to the Mark V-B.

The differences between the Mark II-A and the Mark V-B were small but substantial. The Mark V's engine was only slightly larger than the Mark II's, which meant that there was not that much difference in speed or performance. Armament in the Mark V certainly represented an improvement—four .303 machine guns and two 20 mm cannons. The cannons were much more effective than the 30 caliber machine guns. Their exploding shells not only could penetrate armor plate on enemy bombers but also gave an edge against the Messerschmitts—a machine-gun bullet was seldom fatal, but even a single cannon shell could destroy an enemy fighter. The Luftwaffe had learned this years before.

When the war first began, the 20 mm cannon was more of a hindrance than a help. They always seemed to jam when they were needed most, sometimes after only a few rounds were fired. But when this defect was corrected, the cannon soon proved its worth in combat. A cannon shell could penetrate armor that would have deflected a .303 bullet. The pilot actually had the option of firing just the two cannons, just the four machine guns, or all of the guns at once.

To many pilots, the most important difference between the Mark II and the Mark V-B was the latter's metal ailerons. (Ailerons were responsible for steering a plane up and down.) Metal ailerons made the Spitfire V much more maneuverable and responsive than its elder brother, which came equipped with fabric-covered ailerons.[15] Stick pressure was reduced, along with "heavy response" to the controls. In short, the Spit V was slightly faster, more heavily armed, and much more maneuverable than its predecessor.

The Spitfire was admired by pilots on both sides. According to legend, German ace Adolf Galland infuriated Luftwaffe chief Hermann Göring by saying that what the Luftwaffe really needed was a squadron of Spitfires. Still, no one ever praised the machine for its comfort or luxury; the pilot at the controls of *any* model Spitfire was not the most comfortable man in the world.

According to Wing Commander Miles Duke-Woolley, who would fly with the Eagle squadrons in the future, the pilot of a Spitfire was a "lonely man."[16] The cockpit was so narrow that a pilot's shoulders brushed against the sides whenever he rubbernecked for enemy fighters (which was constantly); his flying helmet, with his radio headset, covered his ears; and the Spitfire's long nose limited his forward vision. Thus the pilot could not hear very well (even the engine roar was muffled), his vision was severely limited, and his entire body was boxed in by the confines of the cockpit. He was, in short, not only lonely but also extremely uncomfortable.

The pilot's position was not improved by the fact that he was traveling at speeds in excess of 300 miles per hour. It became even more awkward when a German pilot in another machine—probably just as uncomfortable—was shooting at him.

When 133 Squadron first saw its Spitfire Mark V-As, the pilots were dismayed. The planes had suffered a great deal of wear and tear: their Plexiglas cockpit hoods were in such bad shape that they could hardly be seen through, and the engines sounded rough and grating. It looked as though Fighter Command was trying to atone for the fact that the squadron had been issued brand new Hurricanes when the unit had first been formed. Just about every fighter needed a complete overhaul before it could be considered combat-ready. When the Spitfires were tuned up and made more air-worthy and presentable, squadron morale improved in direct proportion with the condition of its aircraft.

By the autumn of 1941, all three of the Eagle Squadrons were operational. Fighter Command was glad to have the American volunteers, even though both 121 and 133 squadrons had no combat experience at all, but the behavior of the "wild Yanks" was still a cause for concern. Especially troubling was the rivalry between the three units, which seemed to be worsening.

The future of the Eagle Squadrons was viewed by Sholto Douglas, chief of Fighter Command, as well as his colleagues, with wary optimism. But, if they were as good at fighting the Germans as they were at raising hell and fighting with each other, they ought to have fine combat records.

★★★ CHAPTER SIX ★★★

COLORFUL CHARACTERS AND "OLD SCHOOL TIE BOYS"

T he three Eagle Squadrons certainly had their share of colorful characters—Sholto Douglas and his long-suffering colleagues at Fighter Command headquarters probably thought they had *more* than their share. Because 71 Squadron was the senior unit, and because its members had a knack for attracting publicity, the senior Eagles also received the most attention in the newspapers and the news media.

An American Air Force colonel named James Saxon Childers even wrote a book about 71 Squadron. It was published under the title *War Eagles* in both the United States and Britain. In his book, Childers talked about most of the Squadron's pilots including Gus Daymond, Chesley Peterson, and Red Tobin. But curiously, he left out Bill Dunn. Childers does not even give a passing reference to the Squadron's first ace.

One of the pilots included in the book was Leo Nomis.[1] Of American Indian ancestry, Nomis was nicknamed "the Chief" by his squadron mates and had an Indian chief painted on the side of his Spitfire (which he later blamed on "adolescent" behavior). He was a second-generation flyer; his father had been a pilot in the First World War. After the war, the senior Nomis became a Hollywood stunt flyer and was killed in a 1932 flying accident.

Sam Mauriello, called "Uncle Sam," was one of 71 Squadron's early members and was with the squadron when it flew its first ancient Hurricanes. He lived in New York City where he was a taxi driver. He claimed that driving a taxi made him a better fighter pilot—dodging German fighters was no worse than rush-hour traffic in Midtown Manhattan. Driving in that murderous traffic also gave him an instinct for survival.

Another early volunteer was Newton Anderson from New Orleans. Anderson's story is fairly similar to Andy Mamedoff's, Shorty Keogh's, and Red Tobin's. He had also enlisted in *l'Armée de l'Air*, and he had also escaped to England after France surrendered. But because of his bad eyesight—his nickname was "Weak Eyes"—Anderson was assigned to a training command instead of a fighter squadron. It took a great deal of persistent nagging to convince his commanding officer that he should be posted to a fighter unit. He was finally sent off to 71 Squadron after a long campaign of persuasion.

Red Tobin and Andy Mamedoff were still with 71 Squadron when Anderson arrived. Mamedoff left on September 2 when he was posted to still-in-training 133 Squadron at Coltishall, Norfolk. Mamedoff's squadron mates were sorry to see him go and were especially unwilling to lose him to the upstarts of 133 Squadron.

Five days after Andy Mamedoff left 71 Squadron, Red Tobin was shot down and killed while on a fighter sweep.[2] According to the Squadron logbook, he was "missing over enemy territory," but there was no doubt in anyone's mind that Red would not be coming back.

On September 7, the three squadrons of North Weald Wing, including 71 Squadron, were sent across the Channel to draw the Luftwaffe's fighters into combat. The idea was to tempt the Messerschmitts to come up and fight and then to inflict as much damage as possible on the enemy—"fighter attrition" it was called. But lately, the Luftwaffe had not been taking the bait; the fighters would only come up to attack RAF bomber formations.

Hurricanes of 71 Squadron buzz the field, for the benefit of the photographer, with the Stars and Stripes prominently in the foreground. All American volunteers were assured that they would not be required to swear an oath of allegiance to the British Crown. (Courtesy of the National Museum of the United States Air Force®.)

In an attempt to antagonize the German fighters, the RAF came up with an idea that they called the "Rodeo" mission: a fighter sweep joined by a bomber formation. The target of the Rodeo was usually a German fighter base, and the logic behind it was that the Messerschmitts would have to come up if their own bases were under attack. Sometimes the trick worked, sometimes it did not. When it did not, the RAF would attack the Luftwaffe base and go home.

On September 7, it quickly became evident that the Luftwaffe had a bone in its teeth that day. When the North Weald Wing was about 75 miles inland from the French coast and just about to turn for home, ground control in England warned that large numbers of enemy planes were in the air. The German fighters numbered about one hundred. The RAF were outnumbered by more than three to one.

Number 71 Squadron was flying above the other two squadrons with only nine Spitfires; mechanical problems had grounded the other three. To make matters worse, the Bf 109s had singled out 71 Squadron. They swooped in, made their attacks, and climbed back again. The two lower squadrons were left alone while 71 Squadron took the brunt of the attack.

The Eagles turned in to the attacking Bf 109s and fought back. Chesley Peterson shot down his first enemy aircraft in the ensuing free-for-all. But because of the Luftwaffe's lopsided superiority in numbers, the battle could have only one outcome. As one of 71 Squadron's participants put it, "gradually, they were picking us off."

Two of the squadron's nine pilots were killed. Another bailed out over France and was taken prisoner. Of the six Spitfires that made it back to North Weald, two were so badly damaged that they never flew again.

Hilliard S. Fenlaw was one of the pilots that died that day; the other was Red Tobin. Red had a premonition that he would not survive the war. A year before his death, when he was still flying with 609 Squadron out of Warmwell, he told a squadron mate about this feeling. "I reckon these are a one-way ticket, pal," Tobin said, tapping the pilot's wings on his uniform.[3]

A month later, on October 8, Red's squadron mate Andy Mamedoff was killed. Mamedoff was flying to Eglinton Airfield in Northern Ireland, where 133 Squadron was to have additional training. F/Lt. Mamedoff and thirteen other pilots left England, flying west over the Irish Sea, and ran into bad weather. Of the fourteen pilots, only six of them reached their destination. Four were forced down at other airfields by the weather. The other four apparently became disorientated in the low clouds and crashed; among them was Andy Mamedoff. The squadron's logbook only says that Mamedoff "crashed Isle of Man, 17.10 hrs."[4]

This would not be the last time that the Eagle Squadrons would have trouble with the weather. A few weeks after Andy Mamedoff was killed, three pilots of 121 Squadron lost their way in bad weather while they were ferrying Hurricanes to Wales. None of this group died, but all three were forced to either bail out of their planes or crash-land because they could not find their assigned airfield in the fog.

Clouds and fog were just as much of a threat to British pilots as to the Americans, but the British had two advantages over the Yanks. First, they were more proficient at instrument flying. Second, and probably more important, they were much more familiar with the English countryside. The Brits could pick out landmarks and use them as a reference point, or they could follow roadways and railway lines to their destinations.

Andy Mamedoff was the last of the three original Eagle Squadron pilots. He was also the last of 609 Squadron's "larger than life" Yank volunteers who had fought in the Battle of Britain. David Crook, who had been a pilot officer with 609 Squadron during the summer of 1940, was saddened by the deaths of his former squadron mates but did not really seem all that surprised. "Shorty [Keough] was last seen spinning into the sea near Flamborough Head during a chase after a Heinkel," Crook remembered.[5] "Red crashed behind Boulogne, fighting like hell against a crowd of Messerschmitt 109s, while Andy hit a hill in bad weather and was killed."

Of the seven "official" Americans who fought in the Battle of Britain, the five who had joined the first Eagle Squadron were all killed during the war. Arthur Donahue, who left 71 Squadron in disgust "due to our complete lack of any airplanes at all," was shot down over the English Channel in September 1942. Philip Leckrone was killed in a flying accident in January 1941, and Billy Fiske had been shot down and killed in August 1940 before 71 Squadron was even formed. The only one of the seven Yanks to survive the war was J. K. Havilland who had decided not to join the Eagle Squadron and remained in the RAF throughout the war.

★ ★ ★

At the end of October 1941, the Air Ministry announced to the press that the highest-scoring unit for the month was 71 Squadron.[6] The reaction to this news by Air Marshal Sir Sholto Douglas, the head of Fighter Command, and by Air Vice-Marshal Trafford Leigh-Mallory, the commander of 11 Group, is not on record. However, it is a fairly safe assumption that they were both fairly surprised, if not absolutely astonished, to learn that Fighter Command's problem children had achieved such distinction. The Eagles themselves, needless to say, were not surprised at all. They knew all along that they were the best fighter squadron in the RAF.

The number of German aircraft destroyed by 71 Squadron during the month of October was nine, which represented eleven percent of the RAF's total. This means that the total number of enemy aircraft shot down by every squadron in Fighter Command combined came to eighty-two. These figures give an idea of the state of the war on the western front in the autumn of 1941. It had become something of a sideshow. The Germans and the RAF may have sparred with each other in the air over northern France, but both sides were preoccupied elsewhere. Germany was fully committed to an all-out war in Russia and had been since June. Britain's main efforts were in North Africa against Field Marshal Erwin Rommel's Afrika Korps and against the Italian navy in the Mediterranean.

During the Battle of Britain, the RAF had often shot down eighty-two enemy airplanes in a single week. On September 15, 1940, Fighter Command claimed 185 planes in a single day (a claim that was sharply reduced after the war). But by late 1941, the war had moved elsewhere leaving the fighter pilots with far fewer German aircraft to contend with.

While 71 Squadron was enjoying its status as the RAF's top-scoring fighter unit, the other two Eagle Squadrons were still learning the fundamentals. One of their basic mistakes was firing at targets that were too far away. Two pilots from 121 Squadron sighted a Junkers Ju 88 and began firing at 400 yards out. They claimed to have damaged the Junkers, but both pilots ran out of ammunition and the bomber got away.

Most pilots preferred the 20 mm cannon of the Spitfire Mark V, which could inflict a lot more damage than the rifle-caliber .303 machine-gun bullet, especially at extreme ranges. Some also preferred the De Wilde shell, which exploded on contact like a 20 mm shell. The opinion on tracer ammunition was divided. Those who liked it said that tracer allowed them to see where their bullets were going. Those who did not claimed that the bullet's trail of white smoke only served to warn enemy pilots.

In the Luftwaffe, only the best gunners did the shooting. The other pilots in the flight guarded their leader and helped him to set up his attack, allowing him to concentrate on his target. Legendary German aces, such as Werner Mölders and Adolf Galland, had an incredible talent for marksmanship—they were reportedly able to hit their target from just about any angle and seldom wasted ammunition. But although this "buddy system" was a great help to flight leaders, it was a hindrance to everybody else. The leader scored most of the kills, while his wingmen scored hardly any.

All three Eagle Squadrons were still learning that the Luftwaffe had quite a few nasty little tricks up its sleeve. One was a standard evasion maneuver, simple but effective. The pilot of a Bf 109 would roll the fighter over on its back and pull the stick until it was up against his stomach, putting the airplane in a full power dive. The Messerschmitt was powered by a Daimler-Benz fuel-injection engine, which allowed the German pilot to dive away at full throttle any time he needed to break off combat. The Spitfire or Hurricane pilot did not have this luxury. His fighter's Rolls-Royce Merlin engine came equipped with a carburetor, which meant that it would stall momentarily if he pushed over into a power dive. In order to prevent his engine from stalling, the RAF pilot would have to perform a half-roll before diving, which let the Messerschmitt pull ahead of him and frequently allowed the enemy to get away.

During these power dives, the Messerschmitt's engine would emit a trail of black exhaust smoke as the pilot pushed his engine to full power. This often led to the wishful conclusion of many RAF pilots that the enemy fighter had been shot down—"Last seen smoking and going straight down" was the standard description in filing claims for "probables." This was one of the reasons behind the inflated kill totals submitted by Spitfire and Hurricane pilots.

Another German trick was to tune in on RAF radio frequencies and send pilots false information. In bad weather, German ground controllers would give RAF pilots false positions (what Bill Dunn called "bum fixes") and courses that would take them out to sea.[7] Usually the trick did not work—the British controller would interrupt the German with genuine positions and correct vectors. Both sides used this ruse, but this was just the sort of thing the young Americans had expected from the deceitful Nazis.

Of the three Eagle Squadrons, 71 Squadron saw the most enemy action. Based in the south of England, at North Weald, it flew operations whenever the weather was clear and the opportunity presented itself— which was fairly often, in spite of all the complaining. Besides fighter sweeps and bomber escorts, 71 Squadron also went on "Rhubarbs"— low-altitude ground-strafing jobs.

Rhubarbs were usually flown by two pilots and were generally planned by the pilots themselves. Frequently, the planning was done in a local pub. Targets had to be small enough to be taken care of by two fighters, so rail yards, freight trains (passenger trains were out of bounds), airfields, and small factories were often selected. The pilots would choose the targets, and the squadron would ask permission of 11 Group headquarters before proceeding.

Most RAF squadrons were not all that fond of flying Rhubarbs; they did not think that such small targets were worth the risk. But the Eagles seemed to relish them. The British attributed this to the American love of individual freedom—going off on their own to harass the enemy with no controls or restraints. One former RAF ground crewman thought it had something to do with chasing "Red Indians across the lone prairie."

An American writer said that Rhubarbs "satisfied a desire for individual action that was especially strong for the Eagles."[8] Jean de Crèvecoeur probably would have said that it was the "wild man" coming out in them.

The Rhubarbs could be pretty wild themselves. Even when the pilots were not being shot at by antiaircraft fire, there were other dangers. High-tension wires were one obstacle. One pilot returned to base with a badly mangled wing because he had not pulled up soon enough to avoid a telephone pole. Jack Fessler of 71 Squadron was shooting up the rail yards at Boulogne when a locomotive blew up directly underneath his Spitfire. Debris hit the fighter, forcing it to crash-land just outside the city. As a result, Fessler spent the rest of the war as a POW.

While the senior Eagle Squadron was flying Rhubarbs and providing fighter cover for bombing missions, 121 Squadron was kept busy doing convoy patrols from Kirton-in-Lindsey. The patrols were monotonous, and the weather was "stinko." Once in a while, a pilot would become lost in the overcast and would bail out of his plane when he ran out of fuel.

The "new boys" of 133 Squadron were still at Eglinton, near Londonderry, Northern Ireland. They hated the place and everything about it. The weather in Ireland was even worse than it was in England, which most Americans did not think possible. In England, at least the sun came out on special occasions. In Ireland, it never seemed to come out at all. To the Eagles, the country was a land of endless rain, cold, clouds, and gloom. An American innocently asked a local resident, "When do you get summer?"[9] The Yank was informed that summer came on May 31 and lasted from two o'clock in the afternoon until seven o'clock at night.

One pilot, lost in the fog, bailed out and came down in the Republic of Ireland. Southern Ireland was officially neutral, and the Irish government in Dublin informed the squadron that the pilot would be interned for the duration of the war. At least this was better than being stuck in a prisoner-of-war camp.

In all three squadrons, the strain from the patrols and the practices, along with just the sitting and waiting, built up pressure. The young pilots released this pressure in a variety of ways, most of which were explosive. There were brawls, out-of-control parties, partially destroyed officers' messes, and occasional gunfire, along with other less-than-constructive forms of entertainment.

Losses had hit 71 Squadron particularly hard in September, which was when Red Tobin had been killed. Because 71 was the most experienced of the three squadrons, and because they had the most opportunities for contact with the Luftwaffe, both 121 and 133 squadrons were ordered to supply the senior squadron with replacements when pilots were needed. This did not at all sit well with the two junior units, in spite of orders from Fighter Command headquarters.

Rivalry between the three squadrons was still intensifying. Nobody in either 121 or 133 Squadrons was happy about sending their best men to the stuck-up glamour boys at North Weald. They felt demeaned, as though they were being used as a minor-league affiliate of the big leaguers of 71 Squadron. "P/O Miluck and P/O Stewart of this Squadron have today been posted to 71 Squadron," grumbled the logbook of 121 Squadron. "This is the fourth pilot we have had to lose for the sake of 71 Squadron."[10]

But 71 Squadron also had its own in-house rivalry. The contest between the "fair-haired clique" and those pilots who had not been admitted into their exclusive club was just as hot as ever. On at least one occasion, pilots of the inner circle became highly annoyed when some of the squadron's replacement pilots shot down several German aircraft. The fair-haired crew was not happy about their success.

This particular bit of animosity took place when seven of the squadron's senior pilots, including Gus Daymond, Oscar Coen, and Chesley Peterson, were given a week's leave at the end of September. Bad weather was predicted, and flying for the next week or so seemed unlikely, so the seven of them were given permission to go off the base. A week's rest and relaxation was considered more useful for squadron efficiency than having the pilots stay grounded at North Weald by fog and drizzle.

While the veterans were away, the new replacements continued their practice flying. They went up every day in spite of the weather, doing formation drills as well as simulating combat maneuvers. On one of their practice flights over northern France, Squadron Leader Stanley Meares spotted eighteen to twenty Messerschmitt Bf 109s. The Messerschmitts were flying in three in-line formations right underneath the Spitfires, about 3,000 feet below and climbing—in a perfect position for an attack.

The German pilots did not expect to find the RAF over France in overcast weather and had let down their guard. They certainly did not see the Spitfires attacking. S/L Meares and his wingman went after the last Bf 109 in the formation. "I closed on the rear of one of the nearest," Meares reported, "and gave him a six-second burst from dead astern. He started to pour glycol and I saw strikes all over the fuselage near the cockpit. He turned slowly to port and dived straight for the ground."[11]

The new replacements accounted for four other downed Messerschmitts in addition to S/L Meares's kill. Pilot Officer Carroll "Red" McColpin shot down two, P/Os Newton "Weak Eyes" Anderson and Ross Scarborough teamed up to shoot down another, and P/O Arthur Roscoe was credited with the squadron's fifth kill of the day.

Actually, Roscoe initially claimed only a probable. He emptied his Spitfire's 20 mm cannons into a Bf 109 and saw black smoke coming from its fuselage, but he ran out of ammunition and had to break off his attack. He did not follow the damaged fighter to see if it crashed—pilots were warned never to do this, especially when there were so many friends of the enemy around. But two other pilots saw the Messerschmitt burst into flames and crash, confirming that the fighter had been destroyed. With this confirmation, Roscoe's claim was changed from "probable" to "destroyed."

All the drills and practice flying were apparently paying off. The new pilots executed their attacks on the enemy fighters to perfection. "As we attacked, there was not a plane of ours out of formation," said one squadron member.[12] "We just beat up those [Messerschmitts] according to plan." Squadron Leader Meares was in complete agreement. "Nothing," he said, "could have gone more perfectly."

But when the squadron's senior pilots returned from their week's leave, they failed to see the perfection of the operation. As soon as Chesley Peterson, Gus Daymond, and the others heard that the replacement pilots had shot down five enemy fighters when they were away, they became absolutely livid. They resented the success that the squadron had enjoyed against the Luftwaffe in their absence, and they let everyone know about it.

The senior pilots did not object to S/L Meares's victory, though. Meares had flown with 54 Squadron during the Battle of Britain, which made him a fellow worthy. Besides, he was the squadron's commanding officer. But they were mad as hell that the four little-squirt replacements had shot down four Messerschmitts; these unworthies had apparently encroached upon their private domain. The "fair-haired clique" not only resented newcomers, but also resented any success they might have.

Gus Daymond once complained to American correspondent Quentin Reynolds about all the publicity that 71 Squadron was getting. "You know, they're going to keep flinging that bull at us until some of it sticks," he said. "They're going to keep on telling us that hero rot until we believe it ourselves."[13] Apparently, some of it did stick.

At Fighter Command headquarters, Air Marshal Sir Sholto Douglas was not happy about the various rivalries among the Eagle Squadrons. Neither was Trafford Leigh-Mallory at 11 Group headquarters. The Yanks had shown that they could be effective as fighter units, and a useful part of Fighter command, when they felt like it. The only trouble was that they seemed to spend as much time fighting each other as they spent fighting the Germans.

The Americans who joined the Royal Air Force had been under almost constant scrutiny since they arrived in England—by other RAF units, by the news media, by senior officers at Fighter Command, and by the civilian population at large. While all this was going on, the Yanks had been keeping their own eyes open as well and had a good look at the country, its people, and its customs. They were not always enchanted by what they saw.

One of the many things that came as a surprise to the American volunteers was that England was rather unlike the United States. They never really gave much thought about the differences before they arrived in the British Isles. Most of them just took it for granted that Kent and Sussex would be just like Minnesota and Kentucky and that the people who lived in the villages near their airfields would be the same as the folks back home.

Some aspects of life in Britain went over well. One British custom that the Americans appreciated was the local pub. But they found accents hard to understand, and the weather was beneath contempt. Civilians tended to be polite but distant, which took a while to get used to. In short, the Americans found Britain to be foreign.

Pilot Officer Leo Nomis had been in England for six weeks when he reported to 71 Squadron in the autumn of 1941. During his Operational Training course in Lincolnshire, Nomis had been "fascinated with the countryside and strange customs" of the area.[14] He commented on the "flat checker-board terrain," which was so unlike his native California, but he did not mention which of the strange customs he found so fascinating. When he arrived at North Weald, wearing a brand-new dress uniform, P/O Nomis was presumably taken aback by the land and customs of Essex as well.

Some found England, the country they had left America to help defend, not only strange and foreign but also alienating and depressing. Sergeant Robert S. Raymond, who had come from Kansas to join the "home troops" in Bomber Command, thought that England was "a very small country, and a very old one."[15] He also decided that he would not want to live there, since it "has neither the room nor the aptitude for expansion."

Raymond was not very impressed by the country's inhabitants. "The people are provincial and narrow-minded, self-indulgent and conservative to a degree unbelievable unless you know them intimately." According to Raymond, the basic ingredient lacking in the average Briton was Yankee get-up-and-go: "Nearly every method and thought is at variance with my own background."These opinions were just the result of keeping his eyes open, Raymond insisted; he was not "biased by any unhappy experiences."

But the item that came as a real eye-opener to Americans was the class distinction within the British military system, which was a reflection of British society in general. In the RAF, as well as in the other armed services, the officers and the enlisted men lived in separate worlds, with a barbed-wire fence separating them. No enlisted man would ever dare to invade the officers' domain. American novelist Theodore Dreiser once told an audience that "the British are horse-riding, aristocratic snobs."[16] Except for the part about horse riding, most of the Yanks in the RAF shared this opinion. Officers in the Royal Air Force may or may not have been snobs, but they certainly were extremely class-conscious.

After he received his commission in 1943, Robert Raymond found out just how class-conscious RAF officers really were. The change in his life after he became a pilot officer was striking.

The most immediate change was in his uniform. An officer's uniform was lighter, softer, and much more comfortable than the one he had worn as a sergeant pilot. But, more significantly, people who would never speak to him before decided to become sociable once he wore an officer's uniform. Raymond noticed that other officers—"the old school tie boys"—were suddenly friendly, "now that I wear the same cloth."[17]

Most of the American pilots had no concept of class distinction. There was no real barrier between officers and enlisted men in the Eagle Squadrons. The Yanks treated their ground crews like equals. They cracked jokes with them and called them by their first names or even "Hey, buddy!" This certainly came as an eye-opener to the men in the ranks. In all-British units, fitters and riggers were used to being treated with detached condescension, at best.

Such a demonstration of Yankee egalitarianism came as a source of awe, and frequent ridicule, for other RAF officers based at the same station as the Eagles. It was impossible for them to understand how anybody who held the king's commission could mix with the working class. "US officers did not belong to any sort of 'upper class,'" observed one British officer. "They were merely the best at their job."[18]

The Yanks' irritating ideas concerning class and equality also caused its share of difficulties whenever any British subjects had to deal with members of the American forces. For anyone in His Majesty's service, it was impossible to separate American officers and men by their manner and bearing. "All their ranks had identical table manners and, so far as we could tell, identical accents," Anglo-American interpreter Alistair Cooke recalled, "thereby confronting the British officers with the touchy problem of guessing social station."[19]

Since pilots and ground crews served in the same units, the Yanks saw no reason why they should not drink with the enlisted men when off duty. This was not only frowned upon by British officers, but also thought to be nothing less than subversive, if not downright immoral. Being friends with a rigger or a fitter while on the base was one thing, but drinking with him after hours was against all the known rules of civilized conduct.

The Americans, needless to say, did not see it that way at all. The pilots of 71 Squadron discovered a friendly local pub in Saffron Walden, near their base at Debden, and began to frequent the place. They very quickly discovered that it was an "officers only" bar. As soon as they found out, they stopped going there. One of the squadron's mechanics remembered that "the Eagles would not drink there when they found they could not drink with their ground crews."[20] The reaction of the pub keeper to this bit of democratic equality is not on record—which is just as well, since it was probably unprintable.

The enlisted ground crews were just as puzzled by this brand-new democracy, but they loved it. No officer had ever treated them with so much respect before. And they returned the compliment. One of the British crewmen recalled that the camaraderie between the pilots and the ground crew was much greater than it was in other squadrons.

The official historian of 71 Squadron made the same observation. Whenever an Eagle Squadron pilot came in to land "the ground crews, every damned one of them—fitter, armourer, rigger—would race across the field to ask the pilots what had happened, then hang on the wing tips as they themselves guided the planes to their assigned places."[21] When other units landed, they would only watch and wave from a distance. The British officers just shook their heads. These Yanks certainly were an odd bunch.

Even though they fought against the same enemy, wore the same uniform, and even flew the same kind of airplane, the British and the Americans clearly did not understand each other. Any number of British ways struck the young Americans as strange—a reverence for antiquity and the preservation of ancient monuments and ancient traditions were squarely at odds with the American notion of "progress." Still, the rigid social barriers that kept a person firmly "within his class" were the most foreign thing that Americans found in Britain, and the thousands of US servicemen who followed the Eagles, American soldiers who came to Britain between 1942 and 1945, made the same discovery.

After the war, British social barriers began to break down, and the classes became more equal. Members of the upper class blamed the Americans. They claimed that the Yanks, the two million Americans who had been stationed in Britain during the war, were responsible for this revolution—they gave the masses ideas about rising above their social station. There was probably more than just a hint of truth in this accusation, and the Yanks would have been glad to admit it.

✮✮✮ CHAPTER SEVEN ✮✮✮

NO MORE BLOODY YANKS!

he Air Ministry received yet another surprise (this time a pleasant one) from the American volunteers in the late autumn of 1941. In November, 71 (Eagle) Squadron was named the highest-scoring unit in RAF Fighter Command for the second month in a row. The senior officers at the Air Ministry in London were forced to agree with the senior Eagle Squadron and admitted that 71 Squadron was the best, at least for the time being.

Another important event also took place in November: Chesley "Pete" Peterson became the commander of 71 Squadron when S/L Stanley Meares was killed in a flying accident. This marked the first time that the squadron was truly all-American, with an American commander, since Bill Taylor left in June.

During a training flight on November 15, Meares's plane collided with a Spitfire flown by P/O Ross Scarborough. Meares's Spitfire "burst into flames."[1] Both fighters crashed; both pilots were killed. To make the accident even more bizarre, one of the crippled planes hit a Spitfire from another squadron as it fell to earth.

With Meares's death, Flight Lieutenant Peterson became acting squadron leader. A short time later the appointment became permanent, and Peterson was officially promoted to the rank of squadron leader (the US equivalent would be major). He was twenty-one years old.

Originally, Peterson wanted to be a pilot in the US Army Air Corps. He dropped out of Brigham Young University at the end of his second year, when he was nineteen years old. Nineteen was too young for the Air Corps, so Peterson gave his age as twenty-one. But the Air Corps checked up on him. When they discovered his true age, they washed Peterson out of the service. The reason given was "inherent lack of flying ability"[2]— sympathetic officers thought this would look better on his record than "falsified birth records."

Wing Commander Miles Duke-Woolley, a regular RAF officer who flew briefly with 71 Squadron, called S/L Peterson a first-rate commander, "as good as any of them." He noted that Peterson's main concern was for the well-being of the squadron. He was good at his job, despite having to deal with all of the paperwork and "official correspondence" from the Air Ministry bureaucrats—which usually consisted of filling out endless forms and writing never-ending reports.

On one occasion, Pilot Officer Bob Sprague brought his Spitfire back to base badly shot up after a flight over the Continent. Some high-ranking officer in London thought that the battle damage was excessive and demanded a "detailed report" on what Sprague was doing and how he managed to get his fighter damaged in such a manner. So S/L Peterson obliged with this:

Sir: On yesterday afternoon Pilot Officer Sprague saw that the sun was shining brightly and that there were few clouds in the sky. The beauty of the day caused him and two of his friends to set off for a jaunt over territory usually inhabited by the French, who undoubtedly would have received him most cordially; but the present inhabitants, seeing Pilot Officer Sprague and his friends flying around and enjoying themselves, did not appear to be of a friendly disposition, and such was their dislike that a number of heavily armed fighter planes, marked with swastikas and black crosses, rudely and ungenerously assaulted Pilot Officer Sprague and blew a large hold in his tail, his wings, and the fuselage near his head, which action on their part almost lost Pilot Officer Sprague his life, and caused me the inconvenience of writing this useless bumpf to you.[3]

The report was duly filed and forgotten. (For the uninitiated, "bumpf," also known as "bum fodder" and "bum wad," is a cheap grade of toilet paper.)

While all this was going on, the other two Eagle Squadrons were having troubles of their own. At Eglinton, in Northern Ireland, 133 Squadron were still flying monotonous convoy patrols. The squadron's primary fighter was still the Hawker Hurricane, although they had also inherited a few Spitfire Mark IIs. The Spits were flyable, but were a long way from being in first-class condition. In short, the third Eagle Squadron was feeling bored and dispirited. There were rumors that the squadron might be transferred to England, where they would be issued more modern airplanes. But, as usual, the rumors turned out to be so much hot air.

On the same day that Stanley Meares was killed, two pilots of 121 Squadron, P/Os John Brown and Malta Stepp, attacked what appeared to be a Junkers Ju 88 near York.[4] The airplane turned out to be an RAF Bristol Blenheim, which was also a twin-engined plane. The Blenheim's pilot bailed out, but the rear gunner was killed.

Both pilots from 121 Squadron insisted that they had shot down a Ju 88 and argued that the Blenheim must have been brought down by enemy action, but there had been no reports of "enemy action" anywhere near York on the day in question. Also, no Junkers was found. But the remains of the Blenheim were discovered close by the site where the two Eagles shot down their quarry. The Blenheim pilot was not much help; he claimed that he never saw his attackers and had no idea that he had been jumped until his airplane was on fire.

In spite of these incidents, along with bleak morale and even bleaker weather, the men of all three Eagle Squadrons were brimming with confidence. The three squadrons were operational, although none had seen much enemy action recently, and everybody was overflowing with faith in their own flying ability. A few pilots from Texas even approached the Air Ministry with a brand-new idea: How about forming a fourth Eagle Squadron, a Lone Star Squadron, made up entirely of pilots from their own state?

When Air Marshal Sir Sholto Douglas heard that one, he probably turned bright red and cursed out loud. Among the British, Texans had the reputation of being even wilder and more unruly than the average US citizen. American writer Clare Boothe Luce recalled an occasion when she heard some British airmen making nasty cracks about Americans. Luce listened to the diatribe for a while, but the longer she listened, the angrier she became. Finally, she turned on the Brits with a rant of her own.

"What have the Americans ever done that the British don't do?" she demanded. "Don't generalize. Be specific. Why don't you like Americans?"[5]

The RAF boys were stunned by this sudden and unexpected offensive. After an embarrassed silence, one of the lads stammered, "Well, as a matter of fact . . . it isn't really the Americans that are bad, it's just those bloody Texans who are so insufferable."

No senior RAF officer wanted anything to do with a fourth Eagle Squadron, from Texas or anywhere else in the United States. Remembering all the problems—the rivalries between the three squadrons, as well as within 71 Squadron alone; the lacking of all discipline, especially during the early days; the wild conduct that broke out with irritating regularity—the Air Ministry turned down the idea, rudely and abruptly. "Hell no. No more bloody American squadrons!"[6]

Ironically, the Air Ministry could have had another all-American squadron without any objections from Washington, DC. In the middle of November, Congress officially repealed the last of the Neutrality Acts. It was no longer against the law for an American citizen to join the Royal Air Force. But even though they could now recruit American pilots without any legal objections from the US Government, the Air Ministry still had no interest in forming a fourth Eagle Squadron.

Repealing the last Neutrality Act did not make much of an impression with the British public, either. British opinion of the United States had hit its high-water mark in March when Lend-Lease was signed into law. But since June, resentment over American nonintervention had deepened. The way Britain saw it, they were fighting for their lives but the complacent Americans were doing as little as possible to help them.

Much of this resentment was based upon ignorance. The United States was actually doing as much to help Britain as its neutrality would allow. They may have been officially neutral, but the US was far from being uninvolved. It was just that most of their activities were carried out in secret, and the British man-in-the-street knew nothing about them. The Army Air Corps, for instance, sent shipments of military aircraft to England, including the Boeing B-17 Flying Fortress. American intelligence was supplying London with information it had acquired from breaking the Japanese code. There were also one thousand Americans in Northern Ireland building naval and air bases.

A fairly typical reaction to American activities took place in August 1941 after the first meeting between President Franklin D. Roosevelt and Prime Minister Winston Churchill. The meeting, which occurred off the coast of Newfoundland aboard the battleship HMS *Prince of Wales*, had been anticipated as a new breakthrough in American participation. Britain was hoping for something dramatic, maybe even a declaration of war against Germany. Instead, they got the Atlantic Charter, which was a joint statement of Anglo-American war aims.

Every newspaper in Britain expressed bitter disappointment. Editors were not exactly sure what they expected from the Roosevelt-Churchill meeting, but they certainly were hoping for a lot more than just another load of American rhetoric.

Americans tended to think of the Atlantic Charter as a noble endorsement of the Rights of Man, addressing such issues as "Freedom from Want." But the British viewed the Charter as nothing more than an empty gesture made up of so many empty words. The editor of the *Times* gave a fairly concise reaction:

> The flood is raging and we are breasting it in an effort to save civilisation. America throws a line to us, and will give us dry clothes if we reach shore. . . . We are frankly disappointed with the American contribution to the rescue.[7]

The three Eagle Squadrons were not mentioned in the editorial and probably were not even thought of by the person who wrote the piece. They were most likely considered too insignificant to mention. Britain wanted more than just thirty-odd American pilots from the United States, a lot more.

★ ★ ★

After the United States entered the war, and over two million American servicemen were stationed in the British Isles, the standard wisecrack about the Yanks was, "They're over paid, oversexed, and over here." The American volunteers in the RAF may or may not have been oversexed (the judgment depends upon which nationality, as well as which sex, is giving their opinion). However, 71 Squadron's medical officer, who was in a unique position to observe, did remark that the men in his squadron "were rather enthusiastic in their search for feminine companionship,"[8] and that they "undoubtedly did more lovemaking than the English pilots." The MO also observed that there was "more womanizing" among the pilots of 71 Squadron than he had ever seen anywhere else.

They Eagles argued that they had a very good reason for this enthusiasm. One of their excuses—if an excuse was needed—was that any

American in Britain was thousands of miles away from his sweetheart, which gave him more of an appetite for sex than the British pilots. In other words, if absence makes the heart grow fonder, then abstinence makes the urge grow stronger.

The Eagles also explained that whenever the British pilots had the urge, they could always go home to renew old acquaintances. But since the Americans had to start every relationship from scratch, and were pressed by the urgencies of war, they felt that they had to move more quickly than their British counterparts. Which is why, they said, they went about pursuing girls with so much energy and drive. Or, as their British girlfriends would have put it, with "typical Yankee hustle." (British men would have had a much less polite phrase.)

In spite of all the explanations, Americans still had a reputation of being preoccupied with sex. One Briton (male) said that the popular myth was that "all Yanks were either near-rapists or irresistibly skilled seducers."[9] They also acquired a reputation—well founded, in many instances—for being cocky and conceited.

A London woman said that the Americans were all damn Yankees with a line a mile long. They were full of vanity and conceit and self-importance. But they all fell in love with them anyway. She should know—she wound up eloping with an American airman.

Conceit, smugness, and arrogance were considered "typical Yankee" traits and were no small source of irritation. "They tended to take some things for granted," said one woman. "It took them a little while to get used to the fact that you didn't just drop everything if they asked you out."[10]

Some Americans fell in love with and married the girls they met in England. Only a short time before his death, Andy Mamedoff married Penny Craven, a member of the cigarette dynasty. Chesley Peterson and Audrey Boyes, an actress born in South Africa, were also married. There were a number of other Anglo-American weddings, as well, but these tended to be the exception, not the rule.

William R. Dunn came to the Eagle Squadrons by way of the army—he went to Canada in 1939 and volunteered for the Seaforth Highlanders. When the Air Ministry invited pilots with more than 500 hours of flying time to transfer to the RAF, Dunn applied as a fighter pilot and was accepted. In 1968, he was given official credit for being the first American ace of the Second World War. (Courtesy of the National Museum of the United States Air Force®.)

Although the pilots were frequently in and out of love, they seldom married English girls. Most had girls back home. Bob Raymond, the Kansas native who flew with Bomber Command, kept up a steady correspondence with his girl, Betty, all throughout his time in the RAF. The letters helped keep their relationship intact during their long separation. When Raymond returned to Kansas, after he transferred to the US Army Air Force, he and Betty were married.

Pilot Vic France, who flew with 71 Squadron, was probably a lot more typical of the "enthusiastic" Yanks. He had the reputation for spreading his charm far and wide, according to one of his friends. His impressive number of kills often had nothing to do with enemy aircraft. After he was shot down and killed, one of his girlfriends said that if he wound up in heaven, the angels had better watch out.

Within a couple of years, just about every corner of the British Isles would have their share of Americans, and the Britons would get to know the Yanks and their ways. But this would be in a different phase of the war. The three Eagle Squadrons were only a preview of things to come.

★ ★ ★

After the novelty of an all-American fighter squadron in the RAF, or even three, had worn off, the Eagle Squadrons still continued to attract publicity. At the end of November, a group of American reporters and photographers descended upon 121 Squadron at Kirton-in-Lindsey. The other two squadrons continued to have their fill of press visitations, as well.

The Eagles usually gave the impression that all the press and media attention did not matter and laughed off all the publicity. But it was having an effect on the pilots, whether they admitted it or not, and was one of the main reasons for the rivalry between the three squadrons. Each resented the other's press exposure.

By the end of 1941, however, newspaper and magazine articles were no longer as frequent and numerous as they had been a year before. Still, news items about the Eagles remained popular on both sides of the Atlantic, and newsmen still managed to get their facts all wrong on a regular basis; exaggerating claims of enemy aircraft shot down was a frequent shortcoming. An American reporter gave one pilot the rank of "squadron commander," never bothering to find out that there is no such rank in the RAF.

Hollywood even made a film about the Eagles and called it *Eagle Squadron*. The people who made the film did even better than the news reporters—they did not bother using any facts at all. *Eagle Squadron* was actually nothing more than a grade-B adventure film. Most film critics said that it was a substandard war film which tended to be awkwardly overemotional about English courage and American determination. It was such a bad film that it actually managed to embarrass some of the Eagle Squadron pilots, which was quite an achievement.

When the film was released in England, the three squadrons were officially invited to London to attend the opening. The men had been led to believe that it would be a documentary, or at least a semi-documentary. It started out respectably enough, with well-known reporter and war correspondent Quentin Reynolds delivering a prologue about the Eagle Squadrons. Reynolds had actually written about 71 Squadron and mentioned Red Tobin in his book *Only the Stars Are Neutral*. There was also some actual footage of 71 Squadron, which was probably the highlight of the film. But most of the movie, which starred Robert Stack and Diana Barrymore, was "bloody awful," in the words of Bill Dunn. "The plot was all BS; to be frank, it stunk to high heaven."[11]

Dunn was actually being diplomatic. The other Eagles were a lot more emphatic, and demonstrative, when it came to showing their opinion. They simply got up and walked out, in twos and threes, while the film was still running. When the movie ended and the lights came up, the Eagles' two rows of seats were empty. The attending VIPs, along with the film's producer, Walter Wanger, were not happy.

After walking out of the cinema, most of the pilots gathered at the Crackers Club for a few drinks. Most of them were still at it when morning came. By this time, some were too hungover to drink. They were also too hungover to fly, even though both 121 and 133 Squadrons were called to do a "rush show"—escorting two bomber formations back from a raid on Abbeville. Luckily for the pilots of 71 Squadron, they were not required to go on the escort mission.

The "show" began at 10:00 a.m. The pilots breathed oxygen to help get them over their hangovers and hoped that the Luftwaffe would stay on the ground that day. But, as was their habit, the Luftwaffe chose not to cooperate. The German pilots came up in force and gave the hungover Eagles a mauling.

Despite not being at their best that morning, the Eagles were credited with three German aircraft destroyed, as well as one "probable." Still, both squadrons suffered losses: 133 Squadron had three of its pilots killed and another badly injured; 121 Squadron lost one pilot, as well as its commanding officer through injuries. Squadron Leader Hugh Kennard was so badly wounded, as the result of both enemy cannon fire and the crash of his Spitfire, that he had to be relieved of his command.[12]

Nobody at the Air Ministry, including Sir Sholto Douglas, received word of why the Eagles' standard of flying was so bad that day. If the truth had been known—that the Yanks had got themselves badly shot up because they had been out drinking the night before—the reaction would have been anger, but not surprise. In the air, the Americans were just three average RAF fighter squadrons, neither outstanding nor awful. But why, Douglas often must have wondered, did they always seem to behave like lunatic cowboys when they were on the ground?

★★★ CHAPTER EIGHT ★★★

BELLIGERENT ALLIES

The Americans who volunteered to uproot their lives and leave home to join the Royal Air Force were subject to a wide range of reactions both in Britain and in the United States. Young men in their late teens and early twenties envied them. The public at large was curious about them. Most members of the isolationist group America First resented them. To the press and the news media on both sides of the Atlantic, the Yanks in the RAF had become just another story by this time, like a political campaign or an earthquake.

In Germany, the American volunteers were considered more than just oddities or topics of conversation. They were certainly very strange men. It was very difficult to understand why an American would want to fight for the British, especially considering the hostile past shared by Britain and the United States. Nobody could figure out why they would want to get involved in somebody else's war.

A captured German flyer was incredulous when he found out that Pilot Officer Byron Kennerly was American. "You mean you are going to fight for the fun of it?" the German laughed in amazement.[1]

Whenever an American was shot down over German-occupied France and taken prisoner, he presented a very thorny diplomatic problem. As a US citizen, he was a neutral and a nonbelligerent, and was to be afforded every consideration. But as a pilot wearing the blue uniform of the Royal Air Force, he was also an enemy of the Third Reich.

By the autumn of 1941, a handful of Yank fliers had fallen into German hands—including three members of the Eagle Squadrons. These Americans were kept in prisoner-of-war compounds, but were given treatment by their captors that can only be described as extraordinary.[2] German guards went out of their way to be as considerate as possible toward their American charges. As a special privilege, the Yanks were escorted outside the prison-camp grounds every day and treated to a picnic lunch—which they ate while being watched by armed German guards. The reaction of the other prisoners—or of the German guards—to this kid-glove treatment has never been made known. The Americans certainly could not believe what was happening. They couldn't figure out what was going on, but they decided to enjoy it as long as it lasted.

At the end of November, the American prisoners were given some insight into the situation. A German officer called them all into a room and made a proposal—if they agreed to go along with his offer, they would be sent to Argentina by German U-boat. When they arrived in Argentina, German agents would escort them to the US embassy in Buenos Aires. From there, they would be free to return to the United States as soon as arrangements could be made. All the German authorities wanted in return was for the Americans to tell everyone how well they had been treated when they got back home.

The entire scheme, picnic lunches and all, had been part of a gesture to placate both the American public and the US government, neither of which had been very friendly of late. The idea was to persuade the Americans that Germany bore them no ill will—even when American citizens took up arms against the Reich—and that the Nazis were not such a bad lot of fellows after all.

It was a tempting offer. No one was wild about the prospect of spending the next couple of years in a prisoner-of-war camp. The Americans debated whether or not they should accept it. They were anxious to get back home, but did not particularly like the notion of playing an active role in a German propaganda scheme. They did not have to contemplate for very long, however. At the beginning of December 1941, events on the other side of the world took the decision out of their hands.

★ ★ ★

First reports of the Japanese air attack on the US naval base at Pearl Harbor reached the British Isles on the evening of December 7. It did not take long for the importance of the event to sink in. It meant that the United States, with all of its money and resources, had finally come into the war on Britain's side.

The British public had been hoping for something like this for a year and a half, ever since the British army had been evacuated from the beaches at Dunkirk in June 1940. Still, the news of the Pearl Harbor attack did not trigger any widespread rejoicing. The most common reaction was grim satisfaction—the complacent Americans were finally going to feel the brunt of war at long last.

Harold Nicolson, a former member of Parliament, wrote to his wife that the news of Pearl Harbor was not welcomed in Britain with any kind of fanfare or celebration, which he thought was very strange. He did not see a single American flag flying in the whole of London. Many others throughout Britain also remarked about the coolness shown toward their country's new partners in war, but usually with a good deal less amazement and restraint than Harold Nicolson.

Pearl Harbor brought out all of the pent up anger with Americans for not coming to Britain's aid sooner. A doctor's wife predicted that the Yanks would run in panic after being subject to a few air raids. Another woman's view was that the Japanese should have bombed New York instead of Hawaii and its peaceful natives. (Women, much more than men, seemed to have been particularly vehement in their feelings about the United States.)

The United States and Britain were now "belligerent allies," meaning that the US was now an ally that would fight alongside Britain throughout the hostilities. But as the war went on, he phrase would take on a double meaning. The alliance between Britain and the United States would often become belligerent, quarrelsome, and confrontational, as the two sides would soon find out.

Winston Churchill said that he was overcome with joy at the news of Pearl Harbor and that he knew that Britain would win the war now that the United States was on her side. Many of his countrymen, however, did not share his enthusiasm. Shortly after the Pearl Harbor attack, an opinion poll revealed that many were afraid that America would cut back in sending weapons and supplies to Britain and fearful that the Americans would become preoccupied with Japan. Britain would support the United States and declared war against Japan, but it looked as though the Americans would not be helping Britain in her war against Germany.

The fear that America would be absorbed in a war with Japan did have some foundation. The Pearl Harbor attack galvanized the United States into action, but not against Germany. In his famous "Day of Infamy" speech, President Franklin D. Roosevelt asked Congress to declare war against the Empire of Japan, but there was no mention of Germany at all. On Monday, December 8, 1941, the United States and Germany were still at peace.

In spite of Winston Churchill's relief over American involvement, there was actually a good deal of worry in London about America's position regarding Germany. But there was nothing that Churchill or anybody else could do. The next move would be up to Adolf Hitler.

At that point in time, Hitler did not know what he wanted to do. The attack on Pearl Harbor was as much of a surprise to him as it was to the Americans. His generals advised him to remain at peace with the United States—Germany already had its hands full with the British in the west and the Russians in the east. It was true that American destroyers had attacked U-boats and that there were Americans in the British armed forces. But, the argument continued, the U-boat incidents had only been sporadic, and the number of Americans in the British forces only amounted to a handful. It would be better to leave the Americans out of it, Hitler's advisors warned. After all, Pearl Harbor had nothing to do with Germany.

But Hitler reminded his generals of the Tripartite Agreement, which bound Japan, Italy, and Germany together in the "Pact of Steel." His advisors were well aware of the Tripartite Agreement, but they explained to Hitler that the pact had no bearing in this instance. The agreement stated that Germany was bound to come to Japan's aid if Japan had been attacked by another power. However, since Japan had attacked the United States, not the other way around, Germany was under no obligation to come to Japan's assistance.

The discussion went on for four days. On Thursday, December 11, Hitler finally gave his reasons for wanting to declare war on the United States—by attacking German U-boats, and by allowing its citizens to join the Royal Air Force (Hitler had apparently never heard of the Neutrality Acts), the United States and Germany were already at war.

"They have been a forceful factor in this war," Hitler said about the United States, "and through their actions had already created a situation of war."[3] In his own view, the Americans had already gone to war against Germany. Now, he was going to get even. This means that all of the American volunteers—from Jimmy Davies to Red Tobin to the latest member of the three Eagle Squadrons—had more of an effect upon the war than they ever could have guessed.

Hitler formally declared war on the United States on December 11, four days after Pearl Harbor. Congress reciprocated by declaring war that same day. With his declaration, Hitler had simplified matters for both Winston Churchill and Franklin D. Roosevelt—Roosevelt wanted to take formal action against Berlin, but could not do anything unless Hitler acted first. Dean Acheson, who would one day be US secretary of state, thought Hitler was an absolute fool for declaring war and that he played right into the hands of the allies.

"At last," Acheson wrote, "our enemies, with unparalleled stupidity, resolved our dilemmas, clarified our doubts and uncertainties, and united our people for the long, hard course that the national interest required."[4]

The Pearl Harbor attack did not have any immediate effect upon the Americans in the RAF, including the members of the Eagle Squadrons. The pilots thought that America's entry into the war would instantly change their lives, as well as their careers with the Royal Air Force. But it had no impact at all, at least not at first.

After the initial shock of the attack wore off, the pilots of all three Eagle Squadrons wanted to transfer to the US Army Air Force as soon as possible. The two England-based squadrons, 71 Squadron and 121 Squadron (133 Squadron was still stationed at Eglinton in Northern Ireland), even forgot their mutual animosity long enough to send emissaries to visit the American ambassador in London.

The American ambassador, John G. Winant, spoke with the Eagle Squadron representatives and discussed their transfer to the American forces. Ambassador Winant also telephoned President Franklin D. Roosevelt in their presence and relayed their offer to serve in the US Fighter Command. The best that the president could do, however, was to promise to transfer the Eagle Squadrons to the US Army Air Force as soon as possible.

Leo Nomis of 71 Squadron recalls, "there were rumors that we would be immediately transferred to US command."[5] But all the talk turned out to be "laughably premature." The American forces were not even close to being ready for operations in the European Theatre of Operations and would not be for some months.[5]

The United States was completely unprepared for the war in which it suddenly found itself. Much of the equipment used by the air force was obsolete. There was no American fighter that could hope to compete with, or survive against, the Messerschmitt 109, and there was no "US Fighter Command" into which the Eagle Squadrons could be transferred. The Eagles would have to wait.

★ ★ ★

During the winter months, the weather in the British Isles is not exactly tailor-made for flying. Rain, sleet, snow, and fog sometimes kept all aircraft grounded for days on end. During the winter of 1941–1942, the exploits of the three Eagle Squadrons were, according to Leo Nomis, "forgivably unillustrious."[6] The weather not only grounded the RAF, but also kept the Luftwaffe out of the air.

Not that every day was dull and uneventful. On New Year's Eve, 133 Squadron finally received its long-wished-for posting to an airfield in England, and the squadron flew from Northern Ireland to Kirton-in-Lindsey. Typically for that winter, the unit's Spitfires landed in the middle of a snowstorm. Its first day's operations consisted of shoveling snow off the landing field. But in spite of the snow, everyone was glad to finally be stationed in England. It was better than being buried alive in the heart of darkest Northern Ireland, the land of endless fog and mist.

The station commander at Kirton was not overjoyed at the prospect of having yet another lot of screwy Yanks thrust upon him. The poor fellow could hardly be blamed for this attitude; he had already had his nerve endings unraveled by both 71 Squadron and 121 Squadron. Several colorful events from his past associations with the Eagles must have stuck in his mind. Like the time the playful pilots of 121 Squadron decided to turn on all the bathtub taps and flood the officers' mess. Or when 71 Squadron pilots played a game of indoor football, using a soda siphon for a ball, and wrecked all the furniture. The new arrivals of

133 Squadron were warned not to repeat any of these charming boyish pranks.

When 133 Squadron posted to Kirton, 121 Squadron was moved from Kirton to North Weald. This was greeted with wild enthusiasm. They were now part of 11 Group, the "hot group," and were within striking distance of the German airfields across the Channel. Fog put a stop to most operations in December, but everyone hoped that the weather would improve eventually.

In December, 71 Squadron moved, as well—from North Weald to the small airfield at Martlesham Heath in Suffolk. Originally, the squadron was supposed to have been sent off to Kirton-in-Lindsey to join 133 Squadron, but none of the pilots liked that idea. So S/L Chesley Peterson went to see Fighter Command Chief Sir Sholto Douglas to complain about being banished to the wilds of Lincolnshire.

Air Marshal Douglas intervened on 71 Squadron's behalf and kept the unit from being moved out of 11 Group. This made the pilots happy, but provoked the displeasure of Air Vice-Marshal Trafford Leigh-Mallory, the commander of 11 Group. Leigh-Mallory had never been on friendly terms with the Eagles, not from their earliest days of existence in the autumn of 1940. Now he had something else to hold against them—S/L Peterson had gone outside channels by going over his head to see Sholto Douglas.

This was not the first time Peterson had been in touch with Air Marshal Douglas. Peterson had also approached Douglas shortly after Pearl Harbor, but at that time he was requesting a transfer, not protesting one. Peterson had suggested that 71 Squadron be sent to Singapore, "since what we really want to do is fight the Japanese."[7] The Air Marshal was not impressed with Peterson's arguments. He said that he would not waste a squadron on Singapore, since the city would not be able to hold out for more than six weeks. (Singapore surrendered to Japanese troops on February 15, 1942.)

Although the weather in the United Kingdom was usually not fit for flying, it sometimes did clear long enough for an occasional low-level strafing attack or fighter sweep. On one such Rhubarb mission, near Cap Gris Nez, two of 71 Squadron's pilots were attacked by three unfamiliar German fighters. The fighters turned out to be Focke-Wulf FW 190s, which would be appearing with increasing frequency during the coming months.

Chesley G. "Pete" Peterson (far right) and Gregory A. "Gus" Daymond (standing next to Peterson), along with other Eagle Squadron pilots. Peterson was a Mormon from Utah, and Daymond had been a Hollywood makeup man before the war. Both would eventually be promoted to the rank of squadron leader. (Courtesy of the National Museum of the United States Air Force®.)

The Focke-Wulf was probably the Luftwaffe's best piston-engine fighter of the war. It featured a radial engine and was armed with a 20 mm cannon. It was maneuverable and fast—faster than the Messerschmitt 109—and heavily armed. Some pilots, on both sides, claimed that the FW 190 did not have any weak points at all and that its only limitations were the ones brought by the pilots themselves.

The two 71 Squadron pilots did their best to escape the three strange German fighters, heading back to England underneath the snow clouds, but the Focke-Wulfs stayed right with them. The Spitfires and FWs darted in and out of the clouds, trying to gain the advantage. Eventually, one of the German pilots made a tactical mistake, which allowed one of the Eagle pilots to turn on him and fire a burst of cannon and machine-gun fire. This short burst apparently killed the pilot. The Focke-Wulf did not smoke or catch fire; it just rolled over and dove right into the Channel. After that, the other two Germans kept a respectable distance, allowing the Spitfires to return to Martlesham Heath.

During this dismal winter, the Luftwaffe also went out looking for trouble whenever the opportunity presented itself. Sometimes they livened up a dull convoy patrol for the Eagles. At the end of February 1942, Pilot Officers John Lynch and Leo Nomis intercepted a Junkers Ju 88 that was making a hit-and-run attack on a convoy off the Suffolk coast.[8] "P/O Lynch . . . saw a Ju 88," according to 71 Squadron's logbook, "and he and his No. 2, P/O Nomis, gave chase. The 88 gunner got in a burst, which caused P/O Lynch . . . to give up the chase and make for base." The rear gunner was a good shot. He hit Lynch's Spitfire several times. Lynch was forced to crash-land and suffered injuries.

Nomis's Spitfire was also hit, but not seriously enough to make him break off his attack. He kept at the Ju 88, firing short bursts until he ran out of ammunition. Nomis thought that the bomber "evidently crashed into the North Sea." An observer on one of the convoy's escort vessels confirmed Nomis's suspicions.

★ ★ ★

To nonaviators, pilots are an odd lot. And fighter pilots are the oddest of all, even to other pilots. The fighter pilots themselves would probably say that they were aggressive and alert, which they had to be if they hoped to survive against the enemy. But to non-fighter pilots, they seemed highly strung, nervous, and irritable.

"They ate lightly as a class and couldn't sleep at night," according to one observer.[9] "Sometimes they got so tired they wanted to cry. Their nerves became tatters." They also developed nervous tics like biting their fingernails right down to the quick or exploding in anger at the slightest provocation. "One pilot would sit at the table and bend the knives and forks double."

Luftwaffe ace Adolf Galland thought that the essential elements that made up a first-rate fighter pilot were excellent eyesight, quick reactions, great self-confidence, and good shooting. Another attribute was the ability to withstand the strain of single combat, alone, in a machine several thousand feet above the earth.

"They lived under great pressure," said one writer, "which each man had to endure as well as he could, and by himself. He occupied his aircraft alone; there was only his airplane, the sky and the occasional comfort of his squadron mates nearby, hidden in their machines. On the ground, they relieved the pressure in expectable ways."

Despite the notion that all Americans were wild cowboys at heart, American fighter pilots were probably no worse than their British counterparts when it came to relieving tension. "Every evening was cause for a celebration, because you had succeeded in living through the day, and the celebrations were generally loud and alcoholic." This went for *all* fighter squadrons. British squadrons also got drunk and broke up the furniture in the officers' mess (so did Belgian, Polish, Canadian, and French squadrons).

But it took a lot more than just the ability to withstand stress and strain to be a fighter pilot. Successful fighter pilots—that is to say, the ones who managed to survive in combat—needed many other qualities, as well. Besides the attributes mentioned by Adolf Galland, there was also the matter of what actors might call "technique." Every pilot has his own ideas of how to get to the enemy before the enemy has the chance to get to him, ideas that have been discussed over and over again in bars and reunions throughout the world. Some of these techniques have been set down in what have been called the "Ten Commandments for Fighter Pilots."

Veteran pilots have said that these "ten commandments" might not save your life, but ignoring them will damn well end it in a hurry. These ten rules were posted in the ready rooms of fighter squadrons in just about every RAF station:

1. Never fly straight and level for more than 30 seconds in a combat area.
2. Always keep a sharp look-out for enemy fighters. Keep your finger out and your head on a swivel. Watch for the enemy in the sun.
3. Height gives you the initiative. Don't waste it.
4. Always turn and face the attacking enemy.
5. Make your decisions promptly. It is better to act quickly, even though your tactics are not the best.
6. When diving to the attack, always leave part of your formation above to act as top cover.
7. Wait until you see the whites of your enemy's eyes. Fire short bursts of one or two seconds, and only fire when your gunsight is definitely on the target.
8. While shooting, think of nothing else. Brace the whole of your body, keep both hands on the control stick, and concentrate on your gunsight and on your target.
9. Go in quickly—punch hard—and get out.
10. Initiative, aggression, air discipline, and teamwork are words that mean something in air fighting.[10]

Knowing how to shoot was also a quality that meant something in aerial combat. The Spitfire's reflector gunsight was accurate enough for targets that were dead ahead, but the pilot still had to use his own judgment when shooting at a target that was passing from right to left (or left to right). He had to estimate his deflection, or "lead" his target, in his head. Deflection shooting was a skill that took time to learn and was a difficult accomplishment, in spite of improvements in gunsights. Excellent shots, including Adolf Galland, could hit their target from any angle of attack.

An enemy airplane approaching from ahead, closing in at speeds of 300 miles per hour, would only remain within machine gun range for about a second. This meant that the attacking pilot had to clear his tail, calculate his deflection, turn into position, and get in a good burst in a lot less time than it takes to tell about it. Learning this trick required good eyesight and the ability to concentrate, as well as a great deal of practice.

Rookie pilots had the habit of opening fire while they were still too far away from the enemy. The .303 machine gun was only effective at ranges of about 100 yards or less. Inexperienced pilots sometimes started shooting at ranges in excess of 400 yards, which resulted in a lot of wasted ammunition and nothing to show for it. Patience, and the ability to close to within realistic firing range, also came with practice and experience.

When everything went right, and the pilot closed to within shooting range, the Spitfire's eight .303 machine guns were able to take their toll on the enemy ahead. The guns could literally tear the plane to pieces. "Soon, big pieces start coming out of him," wrote a pilot from 133 Squadron.[11] "It's nuts and bolts stuff at first, then bigger things, big, ripped-off looking things as if you're tearing arms and legs off him . . ."

However, because the .303 was a light rifle-caliber bullet, the same as used by the army for its Enfield rifles, it took a lot of bullets to knock down an enemy aircraft. German aircraft, fighters as well as bombers, were well protected by armor. They could absorb a lot of punishment and still stay in the air. Peter Townsend of 85 Squadron fired two hundred .303 bullets into a Dornier Do 17, but the bomber managed to get away and fly back to base. And six Spitfires of 74 Squadron fired a combination of seven thousand rounds at a single Do 17 and did not bring it down.

Closing to within point-blank range was only one of many skills needed to be a successful fighter pilot. Others included: knowing how to lead a target and set up a deflection shot; knowing how to break away from an attacking enemy fighter; and knowing both the weak points and the strong points of the Messerschmitt 109 and the Focke-Wulf 190. There were dozens of details that could literally mean the difference between life and death. Without the training needed to perfect the techniques for fighter combat, even the most skilled pilot would not live long enough to bring his talents to bear.

★ ★ ★

Nobody had any idea when the first US Army Air Force pilots would be arriving. Pearl Harbor had only been a few weeks before. American forces had been fighting in the Pacific, but the news had been all bad—Japanese troops had overwhelmed garrisons on Wake Island and Guam, and the Philippine Islands were in danger of sharing the same fate. (The Philippines would surrender in April.)

It did not seem as though American forces had been very well prepared to go to war against Japan. And if they were not ready to fight the Japanese, they would probably not be ready to fight the Germans, either. Newly arrived pilots from the States would be in dire need of practical advice about the enemy when they reached England. They would likely need a lot of additional training, as well, to learn how to survive against the Luftwaffe.

The American volunteers in the RAF—not just those of the three Eagle Squadrons, but also the individual Yanks sprinkled throughout Fighter Command, as well as Bomber Command and Coastal Command—had the sinking feeling that it would be their job to educate their fellow countrymen on the finer points of combat flying. It was not an idea that was met with wild enthusiasm.

An RAF officer recalls hearing an American pilot complain about playing "wet nurse" to a bunch of green pilots. This resentment may have been premature—nobody had been ordered to carry out any sort of training at all—but it was not surprising. The volunteers remembered that they had earned their RAF wings, as well as their combat experience, in spite of their country's hostility and interference. They had become veteran pilots, but only because they violated the US Neutrality Acts and had risked criminal prosecution by joining the RAF. Now the US government would probably want them to train American pilots to fight the Luftwaffe. In other words, the original volunteers thought they would have to make up for the short-sightedness of the American government and the American public. As it would happen, however, things did not quite work out the way they thought.

The Americans who flew in the RAF now shared the same cynical point of view as their British counterparts: it would be best not to expect too much from the untried, and probably unready, US Army Air Force. At least not for a while.

★ ★ ★

By the early part of 1942, senior officers at Fighter Command headquarters had come to rate the three Eagle Squadrons as "average" fighter squadrons: not outstanding, not substandard, but somewhere in between—at least as far as flying was concerned. But Sir Sholto Douglas and his staff must have been the only people in Britain who thought of any American as average, in any way, shape, form, or accent. Britons regarded Americans as any number of things—strange, odd, curious, astonishing—but never average. Americans had no idea how strange they seemed to most Britons. (But, then again, the British had no idea of how strange they seemed to most Americans.)

The first US troops landed in the United Kingdom during the early weeks of 1942. They very quickly discovered what every American volunteer in the British forces had already found out—Britain was a foreign country. They also learned that they had very little in common with the British, including the maddeningly deceptive "common language."

Since most Britons had never seen an American before, it is not surprising that most failed to recognize a Yank when they finally did meet one. First meetings were often awkward affairs. Sometimes the Yanks were even mistaken for German paratroopers and arrested by the police. Near Salisbury, two GIs were kept prisoner at the point of pitchforks until someone identified them as noble allies.

The main source for the mistaken identity was the unfamiliar uniforms, especially the US Army "coal scuttle" helmets, which some people decided looked just like German helmets. GIs marching through Hampshire or Wiltshire caused outbreaks of alarm on more than one occasion. The locals thought that the troops must be part of a German invasion. The panic subsided as soon as the strangers opened their mouths, and out came "queer-sounding" English in an unmistakable accent— the same accent everyone had heard many times in Hollywood films. Word quickly went round that the invaders were only Americans.

"We realized with curling lips that they were Americans," one girl remembers.[12] "We were all disgusted that they had sat on the fence for so long and we were determined to have nothing to do with them"—a resolve that usually lasted until the first GI asked an English girl for a date.

The "getting acquainted" phase, as had happened with the Eagles and the early volunteers with the RAF, would begin all over again, with both sides finding out how foreign they were to each other. When a small English boy saw and heard his first Americans, he was moved to inquire, "Are they real, Mummy?" (Mummy's reply is not on record.)

Throughout 1942, the number of American troops stationed in Britain rose and fell, as manpower was needed elsewhere. During the autumn of 1942, just prior to the invasion of North Africa, the number of Americans fell to about 100,000. This includes members of the US Army Air Force. An American face, and accent, remained relatively scarce while the three Eagle Squadrons were still flying operations in 1942.

Eventually, the American presence would become overwhelming in some parts of England, particularly the south. Two million Americans would be stationed in England (mostly), Scotland, and Wales during the buildup for the invasion of France on D-Day in June 1944. There were so many of them that their music, manners, and "lifestyle" would have a permanent impact on British life. But that was still in the future.

★ ★ ★

In mid-February 1942, both 71 Squadron and 121 Squadron found themselves involved in an operation unlike anything they had ever experienced.[13] On February 12, the German battleships *Scharnhorst* and *Gneisenau*, along with the heavy cruiser *Prinz Eugen*, sailed from the port of Brest. The three warships made their way up the English Channel, confidently and in broad daylight, on their way to a safe haven in Germany. The RAF was sent out to sink them before they could reach their destination. The two Eagle Squadrons of 11 Group would be flying fighter support for the attacking bombers.

Berlin's decision to move the three warships was based upon fear— fear that the RAF would either cripple or sink them if they remained at Brest. During the past year, they had been attacked several times; Brest was an easy target for British bombers. But moving to Germany would involve as many risks as staying in Brest.

In order to reach Germany's North Sea ports, *Scharnhorst*, *Gneisenau*, and *Prinz Eugen* would have to travel by one of two routes. The northern route, sailing north of Scotland and down the east coast of Britain, would mean chancing an encounter with the much larger British Home Fleet. The southern route, making a dash up the Channel, meant facing the RAF. The Channel route was considered the lesser of two evils.

Colonel Adolf Galland, who would command fighter cover in "Operation Thunderbolt," as the Channel dash was called, was asked by Adolf Hitler if he could insure the success of the operation. Galland replied that the success of such an operation would depend largely upon luck and surprise. But he also assured Hitler that his fighter pilots would do their very best when they found out what was at stake.

By sailing through the Channel, the three warships would be coming within range of several RAF bases in southern England—including North Weald and Martlesham Heath—but they would also be within range of Abbeville, as well as other Luftwaffe bases in France. Not only would the Luftwaffe be sending up every available fighter to protect the ships, but the Germans also had one very great advantage over the British—they knew that the ships were coming out, while the RAF did not.

Nobody in Britain had any idea that the German ships were in the Channel until 11:09 a.m.; they had sailed from Brest at 7:.00 that morning. Had it not been for an accidental sighting by two Spitfires on a fighter sweep, they might not have been spotted until much later than that. Most aircraft in England had been grounded by bad weather—a mix of rain and snow, along with dense clouds.

At Martlesham Heath, 71 Squadron was alerted about the three German warships around noon. But the alert was so vague that it did not even provide the exact location of the ships. The pilots headed for the general direction of Ostend, on Belgium's Channel coast. Because of the cloud cover, the pilots were not able to see very much or very far.

They realized they were in the right area when they found themselves surrounded by enemy fighters. "The next thing I knew, there were Me 109s all around the place," one pilot said. Fortunately, the German pilots were just as hampered by the cloud cover. The Luftwaffe was not able to coordinate a group attack, even though there were about one hundred German fighters all around the three warships. Once in a while, a Messerschmitt would dart out of the clouds, fire a burst at the nearest Spitfire, and then hurry back into the heavy overcast. Because of the weather, this was the closest the German pilots were able to come to a massive offensive.

From North Weald, 121 Squadron sent eight Spitfires to provide air cover for the bombers assigned to attack the enemy ships. The attack was uneventful; 121 Squadron's logbook entry said only this: "It is believed that no great damage, if any, was done to those ships." The pilots of 121 Squadron had a frustrating flight that day. They still had not yet destroyed any enemy aircraft, a fact that caused the pilots no small amount of embarrassment and disappointment.

The main action took place during the early afternoon of February 12, when six Swordfish torpedo bombers made their attack on the German ships. The obsolete "Stringbags," as they were nicknamed, were sluggish bi-planes with fixed landing gear. They looked like something left over from the First World War, and with a top speed of 85 miles per hour when carrying a full-sized torpedo, they flew like it, too. Despite having an escort of ten Spitfires, there was not very much that could be done to protect the slow and awkward planes. The six Swordfish valiantly went after *Scharnhorst*, but all six were shot down. No hits were scored.

Neither of the two Eagle Squadrons saw much combat. F/Lt. Humphrey Gilbert of 71 Squadron attacked seven German fighters, which is to say that he fired his guns at them, but he made no claims. Because of the weather, everyone's biggest worry was flying into the Channel at full throttle, or crashing into the white Kentish cliffs, which were almost invisible in the fog. The dangerously limited visibility was the main enemy on February 12; the Luftwaffe was only a minor annoyance.

For all of their efforts, the pilots and crews who took part in the operation might as well have stayed home in bed. By days end, *Scharnhorst*, *Gneisenau*, and *Prinz Eugen* were all safe in German ports. Five days after the Channel dash, Prime Minister Winston Churchill disclosed that 4,000 tons of bombs were dropped on the warships and 3,299 sorties were flown, with a loss of 247 pilots and 42 aircraft. No hits were scored on any of the ships, although *Scharnhorst* was damaged by a mine. *Gneisenau*, and *Prinz Eugen* would survive the war. *Scharnhorst* would be sunk by British warships off Norway's North Cape on December 26, 1943.

In Britain, there was a good deal of name-calling and finger-pointing within the navy and the RAF, though this had nothing to do with the Eagle

Squadrons. Nobody wanted to accept the blame for allowing three enemy capital ships to escape through the Straits of Dover, literally within sight of England.

★ ★ ★

The dismal weather continued to dampen the spirits of everyone. News from abroad was almost all bad—Singapore was captured by the Japanese, just as Sholto Douglas had predicted—but the main culprit was the weather. Rain was followed by snow, which was succeeded by fog and drizzle. When the sun finally did make an appearance, it was usually so subdued and pale that it failed to raise anyone's morale.

In the three Eagle Squadrons, the miserable weather had a more direct role in the lives of the pilots—the mists and fog kept all aircraft grounded. Both 71 and 121 Squadrons went on fighter sweeps over France when weather permitted. Frequent targets were railway stations and locomotives, but the pilots went after anything that looked inviting. Even a distillery was attacked. It might have been of questionable military value, but at least it was something to shoot at.

No enemy aircraft were encountered, or even seen at a distance, on these fighter sweeps. The biggest threat came from antiaircraft fire; the flak gunners were a lot better than anyone expected. Shrapnel from bursting shells damaged Spitfires from both 71 and 121 Squadron, but all of them managed to make it back to base.

For the pilots of 121 Squadron, the absence of the Luftwaffe not only made their fighter sweeps dull, but it also made life annoying and frustrating. Even at this late date—at least it seemed late to them—the pilots still had not shot down any German aircraft. The young bloods of the second Eagle Squadron had hoped to run up one or two victories by this time, so at least they would have something to brag about. They were well aware that 71 Squadron had already produced a couple of aces; it had been in all the newspapers. But they themselves could not even *find* the enemy, much less shoot him down. It made them resent 71 Squadron's success even more.

For 133 Squadron, up at Kirton-in-Lindsey, life was just as frustrating. Operations consisted mainly of monotonous convoy patrols. In the squadron's logbook, the entry "no enemy aircraft were seen," or "no interceptions," was made after each sortie.[14]

Of the two junior squadrons, 133 Squadron could claim the bragging rights for scoring the first kill. They finally got their chance against the Luftwaffe on February 5, when the convoy they were protecting was attacked by a marauding Dornier Do 17. Flight Lieutenant Hugh Johnson and his wingman shared the Dornier with two pilots from 253 Squadron. None of the attacking pilots saw the Dornier crash, but an "escort vessel at the tail of the convoy" saw the bomber go in "with a splatter."[15] It was not very much—a quarter of a Dornier for each of the squadron's two attacking pilots—but at least it was a beginning.

On the same afternoon, Red McColpin "had more or less an interrupted series with one or more Do 217s."[16] McColpin, a recent transfer from 71 Squadron, "shot a large piece off the engine nacelle" on one of the bombers. He returned to base "with all his guns empty and a Do 217 damaged to his credit." All in all, a highly satisfying feeling.

The last of the three Eagle Squadrons to shoot down an enemy aircraft was 121 Squadron. Several weeks after 133 Squadron's Do 217, Pilot Officer John Mooney had the distinction of claiming 121's first German aircraft destroyed on March 23, 1942. The aircraft was a Focke-Wulf FW 190, which was shot down during a fighter sweep near Calais.

On the following day, while escorting eight twin-engine Boston bombers, 121 met the enemy again. Focke-Wulfs came up to attack the bombers, and the Eagles went after them. Pilot Officer Reade Tilley claimed an FW 190 as a probable. "The enemy was seen to be belching forth thick black smoke, and it dived into the clouds upside-down," according to the squadron logbook.[17]

The Luftwaffe was finally beginning to show signs of life. This was seen as a good omen—all three Eagle Squadrons had hoped that the enemy would begin to show himself. But their good fortune did not last long. Fighter sweeps and convoy patrols soon afterward returned to the dull and uneventful. Pilots began to return to base without firing a shot.

Besides the lack of targets of opportunity, another thing on everybody's mind was the lack of an American presence in the war. It had now been several months since Pearl Harbor, and there was still no sign of any American servicemen in the British Isles. The Eagles intended to transfer to the US forces, but there would be no transfer until the Army Air Force came to England. And nobody had any idea when that was going to happen.

There had been rumors that American bomber or fighter units were on their way from the States, possibly both,—but there were always plenty of rumors, especially concerning this particular topic. In the end, nobody ever saw any American planes or pilots. From the point of view of the American volunteers, it was as though the United States had never entered the war.

For over two years, the British had been asking, "When are the Americans coming into the war?" Now the Eagles were starting to ask the same thing.

CHAPTER NINE

YANKEE DOODLE GOES TO TOWN

I t began to look as though the miserable English winter would never end. Rain, fog, low clouds, and drizzle continued to plague the three Eagle Squadrons, grounding all aircraft and dampening the morale of every pilot. Even when the calendar finally announced that spring had arrived, apparently nobody bothered to tell the weatherman. The dismal winter clouds and mists refused to go away.

"How the hell can anyone stand to live in this lousy, stinking climate?" was a question that native Californians, along with residents of some of the southern states, asked over and over again about the weather in the British Isles. Nobody ever managed to come up with a satisfactory answer, however.

When the weather did break for a while, long enough for the pilots to take part in a fighter sweep, regulations prevented anyone from breaking formation to chase after any inviting stray German planes. Everyone knew that this was for their own good—most of the pilots had heard about Mike Kolendorski, even if they hadn't met him—but it still did not help anyone's spirits.

On the rare occasion that an enemy fighter did present itself, RAF regulations could *still* interfere. According to the rule book, a German plane could not be claimed as "destroyed" unless it was seen to crash or the pilot bailed out. Otherwise, it only counted as a "probable." This rule deflated a lot of scores, not to mention egos, and raised a lot of the pilots' tempers.

Pilot Officer Barry Mahon of 121 Squadron ran slap into this regulation after an encounter with an FW 190 over France.[1] Mahon dove on the Focke-Wulf, closed to within about 450 yards—which was actually much too far away—and opened fire with his cannons and machine guns. After giving the FW 190 an eight-second burst, Mahon was satisfied that he had shot it down. He duly claimed the enemy fighter as having been destroyed.

Back at base, however, the squadron intelligence officer did not share Mahon's enthusiasm. He refused to give credit for a "destroyed"— Mahon did not see the enemy pilot bail out, and he did not see the FW crash. "P/O Mahon seems certain that he hit this aircraft," the intelligence officer noted. "The Enemy Aircraft was seen to dive steeply down from 9,000 feet, but there was no evidence that the Enemy Aircraft has crashed, no smoke or any other signs were visible. No claim can therefore be made." And no claim was allowed, even though Mahon was certain that he had shot down the Focke-Wulf. This was worse than being grounded by English weather.

Nobody knew it yet, but there were plans afoot that would liven up the existence of every pilot in Fighter Command. Some of these plans were being made at RAF Fighter Command headquarters, some were being concocted by the Luftwaffe, and some were being formulated in Washington, DC. The course of the war was about to change, although none of the Eagles could have been aware of it at that time. Even if they had known, many of the pilots still would not have been satisfied. Everybody was shouting for "more action," more enemy aircraft to destroy, and it did not look like they were going to get what they wanted as long as they were stuck in regulation-happy, fogbound England.

Since they were not content in England, some of the Americans decided to go someplace else. Seventeen pilots from the three Eagle Squadrons, including Reade Tilley and Leo Nomis, volunteered for duty on the Mediterranean island of Malta. Malta was the site of a vital RAF airfield, strategically positioned within striking distance of both the Italian peninsula and Sicily.

Because of its location, the German High Command wanted Malta and its airfield neutralized—permanently put out of action. The Luftwaffe did its best to comply with Berlin's orders. German bombers pounded the island every day, desperately trying to knock out the RAF airfield. By mid-1942, Malta had endured more than two thousand air raids. The RAF needed fighter pilots to defend its most strategic Mediterranean base.

The Air Ministry's call for volunteers sounded like just the thing for a hot, young pilot—sunshine, adventure, and lots of German planes to shoot down—which is likely why so many Eagle Squadron pilots responded. Presumably, they found everything they were looking for on Malta. There was plenty of sunshine and adventure, and there were more than enough German aircraft in the tropical air above the rocky island to satisfy the pilots' cravings.

Not long after they left England, however, the war over northern Europe began to change. Things began to warm up, and not just in the meteorological sense, although the weather was largely responsible for the change. The sun came out of hiding, and the fog and clouds of the winter months finally disappeared. Conditions became favorable for flying, at long last. Both the RAF and the Luftwaffe took advantage of the improvement, and pilots on both sides suddenly became more active and aggressive.

A large part of Germany's fighter force had been sent to Russia by the spring of 1942, but the pilots who remained in northern France were among the Luftwaffe's elite. The very best of these were the "Abbeville

Boys," still based at various airfields in the vicinity of Abbeville and still making life as hazardous as possible for the RAF's bomber crews and fighter pilots.

British writer and historian Len Deighton claimed that the Abbeville Boys did not really exist, that they were nothing but a loose conglomeration of pilots who happened to paint the nose sections of their fighters the same color. But anyone who flew operations over northern France, British or American, quickly found out that the "yellow-nose boys" were real enough. They also discovered that the Abbeville-based pilots were first rate—excellent shots, persistent, and deadly aggressive against any intruding fighters or bombers.

Probably the most famous of the Abbeville Boys was Adolf Galland. Galland was as well known in Britain as he was in Germany. He was enormously popular among his fellow Luftwaffe fighter pilots, and respected by the RAF, if not exactly admired.

Galland had a weakness for cigars, a friendly manner, and an easy smile. His human qualities helped him in his relations with junior officers, but did not always make him popular with his superiors. He was too outspoken to suit the High Command—Reichsmarschall Hermann Göring still remembered Galland's remark that what the Luftwaffe really needed to improve its fighter force was a squadron of Spitfires. Also, the big shots in Berlin thought that he smoked too many cigars, which meant that he was not being a proper role model for the younger pilots in his command.

"Dolfo" Galland was highly amused by the fact that Adolf Hitler disapproved of his cigar smoking on the grounds that it set a bad example for Germany's pure-hearted Aryan youth. He was forbidden to pose for publicity photos while holding a cigar, and no news reporters were allowed to mention the fact that he smoked. Nevertheless, none of these things discouraged Galland from smoking as many cigars as he pleased. He gave himself permission to smoke while on operations, had an ashtray and an electric lighter installed in his fighter's cockpit, and kept a cigar in his mouth until the moment that it was time to go on oxygen. The fact that Berlin did not approve made the cigars taste even better.

Galland did not become one of the Luftwaffe's top-scoring aces on the basis of his personality. He was not only an outstanding pilot, but was also one of the best shots in any of the air forces (German, British, or American), and he had an unshakable confidence in his own abilities. This confidence was not misplaced—Galland not only shot down more than one hundred Allied aircraft, but he also managed to survive the war.

Because of the Abbeville Boys and the improved weather, fighter sweeps were no longer just uneventful round-trip excursions for the Eagle Squadrons. The Luftwaffe suddenly began to show itself. The "yellow-nose boys" came up looking for a fight, and pilots of all three Eagle Squadrons abruptly stopped complaining about "no action."

On April 27, while escorting a bomber strike to St. Omer, 71 Squadron claimed five FW 190s destroyed as well as a few "probables."[2] They had the advantage of position, which gave them an edge in spite of the Focke-Wulf's superior performance over their Spitfire Mark Vs.

Even though the Focke-Wulf was well protected by armor plate, the Spitfire's exploding 20 mm cannon shells smashed right through it. The cannon shells could have a devastating effect, especially if the attacking pilot closed to within minimum firing range—100 yards or less. Even a single 20 mm shell could destroy an enemy aircraft if it hit a vital spot—it could knock out the engine, blow up the fuel tank, or kill the pilot.

Although 71 Squadron scored an impressive number of victories on April 27, the losses were not entirely one-sided. Among those killed was John Flynn, the same pilot who had been shot down by squadron mate James Alexander a year earlier. In April 1941, Flynn had been 71 Squadron's "first blood," but had managed to bring his shot-up plane, filled with .303-caliber bullet holes, back to England. He was not as lucky this time around and crashed with his Spitfire.

Most of the young American pilots were not the reflective type. To them, the war was a matter of shooting down the enemy before they were shot down themselves. If they had thought about it, they might have regarded the Luftwaffe pilots in the same light as Spitfire pilot Richard Hillary. "I wondered idly what he was like, this man I would kill," Hillary wrote. "Was he young, was he fat, would he die with the Führer's name on his lips, or would he die alone, in that last moment conscious of himself as a man? I would never know. Then I was being strapped in, my mind automatically checking the controls, and we were off."[3]

As has already been seen, the pilots of all three Eagle Squadrons had extremely high opinions of themselves. Not many senior RAF officers, in either the Air Ministry or at Fighter Command headquarters, had any argument with this opinion or with the pilot's technical skills in general at this point. This represented a complete reversal in outlook from 71 Squadron's early days, when RAF Fighter Command had *nothing* good to say about the new Yank pilots. Their opinion of the Eagles' leadership was another matter, however—senior RAF officers never did get over the "cowboy" image of the Yank volunteers. But sometimes there was a pleasant surprise in this department, as well.

In May 1942, the Air Ministry announced that Newton Anderson of 71 Squadron had been promoted to the rank of squadron leader and had been given command of 222 Squadron, an all-British unit.[4] Anderson's nickname was "Weak Eyes;" he had become a fighter pilot in spite of his poor eyesight. His determination to succeed made him an excellent pilot, better than some of the "naturals," as well as a respected officer.

Anderson became the first US citizen to lead a British unit in combat— no other American had ever been given such a promotion. (Cynics would say that it was the first time that the British ever trusted an American that far.) Unfortunately, he held the new post for little more than a month. In June, while leading three squadrons—an RAF wing—on a bomber escort assignment, Anderson was shot down and killed.

★ ★ ★

At the beginning of May, the several members of the Women's Auxiliary Air Force in the Operations Room of Biggin Hill Aerodrome heard a strange noise coming over the radio. It was the "battle song" of 133 Squadron, which featured lyrics that were mostly unprintable and ended with "on me no mercy bestow." The song was sung in a "lazy Texan drawl."[5] (The British tend to classify any unfamiliar American accent, as well as a few Canadian, as a "Texan drawl.") The girls smiled at each other with raised eyebrows—the Yanks had arrived. The members of 133 Squadron had been transferred to 11 Group—Fighter Command's first line of defense, and based at Biggin Hill, at that. God only knew what was going to happen next.

"Biggin on the Bump," so called because the airfield was on top of a hill in northwestern Kent, had acquired an almost legendary status. The station protected the vital southern approaches to London. It had been bombed many times during the summer of 1940 and had been knocked out of action several times. Some of the buildings still showed scars from bomb damage. But even more important to 133 Squadron, pilots stationed at Biggin Hill always seemed to be in the thick of the fighting. The station could claim nearly one thousand enemy aircraft destroyed—the first having been shot down by Jimmy Davies, the American volunteer from Bernardsville, NJ. This impressive score would increase as the war went on.

At about the same time that 133 moved to Biggin Hill, and just before Newton Anderson left to take over 222 Squadron, 71 Squadron left Martlesham Heath for the much more modern facilities at Debden, in Essex. Like Biggin Hill, Debden was a sector station in 11 Group and had also been bombed during the Battle of Britain. A map on display in the Officer's Mess served as a reminder of those grim days. It had been salvaged from a German bomber that attacked the field on August 24, 1940. The map traced the course of the plane, a Dornier Do 17, from its base in northern France to Debden.

The Luftwaffe remained active all throughout the spring and summer of 1942, and both squadrons were needed in the front line. Whenever a fighter sweep was made over northern France, the German fighters always came up to challenge. The Debden Wing—made up of 65 and 111 Squadrons along with 71 (Eagle) Squadron—almost always ran into opposition. During one fighter sweep in early June, "numerous enemy aircraft were encountered," according to the squadron logbook.[6] Squadron Leader Peterson claimed one German aircraft destroyed and one damaged, Flight Lieutenants Gus Daymond and Bob Sprague each claimed one damaged, and Flight Lieutenant Oscar Coen fired his guns at three German aircraft, "but was too preoccupied to notice any results."

At Biggin Hill, 133 Squadron was just as busy with fighter sweeps. Among other activities, the squadron took part in an attack on Abbeville Aerodrome during the month of July. The "yellow-nose boys" rose to the occasion and, as expected, gave the intruders a hard fight. The Eagles of 133 claimed two FWs destroyed and a Bf 109 damaged, but also lost three of their own pilots to German fighters.

The fact that the Germans shot back still came as a shock to some of the newer squadron members. On his first flight over France, one newly arrived pilot found himself in a dogfight with an enemy fighter. It was just like flight training back in England until tracer and cannon shells started whizzing past him. "They're shooting at me!" the pilot blurted into the radio.[7] The entire Operations Room at Biggin Hill burst into laughter.

Replacement pilots were usually kids who had just left an Operational Training Unit and usually still had a lot to learn about flying with a fighter unit. But sometimes a squadron was lucky enough to acquire a pilot with some experience.

An RAF historian commented that the heart of a fighter is its engine, but the pilot is its soul. One of 133 Squadron's more rambunctious souls was F/Lt. Donald Blakeslee, who joined the squadron in June 1942. By the time he joined the junior Eagles, he had destroyed a Bf 109 and had also been credited with several enemy aircraft damaged. He had also been awarded the Distinguished Flying Cross. Blakeslee had gone to Canada in

June 1940 and joined the RCAF. In May 1941, he began flying operations with 401 Squadron. Number 133 was glad to have a replacement with Blakeslee's experience.

Blakeslee's reputation was based upon his talents as an air leader, not just as a fighter pilot. There might have been better pilots and better gunners, but Blakeslee knew how to command. "He was everywhere in battle," one commentator said, "twisting and climbing, bellowing and blaspheming, warning and exhorting."[8] Unfortunately, Blakeslee also had a blunt, blustery manner and had no use at all for tact or diplomacy. His personality frequently offended senior officers and gave them second thoughts about his abilities as an officer. Because of his bluntness, he would find himself in and out of trouble in the RAF and, later on, in the US Army Air Force.

Shortly after Blakeslee joined 133 Squadron, the pilots of 71 Squadron began to hear exciting rumors that they were going to be transferred to Russia. In July, the rumor became an official order—71 Squadron and two other RAF squadrons were being sent to the Soviet Union to help reinforce the Red Air Force at Stalingrad. The "Soviet Wing" would be equipped with the newest and fastest Spitfire, the Mark IX. In fact, the new Spitfire IXs had already been shipped to Russia by the time official word of the transfer came through.

The Squadron had a farewell celebration—unusually wild and raucous, even by Eagle Squadron standards—and was preparing to leave England when the transfer order was canceled. Several reasons were given for this sudden change of plan. One was that the Spitfire pilots would be needed for an upcoming offensive against enemy-occupied northern France. Another was that the freighter carrying the Spitfire IXs had been torpedoed by a U-boat on its way to Murmansk. Whatever the reason, 71 Squadron would be staying at Debden.

★ ★ ★

During the summer of 1942, all three Eagle Squadrons were hearing a rumor of a different sort. And actually, it was more of a vague certainty than a rumor. The topic concerned the transfer of the Eagle Squadrons to the US Army Air Force, news of which was received with mixed reactions. Most of the pilots were glad to be joining the American forces at long last, but many were sorry to be leaving the RAF.

By this time, the pilots of the Eagle Squadrons were not the only American flyers in England. In June, they had been joined by the 31st Fighter Group, the first American unit to operate in the United Kingdom.

Although the 31st FG was a USAAF unit, it came under the operational control of RAF Fighter Command—there was still no "US Fighter Command" in England. The group's three component squadrons— the 307th, 308th, and 309th (a US group was the equivalent of an RAF wing)—were trained in RAF methods, procedures, and techniques. Almost all of the operating procedures of what would become the US Eighth Air Force, right down to the squadron markings on the airplanes, would be Americanized versions of RAF methods.[9]

Some of the methods did not go down very well. For instance, the US Army Air Force pilots did not like the concept of the Rhubarb mission. Air sweeps did not appeal to them, and luring the enemy up from his bases and destroying his aircraft through superior tactics was not direct enough for them. "They had come to Britain to win the war," according to one British observer of the new arrivals, "to chase [the enemy] around and shoot him down."[10]

It took quite a lot of time and effort, as well as quite a few hard knocks, to persuade the new American pilots that the Luftwaffe was a lot better than they had been led to believe. It would take a lot more than bombast and good intentions to beat the Germans, the USAAF were warned.

When the first American pilots arrived in Britain, they did so without airplanes. The USAAF did not have any fighters that could hope to compete with either the Bf 109 or the FW 190, so American units were equipped with Spitfire Mark Vs—courtesy of the RAF. (The British referred to this as "reverse Lend-Lease.")

The Yanks fell in love with the Spitfire. They liked it much better than the fighters they left behind in the US—Bell P-39 Airacobras and Curtiss P-40 Tomahawks. In this, at least, they were in full agreement with their hosts. The RAF had given the Airacobra a try. They even equipped 601 (County of London) Squadron—Billy Fiske's unit—with it. But the fighter was found to be so poor in performance that it had to be withdrawn.

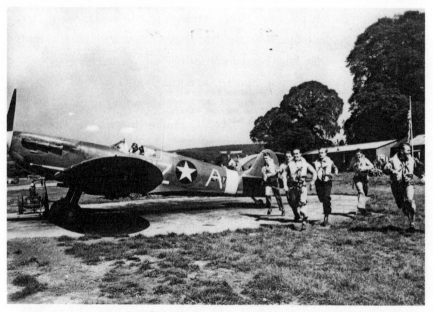

An "American" Spitfire of the 31st Fighter Group. The white US star has been painted over the RAF roundel. The US Army Air Force was completely unprepared for war after Pearl Harbor and had no fighter that could hope to compete with either the Messerschmitt 109 or the Focke-Wulf 190. American fighter units in England flew the Spitfire during its earliest operations, until the P-47 Thunderbolt was ready for service in 1943. (Courtesy of the National Museum of the United States Air Force®.)

The fact that American pilots preferred the Spitfire caused no small amount of disapproval and embarrassment in Washington, DC, as well as among the top brass of the Army Air Force. A remark by one of the new pilots, that he was "glad they had Spitfires instead of P-40s and Airacobras," was quoted in the *New York Herald Tribune*.[11] The same quote also formed the basis for an article in *Time* magazine.

When the story broke in the United States, it caused faces to turn bright red from coast to coast. Neither the War Department nor anyone connected with the aviation industry wanted to hear that any foreign airplane could possibly be better than anything made in the USA—even if it happened to be the truth. Any public official who even so much as hinted at such a thing would have been committing political suicide.

Along with the fighter pilots, American bomber crews were also beginning to trickle into England—just crews, not airplanes. The first American bombing raid against Nazi Germany was flown in airplanes borrowed from the RAF, twin-engine Bostons.[12] Six American crews joined 226 Squadron and took part in a joint USAAF/RAF attack on four Luftwaffe airfields in the Netherlands. All twelve Bostons, including the ones manned by Americans, bore the RAF roundel insignia.

The raid, which was flown on July 4, 1942, can at best be described as a mixed success. Nine of the twelve Bostons bombed their targets; the other three returned to base without hitting their objectives. Of the nine bombers that attacked their target, three were hit by antiaircraft fire and crashed. Two of these were manned by Americans. Another of the American-manned Bostons was damaged by the intense ground fire.

It was a very small beginning, but the raid certainly got its share of publicity, and then some. A great deal was made of the fact that the first American bombing raid had been carried out on the Fourth of July, Independence Day. For security reasons, the British media did not report the exact location of the targets.

Not everyone was impressed by the first American bombing strike, in spite of all the publicity. "In the nine o'clock news was an account of the first US Army Air Corps raid over enemy territory," remarked Kansas-born Robert S. Raymond, "and everyone in the mess smiled when the losses were announced. Two out of six failed to return . . . they'll need a couple of months to forget their glamour propaganda and smarten up a bit. Until then—no cheers from the RAF."[13]

Actually, the BBC announcer had been trying his best to sound encouraging. He wanted his British audience to know that the Americans had arrived and had finally taken the offensive against the Germans, even if it was in a very small way. But Raymond was right—a 33 percent loss was not a very good beginning.

If the Eagle Squadrons heard the news of the first American bombing attack, they did not mention it. They were probably bored by the whole thing. In 121 Squadron's logbook, the intelligence officer did not think that anything noteworthy happened on that particular day. He noted only that the "Squadron released at 13.00 hrs." so that everybody could go to London to celebrate the Fourth of July.[14]

Shortly after this early tentative effort, the first US Army Air Force B-17 Flying Fortresses arrived in the British Isles. In mid-July, the four squadrons of the 97th Bomb Group arrived at Polebrook Airfield, in Northamptonshire. Senior officers of the US Eighth Air Force were anxious to see their four-engine bombers go into action against the enemy, but bad weather kept them grounded for a month—which produced even more curses and complaints about the rotten English climate.

Finally, in mid-August, the weather cleared. On August 17, eleven B-17s took off from Polebrook to bomb the rail yards at Rouen, just across the Channel. Their fighter escort consisted of four Spitfire squadrons, and some of the bombs they dropped were of British manufacture. The strike itself was a success—the target was hit, and railway locomotives and buildings within the rail yards were destroyed. Although this was hardly a major effort—in May, RAF Bomber Command had sent over one thousand bombers against Cologne—it was the first time that American bombers had taken action against the enemy from British bases.

The Rouen mission may not have done all that much damage to the enemy, but it provided a publicity windfall for the Eighth Air Force. The press told the world that the Yanks had arrived, and with a vengeance. More than thirty reporters and photographers were on hand when the B-17s returned to Polebrook. They made prominent mention of the fact that the commander of VIII Bomber Command, Brigadier General Ira Eaker, had flown to Rouen in a Flying Fortress named *Yankee Doodle*. Air Marshal Sir Arthur Harris, the chief of RAF Bomber Command, sent Eaker this message: "*Yankee Doodle* certainly went to town, and can stick another well-deserved feather in his cap."[15]

But yet again, with the exception of Air Marshal Harris, the British were not impressed. As far as the RAF was concerned, the Americans paid too much attention to publicity and not enough to training. By RAF standards, American crews were found to be very poorly trained in the fundamental skills that would be needed to survive over enemy territory. Pilots had trouble flying tight formations. Air gunners could not hit attacking enemy fighters. Some radio operators were thoroughly unfamiliar with sending and receiving in Morse code.

Also, RAF Bomber Command did not have much faith in what the Americans referred to as "daylight precision bombing." The British tried daylight bombing themselves, but had to switch to night bombing because of heavy losses to both fighters and antiaircraft fire. If the Americans were going to try daylight bombing over northern France and Germany with undertrained crews, they wouldn't stand a chance.

Most of the criticism was well meant. The RAF had made many of the same mistakes themselves. British officers were trying to advise the Americans of their own weak points and the enemy's strong points before the Luftwaffe taught them the same lessons the hard way. The RAF also helped to remedy a few training deficiencies. American crews went to RAF schools to brush up on Morse code; target-towing aircraft were provided for air-gunnery practice; British pilots even made mock attacks on Flying Fortresses to simulate air combat. Fighter Command would also be providing escort for the heavy bombers on their first trips over the enemy-occupied Continent, until the Americans could build up their own fighter force.

Officers in the Eighth Air Force accepted both the criticism and the assistance. The commander of the 97th Bomb Group, Colonel Frank Armstrong, followed the advice of British officers and invoked an intensified training program for his pilots and crews. The offer of RAF training facilities was also welcome and appreciated.

But back in the United States, British criticism did not always go down quite so smoothly. As it was told in the American press, the British sounded as though they were faulting the Americans for dragging their feet—shades of the First World War, when the US was criticized for going "over there" much too late in the war and for bringing too little with them when they finally did decide to show up. This did not endear the British to the American public, just as it had not done in 1917.

During the first half of 1942, Americans were especially sensitive about criticism. US forces had been on the defensive for seven months— since Pearl Harbor—and had suffered heavy losses in the early months of fighting. They had not been prepared for war and did not like having their noses rubbed in it. Especially not by the British, who always seemed so willing to criticize, even though the criticism had been constructive—or at least was *meant* to be constructive.

The double meaning of the phrase "belligerent allies" was becoming more evident.

✯✯✯ CHAPTER TEN ✯✯✯

LIKE A GREAT SUSTAINED ROAR

Sergeant John Ellermann, a ground crewman with the US 31st Fighter Group, had an uneasy feeling that something was going to happen soon. It had been much too quiet lately to suit him. There had been nothing but routine patrols for the pilots and a nice, easy work schedule for everybody else.

Ellermann had only been in the Army for two years and in England for less than a month, but he was enough of a veteran to know that a quiet stretch was usually followed by all hell breaking loose. The first two weeks of August were not just quiet, they had been positively boring. It was obvious that something had to be up, and probably something big.

As it turned out, Sergeant Ellermann's instincts were absolutely correct. The calm interlude came to a sudden and dramatic end toward the middle of the month—not only for the new units of the US Eighth Air Force, but also for every unit in RAF Fighter Command, including

the three Eagle Squadrons. The senior Eagles, 71 Squadron, found themselves transferred from Debden, Essex, to Gravesend, Kent. Number
133 Squadron was shifted south from Biggin Hill to Lympne, and 121
Squadron was moved to from North Weald to Southend-on-Sea.

All three bases, along with every base in the south of England, were
then cut off from the rest of the world. All personnel became incom-
municado, all leaves were canceled, and even outside telephone calls
required the permission of the station commander.

On August 19, the reason behind all the movement and secrecy was
finally made known—it was all part of the preparation for an Allied hit-
and-run raid on the French port city of Dieppe, on the Channel coast.
A communiqué from Combined Operation headquarters described
"Operation Jubilee" as a raid on Dieppe, along with all military and air
objectives. Among the objectives was the destruction of "aerodrome
installations," as well as luring the strangely hesitant Luftwaffe off the
ground and into battle.

According to the plan, Dieppe would serve as a sort of dress rehearsal
for future landings. The attacking ground forces would be made up of
5,100 Canadian troops, 1,000 British commandos, and 50 US Army
Rangers. These would be supported by 252 naval vessels—none larger
than a destroyer—as well as 69 air squadrons.[1]

Among the units providing air cover were 48 Spitfire and 8 Hurricane squadrons, as well as the 97th Bomb Group, US Army Air Force. The
B-17s of the 97th BG had been given the assignment of knocking out the
Luftwaffe fighter base at Abbeville for several critical hours at the height
of the Dieppe raid. The objective was, simply put, to make a landing,
carry out as much destruction as possible, and withdraw. It was a raid, a
hit-and-run attack, not an invasion.

The Russians, as well as a few overzealous Britons and Americans,
had been shouting for a "Second Front" for several months. The Russians
had been demanding any sort of invasion, in France or anywhere else,
since June 1941, when German forces invaded the Soviet Union. It was

hoped that Operation Jubilee would not only silence the critics, but also give Anglo-American planners some useful information on the strength and deployment of enemy fortifications for future operations—a major landing on the coast of France was already being considered (D-Day would occur two years later).

The raids would be the first real test of German coastal defenses— were they really as good as Berlin had been saying? The German Propaganda Ministry had been boasting about its "Atlantic Wall" since 1940. The Dieppe raid would test how solid it really was.

Dieppe would also be the first operation in which all three Eagle Squadrons would take part. What has been described as an "air umbrella" of fighters would fly cover over the French coast. This fighter cover would have two purposes: to keep the Luftwaffe away from the landing beaches and—it was hoped—to destroy the maximum number of enemy aircraft.

The resulting combat between German and Allied fighters, which began in the early hours of August 19 and went on until evening, has been called the most hectic day of the war so far for Fighter Command. It would be an extremely busy day for the Luftwaffe, as well.

★　★　★

For 71 Squadron, the operational day on August 19 began at 4:45 a.m. Along with the Spitfires of 124 Squadron, the Eagles prepared to take off from Gravesend at that uncivilized hour. Pilots hurried toward their fighters in the predawn blackness and spent the next few minutes preparing for takeoff: stepping through the cockpit opening and then squeezing into the cockpit's confining smallness. Then the rigger began his routine—parachute straps across shoulders, Sutton-harness straps adjusted and tightened, oxygen mask fastened on, cockpit door closed and locked.

After being strapped in, the pilot's next task was to prime the engine, adjust the switches, and signal "thumbs up" to the mechanics. The Rolls-

Royce Merlin sputtered to life, and its twelve cylinders roared into full song. Wind from the three-bladed airscrew flooded the cockpit. The engine's noise drowned out all other sounds. Finally, the ground crew pulled away the wheel chocks. The Spits began taxiing out behind their leader, S/L Chesley Peterson.

The noses of the twelve Spitfires tilted up sharply, and the fighters began climbing at a rate of 2,500 feet per minute. Pilots had hoods closed and oxygen turned on. Today, everybody was more tense than usual. They realized that this was no small fighter sweep they were flying—this was the "big one." They would be taking the war to the enemy in his own territory.

From Gravesend, both 71 and 124 Squadron flew to Beachy Head to rendezvous with four other Spitfire squadrons. All six squadrons—72 Spitfires in all—then headed cross-Channel to Dieppe.[2]

For Harold Strickland, the old man of the squadron at the ripe age of thirty-nine, the day did not begin on a very encouraging note.[3] His wingman was having trouble retracting his undercarriage, and Strickland had to keep throttling back to stay with him. After several unsuccessful attempts at cranking his wheels up, the other pilot finally gave up and headed back to Gravesend. All alone now, Strickland pushed his throttle all the way forward, trying to catch up with the rest of 71 Squadron.

Strickland never did find his squadron but, in the predawn half-light, he did happen across a gaggle of FW 190s flying in "finger four" formation. He closed in on one of them and, when he came within range, fired a burst at the German fighter.

"People write about the rattle of the guns," one Spitfire pilot reflected. "It's never a rattle, more like a great sustained roar." Strickland's Mark V-B was armed with four .303 machine guns and two Hispano 20 mm cannons. The 20 mm cannon had become a favorite with the Spitfire pilots, at least after its nasty habit of jamming was corrected.

Strickland's cannon shells hit their target; the stricken Focke-Wulf went into a sudden dive. Strickland climbed, trying to get away from the other three FWs, but the three German pilots climbed after him, looking for revenge.

The French coast was covered by eight-tenths clouds that morning, and Strickland used this to his advantage. Ducking into heavy cloud to lose enemy pursuers may not have been a very original trick, but it worked. The three Focke-Wulfs could not find him inside the thick layer of gray. But Strickland could not see, either—not the ground or anything else. Every time he popped out from the clouds to take a visual bearing, the German pilots spotted him immediately and came after him.

Strickland managed to survive the deadly game of hide and seek with the three Focke-Wulfs. He dodged all their attacks and landed back at Gravesend just after dawn—slightly shaken, but still alive. He did not realize it, but he had just taken part in one of the first air combats of the day, one of the first of hundreds.

Radar stations on England's southern coast began to pick up large plots of enemy aircraft at about 7:00 a.m. Most of the activity was in the vicinity of Abbeville and St. Omer—the yellow-nose Abbeville Boys. It looked as though one of the Allied objectives had already been reached—the Luftwaffe was coming up, and coming up in force, to meet the attack.

And the Luftwaffe was getting the better of the Spitfire pilots. In one particularly furious action, five Spitfires were shot down, and a sixth pilot was wounded when his fighter was mauled by cannon fire. The Luftwaffe lost two, or possibly three, FWs. The Focke-Wulf 190 was enjoying a clear-cut superiority over the Spitfire Mark V.

The "second Eagles," 121 Squadron, reached Dieppe at about 9:00 a.m. By that time the Luftwaffe had its "first team" up. The pilots met "a good deal of opposition," according to the squadron logbook.[4] The twelve Spitfires were headed by Squadron Leader Bill Williams, a British officer. The American commander, Hugh Kennard, had been grounded by illness for more than two weeks.

When 121 arrived at Dieppe, the Luftwaffe was waiting for them. "Dogfights ensued," the logbook noted, "and the Squadron became split up and returned to base in ones and twos." It would have been more accurate to say that a melee ensued. Air combat over the French coast was as furious as it had been over southern England two years before when the Luftwaffe attacked British aerodromes at the height of the Battle of Britain.

The Focke-Wulf FW 190 was the Luftwaffe's best piston-engine fighter of the war. Some pilots claimed that the Focke-Wulf did not have any weak points, except for the limitations brought by the pilots themselves. Pictured is a captured FW 190 with American markings. (Courtesy of the National Museum of the United States Air Force®.)

Three of 121 Squadron's pilots did not return to Southend—one was killed, one was shot down over France and taken prisoner, and one was rescued from the Channel. At least one of the pilots managed to nurse his Spitfire back to base in spite of bullet holes that almost literally covered the fighter—there were cannon-shell holes in its wings and fuselage, its glycol pipe, its Plexiglas hood, and even its instrument panel.

The atmosphere in the pilots' dispersal hut must have been dismal that morning. For months, everyone had been waiting for the Luftwaffe to show itself. But when the long-awaited event finally arrived, the squadron lost one-quarter of its pilots to enemy aircraft in the first sortie, and several others came back to base with badly damaged Spitfires.

The squadron could only claim one enemy fighter destroyed, two probables, and one damaged. These results certainly came as a letdown and were a long way from what the pilots were expecting to accomplish when they finally got their chance against the enemy.

This gloom and disappointment was apparent in the squadron's logbook. One entry noted, "A number of pilots fired their guns but made no claims."[5] Even when an FW was caught, it could not be kept in the gunsight long enough for the pilot to get off a good shot.

Radar stations on the south coast were keeping a steady watch on enemy air activity. By 9:30 a.m., there was a lot more activity to monitor. Twenty-plus planes were picked up near Abbeville at 9:41, and at least twenty more blips appeared on the screen only five minutes later.

The Luftwaffe base at Abbeville, as well as at St. Omer and elsewhere nearby, were only about 30 miles away from Dieppe. This put the German pilots only a few minutes' flying time from the beachhead, which allowed them to use most of their fuel for maneuvering against the incoming Spitfires.

Not all German aircraft in the vicinity of Dieppe were fighters. Luftwaffe bomber units were also in the area, sent out to attack Allied ships just offshore. The first of the Eagle Squadrons to come into contact with enemy bombers was Number 133, led by Don Blakeslee. The encounter took place during 133's second sortie of the day; the squadron had already claimed two FW 190s destroyed and one probable on its first trip over to Dieppe.

On their second trip, 133 Squadron's pilots were assigned to fly top cover for the ships off the beaches. The navy was trying to get in as close as possible to pick up survivors. German bombers were doing their best to break through the Spitfires and attack the ships as they closed in on the beaches.

At 12,000 feet, 133 Squadron and several other Spitfire units confronted a very large flight of enemy aircraft preparing to attack—Ju 88s and Do 17s bustling toward the beaches along with a swarm of escorting fighters. As the Spitfires went after the bombers, the German fighters swooped in to intercept the Spitfires.

The Spitfires reached the bombers first and began shooting as soon as they were within range. Thumbs pressed firing buttons, bursts of cannon and machine-gun fire converged on the fast-moving Junkers and Dorniers. A Ju 88 fell out of formation trailing smoke, followed by several others. Pilots of 133 Squadron claimed one Ju 88 and two FW 190s destroyed, along with several other German aircraft damaged.

One of the German planes was claimed by Don Blakeslee. At the end of the fighting of August 19, he would be credited with one enemy aircraft destroyed and two probables. This would later be changed to one destroyed and two damaged.

Although 133 Squadron was having a good day, not many other units could make that claim. Most RAF squadrons were running into stiff opposition from the Luftwaffe. The German pilots smelled blood and were coming after the Spitfires with fury and determination—and the Abbeville Boys were the best in the German air force.

Allied ground forces were not faring very well either. Infantry units were being mauled by German troops before they could get off the landing beaches. The raid on Dieppe was already in trouble, and the situation was getting steadily worse.

Landing troops ran into heavy opposition from the Wehrmacht. Spies in England had tipped the German High Command about Operation Jubilee, and the German army was waiting. With no heavy naval gunfire to support them, over two-thirds of all Canadian troops who came ashore at Dieppe were either killed, wounded, or taken prisoner within six hours. Because of these heavy losses, it was decided to withdraw all troops from the beachhead by 11:00 a.m.

"Two ships were seen on fire in the harbor," noted 71 Squadron's logbook.[6] Pilots over the beach area and the port of Dieppe had a better idea of what was going on than anyone either on the ground or aboard the ships offshore. "The general scene over the beaches was pretty chaotic," reported an RAF wing commander, "the sky was covered in the black smudges of bursting antiaircraft shells. Most of the time, at least one aircraft could be seen spinning or diving down somewhere, in a trail of smoke or flame."[7] Chesley Peterson, commanding 71 Squadron, gave a more pointed description as he stepped out of his Spitfire: "It's like a goddamn Fourth of July."[8]

The three Eagle Squadrons were not the only American fighter units in the air over Dieppe. The 31st Fighter Group, US Army Air Force, flew 123 sorties over the invasion area. It was the first time that the American pilots had been in combat, And it turned out to be a harsh indoctrination: Eight of the unit's Spitfires were shot down, and five of its pilots were missing.

The new pilots did enjoy some measure of success that day. Second Lieutenant Sam Jankin of the 31st FG shot down an FW 190—the USAAF's first enemy aircraft destroyed over Europe. Unfortunately, Lt. Jankin was shot down himself a few minutes later. He was later rescued from the Channel, along with many other pilots from both sides.

German intelligence apparently did not realize that the Americans were flying Spitfires, which were marked with the white US star in place of the red, white, and blue RAF roundel. After Oberleutnant Rolf Hermichen of Jagdgeschwader 26 shot down a fighter marked with the US insignia, he claimed a P-39 Airacobra destroyed, but no P-39s were in the air over Dieppe.

Along with the 31st Fighter Group, the 97th Bomb Group's B-17 Flying Fortresses were also flying operations on August 19. The 97th had flown its first operational sortie only two days before. Its target had been the rail yards at Rouen—an easy trip, a "milk run," in USAAF jargon. The August 19 operation was officially known as "Circus No. 205"—a harmless-sounding name that masked a potentially lethal assignment: a daylight bombing attack on a Luftwaffe fighter base. With four squadrons of RAF Spitfires for an escort, the Flying Fortresses were given the job of bombing Abbeville Aerodrome from high altitude and knocking it out, at least for several critical hours.

Senior officers in the USAAF had high hopes for their top-secret Norden bombsight. According to the experts, the Norden bombsight would allow a bomb aimer to drop a bomb into a pickle barrel from thousands of feet above its target. Now all the generals and planners would be given the chance to put their faith, and their bombsight, to the test.

The Fortresses arrived over the French coast shortly after 10:00 a.m. Surprisingly, hardly any fighter opposition was met. A Bf 109 was chased away by the tail gunner of one of the bombers; the top-turret gunner fired a burst at another fighter that the gunner could not identify. A few Focke-Wulfs hovered nearby for a while, but none of them seemed overly eager to attack. Their reluctance was partly because they had their hands full with activities at lower altitudes—RAF Boston medium bombers were also in the area—and partly because of their unfamiliarity with the big American bombers.

All anybody knew about the Flying Fortress was its reputation, and its reputation was formidable: it was said to be very large, very fast, and, with eleven or twelve machine guns, able to dish out as much damage as it could take. The pilots could see that the four-engine bombers were fast and well-armed and intimidating. Nobody wanted to get too close to those dozen or so machine guns.

This reluctance would change in the not-too-distant future after the Luftwaffe learned the Fortresses' weak points and how to take advantage of them. But over Abbeville on August 19, the bombers lived a charmed life, and the wariness of the German fighter pilots allowed the Flying Fortresses to do their job. Although the bombing accuracy from 23,000 feet did not even come close to the pinpoint precision hoped for by senior air force officers, it was good enough to knock out the fighter base at Abbeville for two hours.

A Messerschmitt Bf 109, caught in the gun camera of an American fighter. Although the Spitfire could outturn the Messerschmitt, the two fighters were basically comparable. (Courtesy of the National Museum of the United States Air Force®.)

The bombs not only prevented fighters from taking off and landing during this time, but also cratered two of the three runways, destroyed or damaged a number of buildings, and blew up three FW 190s on the ground. Unfortunately, the Fortresses did not always hit their target. Bombs also fell on the nearby village of Drucat, and several fell harmlessly into the woods.

At about 1:00 p.m., the pilots of 71 Squadron took off on their third sortie of the day. They did not have to venture very far into France to find trouble. In the vicinity of Dieppe, they came across a flight of three Ju 88s. Oscar Coen and his wingman, "Wee Michael" McPharlin, teamed up on one of the Junkers. They set the bomber on fire, but they did not see it crash and could only claim it as a "probable."

The squadron's leader, Chesley Peterson, singled out a second Ju 88.[9] He approached from behind and opened fire with his cannons and machine guns. The bomber tried to get away, but Peterson managed to stay with the Junkers and kept on firing. The Ju 88's tail gunner started shooting back. Peterson hit the bomber, but the tail gunner showed that he knew his business, as well. Peterson could feel machine gun bullets thud into his Spitfire.

"I knew I was hit and would have to bail out anyway," Peterson recalled, "so I kept firing up to 150 yards, when I had to quit as there was so much steam and smoke in the cockpit."

He got his Junkers. Wing Commander Miles Duke-Woolley, commanding the Debden Wing (squadrons 71, 124, and 232), confirmed that the German bomber crashed into the Channel. But the Junkers' rear gunner also got Peterson—Duke-Woolley also watched him bail out of his Spitfire.

Peterson jettisoned the cockpit canopy (which instantly cleared the cockpit of all the smoke and steam), clambered out of his stricken fighter, and jumped. He pulled his parachute's ripcord and began the long descent—about ten minutes—into the cold Channel water.

On the way down, Peterson remembered that he still had his revolver in his flying boot. He took it out of his boot and was about to toss it away when it occurred to him that he had never fired the thing, not even once. While floating down in his parachute, he decided to remedy the situation—he fired every round into the air, until it was empty. Satisfied, he dropped the revolver and watched it plummet toward the icy, gray water. A few minutes later, Peterson was in the Channel, as well.

After drifting for what must have seemed like forever, Peterson was rescued by a navy patrol boat. But even though he had been picked up, he was still not out of danger. On its way back to England, the boat was strafed by a German aircraft. Another rescued RAF pilot was killed in the attack, but Peterson made it back to England, and eventually, to Gravesend.

A few weeks later, Peterson was released from 71 Squadron and sent to London. From London, he was sent on to the United States to test fighter planes. Before he left England, Peterson was awarded the Distinguished Service Order for his part in Operation Jubilee and previous operations against the enemy.

Another member of 71 Squadron, "Wee Michael" McPharlin, was also shot down by the tail gunner of a Ju 88.[10] While he was double-teaming a Junkers along with Oscar Coen, the German rear gunner hit McPharlin's Spitfire and knocked out the compass. A flight of FW 190s forced him to take cover in a cloud bank. When he came out of the clouds, he had no idea where he was.

Completely disorientated, and with compass gone, McPharlin had no way of knowing how to get back to England. He circled over the Channel for quite a while, trying to get his bearings, but to no avail. When his Spitfire finally ran out of fuel, McPharlin was forced to bail out over the Channel. When he splashed down, McPharlin discovered that he was only about three miles from the French coast, and much too close to the Germans for comfort. He inflated his dinghy and began paddling toward England—a cross-Channel trip that very quickly turned out to be a lot longer than it looked.

McPharlin was not called "Wee Michael" for nothing—short of stature, slight of build, he was anything but a candidate for the Olympic rowing team. After only a few minutes of paddling, it became clear that he was going to need a massive dose of energy and endurance if he was going to complete his cross-Channel journey. Luckily, he knew exactly where he could get an immediate supply of these necessary items—both energy and endurance were to be had in the Benzedrine tablets that had thoughtfully been included in his emergency kit. He opened the kit and downed the entire supply.

The pills certainly did the trick. He was soon bursting with energy and paddling full tilt toward southern England. He was picked up by Air-Sea Rescue within about twenty minutes and was able to return to base that night. But even though he was now safe on dry land, the effects of the Benzedrine did not wear off. This was not surprising, considering the dose he had taken. McPharlin did not go to sleep for two days and two nights. At two o'clock on the third morning, he was still sitting at the bar, wide awake. The pilots took turns keeping an eye on him—nobody knew when he was going to collapse.

McPharlin's energy finally gave out as the third night was approaching, which was when he finally conked out, right onto the floor of the bar. His squadron mates picked him up and, according to an eyewitness, "poured him into bed."

He slept for twenty-four hours straight. When he finally did wake up, everybody was absolutely astonished that there were no side effects from the pills—no headache, no hangover, no nausea, nothing. McPharlin was as bright as a button. Everyone's respect for Benzedrine as "an escape aid" reached new heights.

★ ★ ★

Both 71 and 133 Squadrons flew four trips over Dieppe; 121 Squadron made three trips. By the time 71 Squadron arrived over the landing area at about 5:45 p.m., as part of Duke-Woolley's Debden Wing, all the assault boats were away from the beaches and heading back toward England. A large formation of FW 190s flew into sight, and the Spitfires maneuvered into position to attack. But as soon as the three squadrons turned toward the Focke-Wulfs, the Germans retreated toward Le Touquet.

It was nearly dark, so the Debden Wing set course for Gravesend where the Spitfires were rearmed and refueled in preparation for night operations. As it happened, there were to be no night operations, but the day's operations were not over yet. Don Blakeslee took 133 Squadron back to Dieppe at 7:55 p.m. By that time, there was not much traffic in the area. What was left of the landing force had already been evacuated, And most of the Luftwaffe had returned to its airfields.

There were still a few German pilots up and looking for a fight. Two FW 190s materialized and came after the Spitfires. One of the Spit pilots fired "a good burst" into one of them and claimed the FW as "probably destroyed." This was very likely the last action of the long, harrowing day. The Spitfires of 133 Squadron were the last ones down, landing at Lympne at 8:55, and actually, things had not been that bad for them. They had enjoyed themselves hugely. "Every dog has its day," crowed the Squadron's logbook, "and on August 19, 133 was the dog."[11]

As a unit, the pilots claimed six enemy aircraft destroyed, two probables, and eight damaged (claims that would later be "officially" changed), with no losses or casualties of their own. These were the numbers given in the Squadron's logbook, but would be changed after the battle. Number 133 Squadron was one of the few RAF units to come out ahead on that particular day.

The Eagle Squadrons probably flew both the opening and the closing sorties of Operation Jubilee. At dawn, 71 Squadron was the first squadron in combat, and 133's encounter with the FW 190s came after dark.

★ ★ ★

Dieppe marked the first time in two years that a major air battle had come so close to Britain's shores. Not since the Battle of Britain in the summer of 1940 had such heavy aerial fighting, by masses of airplanes on both sides, been visible from England. Crowds of spectators gathered along the Channel coast to watch the planes twisting and weaving in their deadly maneuvers. The best place to see the action was from the high ground at Beachy Head in Sussex. From there, the intricate white contrails were plainly visible against the blue summer sky.

"The planes in their hundreds made the sky alive with action, speed and noise," wrote a news reporter from the southern coast. "Bombers and fighters were seen, some engaged with enemy planes, and many a swift aerial battle was fought out within sight of the eager, watching crowds."[12]

The Dieppe raid had certainly succeeded in one of its aims—it did bring the Luftwaffe out. Nearly 1,000 sorties had been flown by the German air force—145 by twin-engine bombers and the rest by fighters. Most of the German force was concentrated over Dieppe. This bunching of so many fighters over so small an area often gave the Germans numerical superiority even in small encounters with the RAF—which resulted in "one of the happiest days since the Battle of Britain," according to Hans Ring, a German historian.[13]

Total German claims for the day were 112 aircraft shot down, though the British Air Ministry only admitted to 88 airplanes and 57 pilots lost.[14] Top scorer was Lieutenant Josef Wurmheller of Jagdgeschwader 2, who was credited with six Spitfires and one Blenheim bomber destroyed.

In the three Eagle Squadrons, losses came to six Spitfires destroyed and four damaged.[15] One pilot was killed; another was shot down and taken prisoner. The hardest hit had been 121 Squadron, which had four of its twelve Spitfires destroyed and two others damaged. One of 121's pilots had been killed, and another fell into enemy hands.

As far as claims were concerned, the official score of the three Eagle Squadrons was seven enemy aircraft destroyed (one by 71 Squadron, one by 121, and five by 133); four probables (one by 71 Squadron, two by 121, and one by 133); and fourteen damaged (three by 71 Squadron, one by 121, and ten by 133).

The air battle over Dieppe marked the first time that the Eagle Squadrons had encountered the enemy in such force. They had been used to seeing Focke-Wulfs and Messerschmitts in small numbers on their fighter sweeps over the Continent. This confrontation came as a sobering experience.

For the pilots of the US 31st Fighter Group, who lost eight Spitfires, the air battle also came as a nasty shock. They found out that they had a great deal to learn about air combat and that flying against the Luftwaffe was a lot different from flying training sorties over the green fields of southern England.

Military historians generally consider the Dieppe raid a failure, if not a total disaster. About the only consolation were the lessons learned from the landing: there is a vital need for heavy naval gunfire support to soften up the landing beaches, and intelligence and air superiority in preparing for such an undertaking are of great importance.

That the losses of Dieppe prevented even heavier losses in subsequent operations, notably the Normandy landings on D-Day, June 6, 1944, was the orthodox point of view. But it was of little value or consolation to the thousands killed or captured during the Dieppe landing, or to the pilots shot down trying to protect the landing force.

Pilot Officer Harold Strickland of 71 Squadron would take a more optimistic view—that Dieppe was instrumental in the *success* of the D-Day landings. "Operation Jubilee in 1942 had conditioned the German strategists to believe that the logical site for the main landing . . . would be in the Pas de Calais area, and Normandy was a diversion."[16]

But Wing Commander Duke-Woolley, who had flown with 71 Squadron over Dieppe, thought "the whole operation was an extraordinary nonsense. It was large enough to invite heavy casualties, but too small for the Germans to consider it an 'invasion' of any sort."[17] He also believed that anchoring the fighters to Dieppe was a bad mistake. Instead, he wished they had attacked the Luftwaffe bases "in a big way," especially the fighter bases in the Abbeville area.

The British press played down the losses suffered at Dieppe. Newspapers emphasized the fact that the Allies had finally staged a landing on the enemy's coast and hinted that this was only a dress rehearsal for a much more ambitious invasion in the not-too-distant future.

★★★ **CHAPTER ELEVEN** ★★★

A MOST DEMOCRATIC ARMY

F ollowing Dieppe, the three Eagle Squadrons were not given any time off. On August 20, the day after the raid, 71 Squadron escorted bombing raids over northern France. Bomber escorts were the Eagles' main activity during the latter part of August, along with convoy patrols.

The Luftwaffe stayed out of sight most of the time. A frequent entry in squadron logbooks is "no enemy aircraft seen." It was as though the German air force had made its point—it was still full of fight and was more than capable of challenging either the British or the Americans any time it chose—and was satisfied to let it go at that.

Once in a while, though, the enemy did decide to make his presence known. When that happened, the result was a short, violent combat. On August 27, for instance, 71 Squadron took part in what started out as another routine escort mission. But this time the Luftwaffe made up its mind to come up and fight. In the ensuing melee, 71 Squadron claimed two enemy aircraft destroyed and one probable. The squadron also lost one of their own Spitfires to enemy fighters.[1]

In addition to the Luftwaffe, the coming transfer to the US forces was also on everyone's mind. The pilots in all three Eagle Squadrons knew that their days in the RAF were numbered and that it would only be a matter of a few weeks until they were absorbed into the growing Eighth Air Force. Handwritten across the top of 71 Squadron's operations record book was the note, "Now No. 334 Sq. USAAF."

The impending move was not being anticipated with any particular enthusiasm, however. After taking a look at the Eighth Air Force in combat, many of the Eagles wondered what they were getting themselves into. No one was impressed by what they had seen so far. Robert S. Raymond, the Yank from Kansas in Bomber Command, considered the American crews poorly trained, poorly equipped, and not very well prepared for living in Britain.

Not many of Robert Raymond's colleagues would have disagreed with this judgment. From what the RAF had been able to observe so far, the Americans did not seem to be able to do anything right. When the Eagles escorted B-17s over France, the bombers had a habit of showing up either too early or too late at their rendezvous. Also, the crews frequently displayed faulty navigation, failed to hold tight formations, and sometimes even flew right past their target.

One thing the Eagles—as well as other Spitfire pilots—learned very quickly was not to get too close to the Flying Fortresses. The American gunners shot at any fighter that came within range—they did not care if the fighters were German or Allied. Stories began circulating that some of the Spitfires of 133 Squadron returned to base with .50 caliber bullet holes in the wings and fuselage, but Carroll McColpin of 133 does not agree.

"They shot at Spits many times," McColpin recalled, "but I have never heard of a Spit complaining of being hit."[2] As an afterthought, he said, "I wonder how they are shooting the Jerries if they never hit the Spitfires?"

That raised another sore point—the wildly extravagant victory claims made by American gunners. RAF pilots, including the Eagles, were absolutely astonished by the number of enemy aircraft the bombers claimed as shot down. On one particular mission, Flying Fortress gunners claimed a total of forty-eight enemy aircraft, along with twenty-five probables and thirty-two damaged. But the RAF fighter escort did not see that many German aircraft in the air.

One of the British flyers at Biggin Hill sarcastically asked a 133 pilot, "Why no claims? The bomber boys have claimed something phenomenal, at least ten destroyed and fifteen probables."[3]

The Eagle pilots seemed alternatively furious at and ashamed of their fellow countrymen, and were disgusted by their evident lack of training and discipline. Among the more diplomatic phrases used to describe the B-17 crews were "pretty sickly" and "hopeless." In private, they wondered how the top brass in the USAAF could be so short-sighted and unprofessional as to send such undertrained crews into combat.

A fairly typical escort mission took place on September 9. The Spitfires of 133 Squadron were scheduled to rendezvous with thirty-six Flying Fortresses over the southern coast of England. "The Fortresses were seven minutes early, but 133, being wise guys, were seven minutes early, too," cracked the Squadron's logbook.[4] Ten Focke-Wulfs hovered near the bombers but did not seem overly keen to engage in combat.

When the B-17s recrossed the French coast on their way back to England after bombing their target, their gunners, "for some reason or other," began shooting at the Spitfires. "This did not please the pilots at all," the squadron's intelligence officer recounted, "so they dived down to sea level and came back alone, leaving the bombers to themselves."

Opinions of American bombing techniques were as uncomplimentary as those of American gunnery and navigation. On another bombing mission, the Flying Fortresses showed up twenty minutes late for their rendezvous with 133 Squadron, proceeded to drop their bombs "all over the place," and then "made for home." This sort of performance was not even close to the standards demanded by the Royal Air Force.

From what the RAF had seen, the American bomber crews were not going to be much of an asset. Their navigators could not steer a course, their bomb aimers could not hit their targets, and their gunners could not hit anything.

Even though most Britons had never met an American before, their mental image was of a people who were always thorough and efficient, in a ruthless sort of way—"typical Yankee efficiency" was one transatlantic trait that was given enthusiastic admiration. It did not take very long for the myth of the efficient, energetic American to come crashing to earth.

The British view of American involvement in the war to date went something like this: First, they had been caught sleeping at Pearl Harbor. After being kicked into the war, they found themselves without any fighter aircraft that could hope to compete with the Luftwaffe's Focke-Wulfs and Messerschmitts. When they finally were able to send aircrews to Britain, the men were either undertrained, incompetent, or both.

And this did not apply to just a few untrainables who somehow slipped through the net. The majority of American aircrews were inadequate, at least by RAF standards. But it was not the men who were to blame; senior air force officers back in the States were pushing them through training and sending them off to war before they were ready.

It seemed to the RAF that the United States was planning to fight the war with half-measures and excuses—a program that was certain to kill a good many Americans in the sky above the German-occupied Continent. They came to England bragging, "We're going to win the war for you," but could not even do their jobs properly. So much for "typical Yankee efficiency!"

Dissatisfaction with the performance of American pilots and aircrews was widespread throughout the RAF, and Eagle Squadron pilots criticized them just as loudly. Although the Eagles probably did not realize it, their reaction to the newly arrived Eighth Air Force was filled with irony. When the first Eagle Squadron had been formed two years before, the Yank volunteers were bitterly faulted for being unmanageable, undisciplined, and generally of little use against the Germans. Now, the pilots of the Eagle Squadrons were making the same sort of remarks about another group of Americans who had recently come to England to fight the Germans. The course had run full circle.

A dramatic photo of the Mighty Eighth, in all of its glory: a formation of B-17 Flying Fortresses escorted by fighters, somewhere over the enemy-occupied Continent. In 1942, the Eighth Air Force was just starting operations from British airfields. Bomber pilots and aircrews lacked training and experience and would learn many things about the Luftwaffe the hard way. (Courtesy of the National Museum of the United States Air Force®.)

Members of the three Eagle Squadrons did not confine their criticism to just the Eighth Air Force. They were also still busily finding fault with each other.[5] The rivalry among the three units had not diminished with

time, as RAF Fighter Command had hoped. If anything, it had grown—
"to the point where it was causing concern to various wing commanders,"
one historian noted. Keeping the three squadrons separated, basing them
at three different airfields was the only way to keep the problem at bay.

Besides troubling senior RAF officers, this unfriendly rivalry was also
causing increasing concern among officers in the Eighth Air Force. Once
the three Eagle Squadrons had been absorbed into the American forces,
the plan was to station all three units at one base and incorporate them
into one group: the US 4th Fighter Group. If the three squadrons kept
squabbling with each other, such an arrangement would be out of the
question.

The negative attitude of the squadrons toward each other once again
came into plain view after Dieppe, when 133 Squadron was reequipped
with the new Spitfire Mark IX. The Mark IX was the most up-to-date
and sought-after British fighter. Number 133 had been issued the newest
model Spitfire (along with the other two Biggin Hill squadrons) and
claimed this as a sign of superiority over both 71 and 121 Squadrons,
which still had the old Mark V Spits. The other two Eagle Squadrons,
needless to say, resented this.

"We had the best planes," said one member of 133. "We had dawn
readiness—71 didn't. . . . We considered ourselves the best without question. One-three-three was number one among the Eagle Squadrons."[6]

This latest version of the Spitfire had been designed to match the
Focke-Wulf 190 in performance. It had a much larger and more powerful
engine than the Mark V, giving it a higher speed and faster rate of climb.
The Mark IX was also more heavily armed; it came from the factory with
mountings for four 20 mm cannon and four .303 machine guns. The
pilots of 133 only used 20 mm cannons, however. Adding four machine
guns would have meant carrying an additional 300 pounds, which would
result in a loss of maneuverability at high altitudes.

Getting the Mark IX was certainly a status symbol. Every fighter
squadron in the RAF wanted them, and only the Biggin Hill wing had

them. But although 133 Squadron now had a more advanced fighter, the other two squadrons did not agree that this made them the best of the all-American fighter units. (Neither did senior officers in the Eighth Air Force, who still considered 71 Squadron the best.)

The pilots of 71 Squadron shared the Eighth Air Force's opinion. Their claim was based upon the number of enemy aircraft they had shot down—more German planes than the other two "junior" squadrons combined. And 121 Squadron did not want to hear that either of the other two Eagle Squadrons thought that they were better flyers.

All of this sounds petty and carping, but the resentment among the three Eagle Squadrons was bitter and deep-seated, enough to frighten officers in both the RAF and the USAAF. Even though all the pilots were American, the only thing they seemed to have in common was animosity. There could not be any possibility of forming an all-American wing; at least not with these three squadrons. If they were all based at the same airfield, the pilots would spend more time fighting each other than the Luftwaffe.

★ ★ ★

By September 1942, the problem was more of a concern for the Americans than for the British. On September 15, 1942—more than nine months after the United States entered the war—the first group of Eagle Squadron pilots was commissioned into the US Army Air force.

"We went to London in ones and twos during our precious 24-hour passes to transfer and pick up our US uniforms," recalled James Goodson of 133 Squadron.[7] Before they could transfer officially, every pilot had to travel to London for an examination by a board of American officers. Among those asking questions were two of the highest-ranking officers in the USAAF: Major General Carl A. Spaatz, commander of the US Army Air Forces in Britain; and Brigadier General Frank O'Driscoll Hunter, in command of US Fighter Command.

James Goodson, sitting at the controls of his P-51 Mustang.
He had been on board the British liner *Athenia* when it was
torpedoed by a U-boat in September 1939 and volunteered
to join the Royal Canadian Air Force when he recrossed
the Atlantic and made his way to Canada. (Courtesy of the
National Museum of the United States Air Force®.)

After their examination, the pilots were sworn into the US forces.
Most entered the American air force with the rank that corresponded
with their current RAF grade: flight lieutenants became captains,

squadron leaders became majors. Sergeant pilots were given commissions, entering the USAAF as second lieutenants.

Not every pilot was fully prepared to go along with this scheme, however. Squadron Leader Carroll McColpin told his examiners that he ought to be promoted to brigadier general—after all, the American forces would be acquiring a seasoned combat veteran and a proven combat leader—but allowed himself to be persuaded into settling for the rank of major.

Most of the pilots did not ask for a promotion, but they did make one special request—permission to wear their RAF wings on their American uniforms. They felt that they had earned the right to wear them. To almost everyone's surprise, the Eighth Air Force agreed with them. Transferring pilots would be allowed to wear miniature copies of their RAF wings over the right breast pocket of their tunic. Full-sized US silver wings would be worn over the left pocket. It was a small concession, but it raised everyone's spirits—while serving in the American forces, the former Eagles would be able to wear a symbol of their time in the RAF.

The most significant changes in the pilots' lives involved issues that were much more basic than their uniforms or rank. When transferring to the US military forces, pilots became eligible for American-style food, as well as American-style pay.

The change in food constituted a gigantic improvement, at least in the opinion of most of the pilots. No more "bubble and squeak"—cabbage and potatoes—in the officers' mess. From now on, there would be real vegetables, real American coffee, ice cream, pork chops and other red meat, along with other items they had not seen since they left the States. The British Isles had many pleasant attributes, even in wartime; the food, however, was not one of them.

But the most profoundly felt change, the biggest and best, was in the rate of pay between the US forces and the RAF. Once they were in the American forces, the pilots would be receiving somewhere between two and three times the amount of their RAF pay. A pilot officer in the Royal Air Force was paid roughly $67.00 per month; an equivalently ranked second lieutenant in the USAAF earned $162.00 per month. By joining the American air force, the pilots would be getting a promotion (in pay, at least), whether they received an increase in rank or not.

During 121 Squadron's farewell party, a departing pilot told an RAF wing commander, "We can't afford *not* to go. Do you realize, Wingco, as of now, I'm being paid about twice as much as you if not more—and I'm only a lootenant. Too bad you don't qualify to come with us, your accent would be worth every cent of your pay—what, what, old boy?"[8]

But in spite of all the incentives, some American pilots were reluctant to leave the RAF. Leo Nomis, who had been with 71 Squadron until he transferred to duty in Malta, was still in the Middle East when he joined the USAAF. He admitted that he was reluctant to leave the British forces, "because by that stage I had become immersed in RAF tradition, and American procedures seemed quite foreign to me."[9]

Others felt the same way. Robert S. Raymond had been in RAF Bomber Command for two and a half years when he transferred to the US forces. "It's a bit depressing to leave a service I've grown to like," he reflected, "to leave familiar ways."[10]

Raymond had flown thirty missions over Germany between January and April 1943, including strikes against Düsseldorf, Nuremberg, and five trips to Berlin. After finishing his tour of operations, he was sent to an Air-Sea Rescue unit as a "rest" posting. Raymond was not happy with his new job, however, which consisted mainly of saving downed flyers from the freezing waters surrounding the British Isles. So, when the opportunity presented itself, he left the RAF to join up with the Eighth Air Force.

Although he was now back among his own countrymen, Raymond did not feel at home. "It seems strange to be an officer in an army and know nothing about the methods, customs, and procedures they use," he said. Even some of the language was foreign to him. He had seen the well-known initials "G.I." stenciled on army equipment, but he had no idea what they meant. . Somebody had to tell him that they stood for "Government Issue."

Like the pilots of the three Eagle Squadrons, Raymond also had a less-than-glowing opinion of the American Flying Fortress crews and their sub-RAF standards. He observed several cases of "battle fatigue" in his new unit, an affliction that was very rare in the RAF (where it was known as "operational nerves"). He blamed the common combat nerves of American crews on their "typical" temperament—Americans always seemed shocked whenever they were faced with unpleasant situations.

Most of the American servicemen he met also seemed rudely surprised to discover that the Germans were very aggressive opponents. Raymond blames this shortcoming on the US high command, who did not prepare pilots and crews for what they would be facing when they went into combat—an irresponsible omission, since it meant that the men would have to find out for themselves.

But Raymond also encountered a few pleasant surprises. During the last two and a half years, he had forgotten what Americans were really like. He quickly rediscovered American ways and also learned first-hand how foreign the British and Americans are to each other—especially where the separation of rank and class are concerned.

The American forces, Raymond observed, were "a most democratic army." Enlisted men displayed a singular lack of deference to officers—which they never would have got away with in the British forces. The men also tended to add individual flourishes, such as baseball caps, to their uniforms. Raymond had become accustomed to the "class-conscious British way" and found the New World difference in attitude refreshing.

Another welcome change was the American get-up-and-go—they may not have done things right all the time, but at least they did them in a hurry. Everybody seemed to do everything on the run; nobody ever seemed to walk anywhere. "The Yankee energy here displayed is infectious," Raymond remarked. "It makes me feel like I've been sleepwalking."

William Dunn, the first ace produced by the Eagle Squadrons, had an entirely different reaction toward transferring out of the RAF.[11] By the autumn of 1942, he had fully recovered from his combat wounds and was serving as acting squadron leader of 130 Squadron, stationed in Canada. Dunn knew that most American pilots in the British forces were changing their RAF blue uniforms for US khaki, but he had no real desire to do the same.

A letter from an organization that called itself the United States Inter-Allied Personnel Board changed his way of thinking. The letter was not a friendly one; the board pulled no punches. "It was sort of implied that if I didn't agree to a transfer, they'd come and get me," Dunn recalled. He was not intimidated by the nasty letter, but, like most Americans, he was won over by the generous US pay and allowances. Squadron Leader Dunn agreed to the transfer and was released from the Royal Air Force in June 1943.

When he became a member of the US Army Air Force, however, Dunn was unpleasantly surprised to find that at he had been sharply reduced in rank. He would enter the American forces as a second lieutenant—three notches below his current rank.

Dunn was not happy about being "busted," to put it mildly. He complained about the situation and had his rank increased to captain—still one notch below his RAF rank—which is what he had to settle for. The next time he flew against the enemy was as a member of the 406th Fighter Group, USAAF. While with the American forces, Dunn shot down another German plane. He finished the war with a score of six victories.

In reality, neither Dunn nor any other American citizen was compelled by any law to transfer to the American military forces. Anyone could stay in the RAF if they chose to. And a number of Americans did elect to remain with the British forces. Nobody knows exactly how many since, because of the Neutrality Acts, nobody knows how many Americans served with British military units to begin with. For any number of reasons, these men were not influenced by the incentives of added pay and better rations.

Some likely had practical reasons for remaining in the RAF. There were probably more than a few who entered the British services by way of forged passports or other documents who had to keep their mouths shut regarding their true citizenship. Some "secret Americans," who went to Canada in 1939 or 1940 under forged passports or assumed identities, might have felt hesitant about leaving the RAF after having gone through so much trouble to get into it. Others may have simply elected to stay in the RAF because they had already served two or three years. They had thrown in their lot with His Majesty's forces and decided that they might as well stay for the duration.

J. K. Havilland, one of the seven "official" Americans who fought in the Battle of Britain, remained in the RAF throughout the war.[12] He survived the fighting, and after the war, he moved to Canada and became a teacher. James C. Nelson of 133 Squadron also elected to stay in the RAF when the Eagle Squadrons transferred. When the war ended, he returned to the United States.

The American in the RAF with the most enemy aircraft shot down was Lance C. Wade, who scored twenty-five victories in North Africa, Italy, and Sicily. Wade was given the nickname "the Arizona Wildcat," which he probably hated—he was also described as being "unusually modest" for an American. Wade was the commanding officer of 145 Squadron and scored the units 200th victory. Shortly after this, he was promoted to the rank of wing commander. On January 12, 1944, Wade was killed in a flying accident.

John J. Lynch, formerly of 71 Squadron and hailing from Alhambra, California, rose to the rank of squadron leader and is credited with shooting down thirteen enemy aircraft. All of his victories were scored over Malta. He is credited with Malta's 1,000th German aircraft destroyed, which he shot down on April 28, 1944.

Wing Commander James H. Little of New Orleans commanded 418 Squadron, a night fighter unit. Little is officially credited with four enemy aircraft destroyed.

David C. Fairbanks, a native of New York, destroyed fifteen enemy aircraft during the course of the war. Two of these were Messerschmitt

Me 262s, the revolutionary German jet fighter, which Squadron Leader Fairbanks shot down in February 1945.

Two Americans who left the United States soon after the war began in 1939 were Alger Jenkins of Montclair, New Jersey, and Alan Reed, who graduated from Princeton University in 1940. No trace of either of them exists after their departure for Britain—which, presumably, was via Canada. They simply left the country and disappeared. No one knows how many of their fellow countrymen shared the same fate.

★★★ CHAPTER TWELVE ★★★

MORE ENGLISH THAN THE ENGLISH

The last half of September 1942 was a strange time for the Eagle Squadron pilots. They had been commissioned as officers in the United States Army Air Force, but they were also still on "detached service" with RAF Fighter Command. The pilots still wore their RAF uniforms; some had not even got around to buying American uniforms. They still flew Spitfires, which were still marked with the RAF roundel insignia. Although they were now in the American services, at long last, the men were not yet out of the British forces.

Most of their trips over to France were uneventful. Fighter sweeps hardly ever encountered any enemy aircraft. The most common entry in Squadron logbooks was the all-too-frequent "nothing to report." Once in a while, though, there was something worth mentioning in the logbook.

On September 5, P/O D. A. Young of 121 Squadron spotted a Ju 88 over Southend-on-Sea.[1] The bomber was already being attacked by two

Spitfires from another squadron when he joined in on the kill. Young chased after the Junkers, which had been set on fire, and gave it two bursts of cannon fire. The German bomber crashed into the Thames Estuary "with a huge splash" according to 121 Squadron's ORB. This was the last enemy aircraft that 121 Squadron would shoot down. A few shots were fired at FW 190s during fighter sweeps, but no further claims were made.

Preparations were already under way to absorb the three Eagle Squadrons into the US forces. On September 23, both 121 and 133 Squadrons joined Number 71 at Debden Airfield, in Essex. This was the first time that all three units had ever been based at the same station. Senior officers within the Eighth Air Force had heard about the bad feelings between the three squadrons and wanted to see what would happen when they were thrown together.

The operations record book of 71 Squadron remarked, "The nearby village of Saffron Walden [about three miles away from the fighter base] would not be losing its boisterous Yanks." On the contrary, with all three squadrons now at RAF Debden, there would actually be three times as many Yanks in Saffron Walden as before, for better or worse.

Three days after arriving at its new base, 133 Squadron was temporarily sent off to the RAF airfield at Bolt Head, near the city of Exeter. From Bolt Head, the Squadron was to fly a routine escort mission, giving fighter cover to the 97th Bomb Group on a raid on Morlaix, in Brittany.[2] Morlaix was the site of a Focke-Wulf maintenance plant, as well as a center for rail yards and railway facilities.

It was considered such a routine assignment—just fly to the target with the bombers and fly back again—that hardly any of the pilots bothered to attend the preflight briefing. They had done this sort of run so many times before, and they knew the coast of Brittany almost as thoroughly as they knew the coast of southern England. Going to the briefing seemed a waste of time.

The operation turned out to be anything but routine—it went wrong from the very beginning. According to plan, the twelve Spitfire Mark IXs of 133 Squadron, along with the Spitfires from 66 and 401 Squadrons, were to rendezvous with the Flying Fortresses over the English Channel, which was roughly halfway between Bolt Head and Morlaix. But the bombers arrived at their rendezvous point early. Not bothering to wait for the Spits, they went on to the target without an escort.

While the Flying Fortresses went on toward Brittany, the Spitfires kept orbiting the Bay of Biscay, burning up fuel and waiting for orders—should they continue after the bombers or go back home? After orbiting the bay several times, ground control in England finally ordered the fighters to fly after the bombers, which were now many miles away, catch them up, and escort them to Morlaix.

Normally, the mission would have been aborted. It was RAF procedure to call off an operation if the rendezvous was missed by as much as half a minute. But this was a publicity mission, flown to show that the United States and Britain were equal partners in the war and also to give American war correspondents a good story. The most widely circulated rumor was that ground control sent the Spitfires after the Flying Fortresses because of pressure from senior officers in the Eighth Air Force.

Besides being kept waiting over the Bay of Biscay, the pilots were also given an incorrect estimate of wind speed when they were sent off to find the Flying Fortresses—a problem that would soon prove to be extremely costly. The Spitfire pilots had been told that they would be flying into a 35-knot headwind, slowing their forward speed. But the Spits, flying at 28,000 feet, were actually in the jet stream, a high-speed wind current that was all but unknown in 1942. Instead of a 35-knot headwind, the jet stream gave the fighters a 100-knot tailwind. This added up to a 135-knot miscalculation.

According to their estimated airspeed, counting the 35-knot headwind, it should have taken them thirty-three minutes to fly to their destination. But because of the jet stream, the Spitfires actually flew more than 100 miles to the south of their projected destination during the thirty-three-minute flight. And because of the heavy overcast (cloud cover was about 80 percent over most of northern France), nothing but solid gray-white clouds could be seen underneath. Blown well to the south by the jet stream, and unable to identify anything on the ground, nobody had any idea where they were.

Ground control in England could see the Spitfires on radar, but could not give the pilots their position—the Luftwaffe might be listening. Eventually, the three Spitfire squadrons ran into the Flying Fortresses they were supposed to escort—the bomber pilots had given up trying to find Morlaix through the thick cloud and had turned back for England. The fighter pilots latched on to the Fortresses, hoping that their navigators would lead them home.

Low on fuel, the pilots began to descend below the clouds after only half an hour with the bombers. They were thoroughly disorientated and thought that they must be over southern England by that time. By dropping through the clouds, they hoped to spot an emergency airfield and make an unscheduled fuel stop. But they were not over England, they were still over Brittany. As soon as they dropped through the cloud layer, the Spitfires came under immediate attack—first by antiaircraft fire, then by FW 190s.

With no fuel to spare, there was not very much the pilots could do in the way of evasive action. Each pilot called out his situation over the radio and tried to do what he could to save himself. Some bailed out. Others crash-landed. One pilot was shot down and killed over Brittany. Only one managed to make it back to England—Richard N. Beaty ran out of fuel and crash-landed his Spitfire a few miles inland from the south coast.

Of the thirty-six Spitfires that took part in the "routine" operation, twenty-two were lost. Number 133 Squadron fared the worst. Four pilots were killed; six bailed out or crash-landed in enemy territory and were taken prisoner; another pilot managed to evade capture and eventually returned to England; and Richard Beaty belly-landed his fighter in England. All twelve Spitfires were gone.

Except for on paper at the Air Ministry in London, 133 Squadron no longer existed. Replacement pilots were sent to Debden to take over for the pilots who were lost in that disastrous mission. Replacement aircraft were also sent—but there were no more Mark IX Spitfires available, so 133 Squadron was reequipped with the older Mark V.

P/O James Goodson, a replacement who happened to come to Debden on the same day as the Morlaix raid, arrived at a nearly deserted airfield. The only pilot he met was P/O Don Gentile, who had not gone with the squadron to Morlaix. Gentile told Goodson and another new arrival, "I sure am glad to see you. I'm all alone here."[3]

Gentile explained to the two new men that none of the others had come back. There had been a Fortress raid on "Brest," he told them—he obviously had not been to the briefing either. "There was a lot of cloud, and maybe the wind changed," Gentile continued. "I guess the Forts kept going, and our guys stayed with them. On the way back, they were already short of gas when they were bounced by Jerries. They couldn't get back across the Channel." A fair thumbnail description, although not entirely accurate.

Dr. Goebbels's Propaganda Ministry in Berlin immediately announced that twenty-two RAF Spitfires had been brought down by the Luftwaffe and that several Americans had been among the pilots that were killed or captured. Both the British and the American press asked questions about the mission. In response, the Air Ministry and the Eighth Air Force declared that the fighters had been lost because of wing icing and adverse weather conditions. The press, having no other source of information, printed the only information they had, and reported that twenty-two Spitfires crashed because of heavy icing on the wings.

"I guess you can take any room," Gentile told Goodson. "They're all empty."

Goodson found a room that suited him, but quickly discovered that its previous occupant's personal belongings had not been removed. Besides uniforms, a shaving kit, and toilet articles, there were also letters and family photos. On the desk was an unfinished letter to the pilot's mother. Goodson felt like an intruder.

One good thing did come out of the Morlaix disaster—it played a large part in dispelling the bad feeling and rivalry among the three Eagle Squadrons. The "third Eagles," which had been ridiculed as "junior," had been wiped out—killed or taken prisoner, except for one pilot. The catastrophe abruptly ended all the name calling. Bad feelings were instantly replaced by sympathy; the rivalry of the past year, along with all the criticism and cutting remarks, was forgotten. Both 71 and 121 Squadrons knew that the same thing that happened to 133 could just as easily have happened to them.

★ ★ ★

For many years after the event, pilots speculated on who was at fault in the Morlaix tragedy: ground control in England; the Flying Fortress pilots; the meteorological officers. The remaining Eagle Squadron pilots had good reason to complain about the chain of events that led to the loss of an entire fighter squadron. But in the late summer of 1942, they seemed to be finding fault with everything, including anything connected with the US Eighth Air Force.

It seemed that all the "glamour boy" publicity really *had* gone to their heads. The Eagle Squadrons, now the 4th Fighter Group, acquired a reputation for being a clique of prima donnas (the old phrase was still being used) who looked down their noses at the rest of the world—including all news reporters and the entire US Army Air Force.

One incident that helped to reinforce this image took place shortly after the Eagles became part of the Eighth Air Force. About forty news reporters, British and American, gathered at the US embassy in Grosvenor Square to interview Chesley Peterson, executive officer of the 4th Fighter Group (former commander of 71 Squadron).[4] His behavior at the news conference lowered the press corps' opinion of the 4th Fighter Group "Eagles" to new depths.

Before the interview began, Peterson was scheduled to pose for a group of newspaper and magazine photographers. The cameramen thought that the American flag would make an appropriate backdrop for the photo session, and asked Peterson to stand in front of a large flag. Peterson was annoyed by the request. "I take a dim view of this corny stuff," he told the photo crew. He deigned to stand near the flag when someone informed him that General George Marshall, the US Army chief of staff, had agreed to a similar pose.

Having done his bit to offend the photographers, Peterson then went to work on alienating the other members of the press. "I want to say right in the beginning that I'm going to be damn careful in what I say to you," he growled. "I expect you people to misquote me. I don't trust reporters."

The reporters were anything but charmed by Peterson, and the news conference was anything but a success. A number of reporters walked out on him. All of them would remember his little performance. During the aerial fighting over the enemy-held Continent in 1943 and 1944, when the 4th Fighter Group was competing with Hubert Zemke's 56th Fighter Group for most confirmed victories, reporters and editors at the *Stars and Stripes* showed their feelings for Peterson's 4th FG by running stories about that group in 12-point type. Stories about Zemke's unit were run in the much more commanding 24-point type. The *Stars and Stripes* made no secret of which unit it favored.

The editorial staff struck its first blow in response to Chesley Peterson's conduct even before Hubert Zemke and the 56th Fighter Group arrived in Britain. The occasion for its first retaliatory gesture was the 336th (formerly 133) Fighter Squadron's first fighter sweep over German-occupied territory.

It did not amount to much of an effort—only a low-level strafing attack by two pilots, Richard L. "Dixie" Alexander and James Goodson.[5] The weather was too overcast and unpredictable for normal fighter operations, so the two were allowed to go off on their own "unofficial" free-hunt over France and Belgium. Their Spitfires were marked with brand-new US Army Air Force white stars.

Once they reached the enemy coast, Alexander and Goodson came in at a very low level, surprising all the antiaircraft gunners. Flak batteries did open up on them, but everything arced right over the two fighters. As the two pilots skipped from Gravelines to Dunkirk, they shot up any boats and barges they happened to come across. They also blasted away at a couple of locomotives in the Bruges rail yard.

Apart from boosting their own morale, Goodson and Alexander did not accomplish very much. Goodson's report to the squadron's intelligence officer was, in his own words, "duly modest, if not laconic."

When the staff at *Stars and Stripes* heard about the sweep, they wrote their own version of what happened. In sarcastic retaliation for Chesley Peterson's less-than-charming behavior at the Grosvenor Square news conference, the writers at the newspaper made the two-man impromptu fighter sweep seem as though thousands of aircraft had more or less destroyed all enemy transportation on the Continent. (Although Goodson was of the opinion that the exaggerated story had been concocted by "the newly arrived public relations corps" that was "hungry for news" about the first US fighter mission over France and Belgium.)

Goodson remembers the account beginning something like this: "At dawn today, fighter planes of the US Eighth Army Air Force carried out daring low-level attacks on rail, road, and water transport in northern France and Belgium, leaving behind them a trail of destruction. . . ."

When Squadron Leader Don Blakeslee, who did not take part in the Morlaix operation, saw the *Stars and Stripes* story, he was not amused. He came looking for the two pilots and found Goodson in the officers' mess. "All right," he demanded. "Where's the other half of the Eighth Air Force?" Goodson replied that Alexander was "taking a pee."

Both pilots managed to persuade Blakeslee that they had nothing to do with what appeared in *Stars and Stripes*. "All I claimed was one bicycle damaged," Goodson said. "I blew the guy off on the way out"—which was the truth. They had flown so low that Goodson actually had to pull up to avoid hitting a man on a bicycle. As it was, the Spitfire's prop wash blew the bike over, sending the man sprawling.

What bothered Blakeslee was not that the story of the fighter sweep had been exaggerated. He was upset by the thought that Goodson and Alexander might have done the exaggerating themselves, which would have made them guilty of the heinous offence of "shooting a line."

In the RAF, pilots were taught that embellishing a story was a crime only slightly less dastardly than murder. "We had been steeped in the RAF tradition that any exaggeration, or line-shooting, was intolerable," said James Goodson, "and, worse still, was 'bad form.'"

This was certainly a dramatic change in thinking and attitude from the early days of the first Eagle Squadron. In late 1940 and early 1941, the members of 71 Squadron seemed to go out of their way to act "American"—shouting and carrying on like refugees from a traveling Wild West show. They enjoyed their reputation as a bunch of crazy bloody Yanks—shooting up their barracks with a machine gun or, like Mike Kolendorski, breaking formation whenever the spirit moved them.

Even after their transfer to the US forces, the Eagles tried to retain as much of their "Englishness"—or at least what they perceived as Englishness—as possible. One of the most noticeable things they retained, something that made them unique from other US squadrons, was their usage of RAF slang and terminology.

The 4th Fighter Group did not fly airplanes like other American units; instead, they flew "kites." An accident, or a crash, was a "prang." A medal was a "gong." Cockpit canopies were "hoods." Missions or sorties were "shows." And, in RAF style, the "th" was dropped from the squadron's designation—instead of saying "the three hundred thirty-fifth squadron" it was "three-three-five squadron." "Three-three-five squadron went on a show."

"The 4th FG was still very much the 'Eagle Squadrons' in spite of American uniforms and the star insignia on their aircraft," wrote the Eighth Air Force's British biographer.[6]

Another holdover from the RAF would be the group's commanding officer. Wing Commander Miles Duke-Woolley would retain command of the 4th Fighter Group during its first two months of existence.

Duke-Woolley was familiar with American units, having flown with 71 Squadron in the Dieppe operation, and had more combat experience than any American lieutenant colonel in England (lieutenant colonel being the equivalent of wing commander).

Colonel Don Blakeslee briefing some extremely intense members of the US 4th Fighter Group, including James Goodson (with mustache, sitting in front row). The 4th FG was the top-scoring American unit in the European Theatre of Operations, with more than one thousand German aircraft destroyed. (Courtesy of the National Museum of the United States Air Force®.)

After a period of adjustment, which included a painful stretch of on-the-job-training in the sky over Germany and enemy-occupied France, the Eighth Air Force evolved into "the Mighty Eighth." Its pilots and aircrews overcame their initial lacking of know-how and experience and carried out their campaign of daylight precision bombing with single-minded resolve— their British hosts probably called it "typical Yankee determination." From its rocky start in the summer of 1942, to its total domination of the Luftwaffe in the run-up to D-Day in 1944, to its imposing record of operations against enemy targets on the Continent, the Eighth's combat record made it "one of the most famous military organisations in history."[7]

Don Gentile and John Godfrey, after returning from an escort mission to Berlin. As members of the 336th Fighter Squadron—formerly 133 (Eagle) Squadron, RAF—they became known as the "Deadly Duo" and the "Terrible Twins." Reichsmarschall Hermann Göring, chief of the Luftwaffe, offered to give up two fighter squadrons in exchange for "the Italian Gentile and the Englishman Godfrey." (Courtesy of the National Museum of the United States Air Force®.)

Although the Eagle Squadrons turned out eight aces (William Dunn having been the first), the 4th Fighter Group would produce many. Jimmy Davies of Bernardsville, New Jersey was the first American ace of the war, but he never flew with the Eagle Squadrons. Among the group's best pilots were Don Gentile and John Godfrey.

Both Godfrey and Gentile had been turned down by the US Army Air Force—Gentile for being "unsuitable for pilot training;" Godfrey for not having a university degree. Gentile enlisted in the RAF in September 1940, made his way to England via Canada, and was assigned to 133 Squadron in June 1942. He took part in the Dieppe mission, Operation Jubilee, on August 19, and claimed two German aircraft. He just missed going on the disastrous Morlaix raid. As part of the 336th Fighter Squadron, Gentile would shoot down another nineteen German airplanes for a total of twenty-one.

John Godfrey never flew with the Eagle Squadrons. After having been turned down by the USAAF, he went to Canada and became a pilot in the RCAF. He transferred to the US forces in April 1943 and was also assigned to the 336th Fighter Squadron. Godfrey's total number of enemy aircraft destroyed was eighteen at war's end.

Godfrey and Gentile became wingmen. As members of the 336th, the two of them accounted for thirty-seven German aircraft shot down. They were known in the newspapers as the "Deadly Duo" and the "Terrible Twins," along with other colorful nicknames.[8] They also acquired a reputation with the Luftwaffe. Reichsmarschall Hermann Göring offered to give up two fighter squadrons in exchange for "the Italian Gentile and the Englishman Godfrey."

★ ★ ★

For six months, the 4th Fighter Group was the only US fighter unit in England—the 31st FG left the British Isles for North Africa in the autumn of 1942. The 4th retained their Spitfires until the early part of 1943, when they were reequipped with Republic P-47 Thunderbolts.

This change did not make the former Eagles happy, to put it mildly. They did not like the idea of parting with their beloved Spitfires. As far as they were concerned, no American-built fighter could hope to compete with the Spit. Or, for that matter, with the Messerschmitt or Focke-Wulf, either.

"To the pilots," wrote the 4th FG's historian, "the Spit was a sure-footed, graceful little filly; the P-47 a bull-necked, unwieldy stallion."[9] Besides the differences in size and weight—the P-47 weighed twice as much as the Spitfire—there were also other disparities to contend with. For instance, the propeller on the P-47 turned in the opposite direction; the difference in torque would take some getting used to.

During the early part of 1943, the 4th Fighter Group was equipped with the Republic P-47 Thunderbolt, which replaced the Spitfire. The former Eagles did not like the idea of parting with their beloved Spitfires and were not happy with the change. (Courtesy of the National Museum of the United States Air Force®.)

The Spitfire had 20 mm cannon; the P-47 had eight .50 caliber machine guns. The ex-Eagles preferred the cannon's exploding shells. The P-47's cockpit and rearview mirror were also not very well liked—pilots complained that both made spotting enemy fighters much more difficult. In fact, some replaced the P-47's mirror with a Spitfire mirror.

With time, the pilots would come to value the P-47's strong points: its weight gave it the ability to dive away from any opponent, and its size allowed it to take a lot more punishment than the Spitfire. And the firepower from its eight .50 caliber machine guns was devastating: even a short burst would knock pieces from an enemy airplane.

The loud objections against the Thunderbolt—"it can dive, but it sure as hell can't climb" was the usual criticism—were taken as another example of the 4th FG's knack for complaining about everything and anything. Now, on top of everything else, the glamour boys were even finding fault with their own fighters.

Beginning in February 1944, the 4th Fighter Group would be reequipped again, this time with the P-51 Mustang, which is generally regarded as one of the outstanding fighters of the war. Even the former Eagles did not have very many complaints against the Mustang. The 4th was the first to convert to this fighter, which would not only outperform the P-47 Thunderbolt but also had a longer range. The Mustang could escort the Flying Fortresses all the way to Germany and back.

With the P-51 Mustang, the 4th FG's total of enemy planes destroyed increased dramatically. During March and April of 1944, the group, commanded by Colonel Don Blakeslee, destroyed 189 German aircraft in the air and another 134 by ground strafing.[10] This outstanding number earned the 4th Fighter Group a Presidential Unit Citation, the highest award that any unit could receive.

This performance also earned them the nickname "the Debden Gangsters" from Dr. Goebbels's Propaganda Ministry. (Hollywood gangster films had made their way to Germany, as well, and created their own impression of what American life must be like.) The Luftwaffe was also well informed about the 4th FG, with their red-nosed fighters—the Germans both respected and feared them. The Debden group enjoyed the same reputation among the Luftwaffe's pilots as the yellow-nosed Abbeville Boys had with British and American flyers.

By the end of the war, the 4th Fighter Group had become the top-scoring American unit in the European Theatre of Operations. Their final score was 583 ½ enemy aircraft destroyed in the air and another 469 destroyed on the ground, for a total of 1,052 ½. Hubert Zemke's 56th Fighter Group destroyed fewer enemy planes total—985—but its members are quick to point out that the 56th destroyed more planes in the air (674 ½), in actual combat, than the 4th.

The bitter rivalry among the three Eagle Squadrons, which had caused both British and American officers so much anxiety, had been eliminated by two events—one was deliberate, and the second was an accident that turned out to have produced at least one fortunate result.

The deliberate move was the integration of the three Eagle Squadrons. All three of the former RAF squadrons were mixed up together within the three newly formed US squadrons—not one of the original units was left intact. Each individual squadron of the new 4th Fighter Group incorporated members of all three former RAF units. And the sympathy offered 133 Squadron after the disastrous Morlaix raid probably helped unite the three units more effectively than any program that the Eighth Air Force could have ordered.

★　★　★

The pilots of the new 4th Fighter Group felt foreign and out of place in the US forces. It would take a while to get used to American ranks and to saying *lieu*tenant instead of *left*enant (as the British pronounced it). They also needed to figure out if an officer wearing a gold bar outranked somebody wearing two silver bars (he didn't), Or if a gold leaf was worth more than a silver one (it wasn't). It was all very perplexing, but the

American rates of pay they would now be earning made all the inconveniences worth overcoming.

It was probably no consolation at all to the former Eagles, but newly arrived American officers from the States were having their own problems with adjusting—everything was foreign to them, as well. Sometimes these men had to learn everything from the ground up, and they had to learn quickly. And frequently, in matters such as protocol, they had to find things out the hard way.

Among the six original US Army Air Force officers in England was Beirne Lay Jr., who later coauthored *Twelve O'Clock High*, a novel about the early days of the Eighth Air Force in England. Major Lay described himself as a kind of jack-of-all-trades for General Ira Eaker. General Eaker was the commander of VIII Bomber Command and held extra duties in public relations.

Major Lay was stationed in London during his first few weeks in the United Kingdom. Like most Americans, he was sobered by the bomb ruins he saw—completely burnt-out buildings and free-standing walls all over the city. Also, like most Americans, he was amazed to find everything still functioning, albeit on a reduced scale, including black-market restaurants.

One of his first public relations assignments involved a visit by King George VI to an American bomber base. Lay was given the job of seeing to security details, which had to be arranged through the king's secretary. Among the many items to be ironed out was the timing for the fighter cover to protect the king's train going to and coming from the air base.

All the arrangements were made, and the king arrived at the base as planned. Once he was on the base, all went according to schedule until lunch. Because of a few last-minute details, Lay was a minute late arriving at the mess hall. When he reached the mess, he found the king seated at a select table, surrounded by the group's commanding officer and other senior officers.

Lay's chair was directly opposite the guest of honor. Before sitting down, he waited to be introduced. Protocol dictated that no one address the king first; American officers had been briefed not to say a word until spoken to by His Majesty. But nobody made a move to introduce the major. The king expectantly stared at Lay. Lay, in turn, stared at the group commander, waiting for him to say something. It was an impasse. It was also becoming acutely embarrassing.

Finally, not knowing what else to do, Lay decided to break the silence. It was nothing dramatic; he simply introduced himself as Major Lay. The king smiled, extended his hand, and proceeded to introduce *himself* – as George Sixth. With that minor obstacle out of the way, conversation once again resumed.[11]

Brigadier General Frank O'Driscoll Hunter, commanding general of Eighth Air Force Fighter Command, and Sir Sholto Douglas, the head of RAF Fighter Command, take part in the ceremony transferring the three Eagle Squadrons from the RAF to the US Army Air Force on September 29, 1942. Although Douglas wished the departing Eagles a fond farewell, he had often thought of the Americans as a wild bunch of prima donnas when they had been part of his command. (Courtesy of the National Museum of the United States Air Force®.)

This was not the first time that protocol went wrong between the British and the Americans—and it certainly would not be the last. In late September, a ceremony was held at Debden to send the Eagle Squadrons from the Royal Air Force over to the US forces. Luckily, there were no gaffes during the event. Actually, everything went absolutely right, from first to last. Despite the all-American fighter units having had their fair share of conflicts with the RAF hierarchy during the previous two years, their transfer out of the RAF was letter-perfect, a proper model of decorum.

The three Eagle Squadrons officially left the RAF on September 29—two years to the day after S/L Walter Churchill arrived at Church Fenton to take command of the brand new 71 Squadron, which consisted of three Yanks: Red Tobin, Shorty Keough, and Andy Mamedoff. All three Americans had been killed during their service with the Eagle Squadrons, and Walter Churchill was killed in Sicily on a fighter sweep on August 27, 1942, just one month before 71 Squadron became the 334th Fighter Squadron.

Number 71 Squadron had begun its career in a haphazard way—with only three pilots, no commanding officer, and one airplane, which would not fly. As if to compensate for so much informality, the three Eagle squadrons passed out of existence in a formal ceremony that was filled with speeches and fanfare.

Among the officers present were Major General Carl Spaatz, commander of the Eighth Air Force, and Sir Sholto Douglas, chief of RAF Fighter Command. Both Spaatz and Douglas made speeches, and also inspected the pilots of the three squadrons. Other officers spoke a few words, as well. None of the former Eagles seemed terribly impressed. Generals were always making speeches, especially when reporters and photographers were around.

Douglas's address received the most attention in the press. Besides being the most widely quoted, it was also the most frequently misquoted speech—various newspapers and magazines gave several different versions. But every variation agrees that the Air Chief Marshal wished the departing Eagles a fond farewell and that he expressed regret that they were leaving the RAF—polite words that he could now afford. Since 1941, Douglas had frequently been furious with the Eagles and their conduct. On any number of occasions, he had devoutly wished that he had never heard of the Eagle Squadrons. Now, he was officially seeing them out of his command.

The 4th Fighter Group was the first unit to receive the North American P-51 Mustang, one of the outstanding fighters of the Second World War. Pictured are Mustangs of the 334th Fighter Squadron, formerly 71 (Eagle) Squadron, RAF. The Mustang could out-perform the P-47 Thunderbolt and also had a longer range. (Courtesy of the National Museum of the United States Air Force®.)

Besides making the usual gracious remarks, the sort that are always made on such occasions—"The United States Army Air Force's gain is very much the Royal Air Force's loss"[12]—Douglas also gave a brief history of the Eagle Squadrons, including the total number of enemy aircraft destroyed: "Eagle pilots have destroyed some seventy-three enemy aircraft, the equivalent of about six squadrons of the Luftwaffe." A moment later, he amended the score to 73 ½—the half being a Dornier shared with a British squadron, which was "a symbol of Anglo-American co-operation."

Douglas also mentioned "those of your number who are not here today"—nearly one-third of the pilots who flew with the Eagle Squadrons had either been killed or taken prisoner. Nothing was said about the Americans who had joined the RAF as "Canadians." Jimmy Davies, the first American ace of the war, as well as the first American to win the Distinguished Flying Cross, was also omitted from Douglas's address. So were the many known Americans in other RAF units, since they had never belonged to the Eagle Squadrons.

All three squadrons severely downplayed their formal transfer to the US forces. It seemed that they were deliberately going out of their way to be as casual as possible concerning the event. The logbook of 121 Squadron, which was now the 335th Fighter Squadron, treated the event as a routine matter. "The 'handing over' ceremony of the 'Eagle' Squadron pilots to the US Army Air Corps took place during the morning," it reported and went on to give a few details of the ceremony.[13] By the way the incident was recorded, anyone might assume that such an event took place every day.

But at least 121 Squadron said *something* about the transfer. In 71 Squadron's logbook, no mention was made at all. Not a word. The senior Eagles were apparently trying to out-British the British in stiff-upper-lipped nonchalance.

When the transfer ceremony finally ended, the pilots were dismissed. The last entry in 121 (Eagle) Squadron's logbook reads: "The Squadron then marched from the parade ground as No. 335 (USA) Squadron, under the command of Major W. J. Daley, DFC. (formerly Flight Lieutenant Daley)."[14] The other two squadrons marched off the field along with Major Daley and his pilots. Number 133 Squadron was now the US 336th Squadron, commanded by Major Carroll McColpin; 71 Squadron was now the US 334th Squadron, led by Major Gus Daymond.

The Eagle Squadron memorial in London's Grosvenor Square, just across from the US embassy. It was unveiled in 1986 and commemorates the more than two hundred Americans who flew with the three Eagle Squadrons. In the early part of 1941, many senior RAF officers thought that the pilots of 71 Squadron were too undisciplined to help the war effort and that the squadron should be disbanded and the pilots sent back to the United States. (Photo by the author.)

There were some who felt that a monument more permanent than just words should be dedicated to the three Eagle Squadrons. In 1986, forty-four years after the Eagle Squadrons' last sortie, a stone memorial was dedicated to those who flew with the all-American squadrons—a granite obelisk, inscribed with the names of the pilots of 71, 121, and 133 Squadrons, and topped by an American eagle.

Appropriately, the memorial was installed in the heart of London's West End, which Americans had come to know very well during the war. The exact location is Grosvenor Square, London's most American place, which has been the site of the US embassy ever since the thirteen original colonies won their independence from Great Britain. Directly across the square is the famous statue of America's wartime president, Franklin D. Roosevelt.

☆ ☆ ☆

Another 71 Squadron eventually would be formed, although not until after the war ended. It existed for seven years in the 1950s. From October 1950 until October 1953, the re-formed 71 Squadron flew Vampire fighter-bombers from bases in Germany. In 1953, the Vampires were replaced by F-100 Super Sabre jet fighters, which, in turn, were replaced by Hunters in 1956. The squadron retained its old "Eagle Squadron" badge, complete with bald eagle, even though it had no American members and had no connection with the all-American unit that had flown Spitfires and Hurricanes. This jet-fighter unit was disbanded in 1957.

☆ ☆ ☆

Within a year and a half after the Eagles became the 4th Fighter Group, nearly two million Americans would be in Britain, mostly in southern England. They would be there as part of the buildup for the invasion of the enemy-occupied Continent on D-Day, in June 1944.

For better or worse, the "GI invasion" of Britain would forever alter the relationship between the two peoples. There would hardly be a village in England that would not get to know the nasal twang of an American accent. As one British writer put it, "it was clear that the American invasion rated second only to the bombs as the outstanding feature of wartime life."[15]

Another British author said that the American presence was one of the great social experiments of the war, since it introduced the American way of life to the British. Following the war, the American influence on British life would become even stronger and more pervasive. The Grand Alliance, as Winston Churchill called the relationship between the United States and Great Britain (with the Soviet Union as the third member of the alliance), would develop into the celebrated Special Relationship after the war.

Unknown numbers of Americans would remain in the British armed services; each would have his own private reason for not wanting to join his fellow countrymen in the US forces. But, after September 29, 1942, the Eagle Squadrons no longer existed. In summary: thus ended the "riotous, semi-independent career" of the American Eagle Squadrons.[16]

★★★ CHAPTER THIRTEEN ★★★

YOU'RE AN AMERICAN, I BELIEVE

Hundreds of Americans joined the Royal Air Force between 1939 and 1942. Most were forced to remain anonymous because of the Neutrality Acts. But facts concerning the lives of some of the volunteers, and what made them decide to leave their own country and go to war, did come to light once they were safely in England.

One of the most famous Yanks in the RAF was Pilot Officer John G. Magee Jr.[1] The reason Magee is well known is not because of anything he did as a pilot, however; it is because of a single poem he wrote while in the RAF. The poem, "High Flight," has been included in many anthologies, as well as in school texts. Probably because of his poetic inclinations, Magee's career in the RAF has been the subject of romantic myth, hazy legend, and general inaccuracy.

John Gillespie Magee, Jr. was born in Shanghai in 1922. His mother was English; his father was an Episcopalian minister from Pittsburgh,

Pennsylvania. John was an American citizen, but he lived in China until he was nine years old, when his mother took him to England. He attended Rugby, the famous boys' boarding school, where he discovered the romantic poetry of Rupert Brooke, fell in love, and began to write poetry of his own—not necessarily in that order.

In 1939, when war was clearly imminent, young John was determined to be a pacifist—"That's what Jesus would have wanted," he wrote to his mother. But his father wrote to him from China and told him about the Japanese brutalities against Chinese civilians. His father's letters convinced John that pacifism was not practical in the war that was soon to come.

Shortly after the war broke out, John visited Pittsburgh; it was only the second time he had ever been to the United States. He had planned to spend the summer with his father's family and then return to Rugby for his final year, but when Britain and France went to war against Germany in September, the State Department determined that John would not leave the country—the neutral United States did not want any of its citizens traveling to a country at war. Unable to get back to England, he was enrolled in the Avon School, near Hartford, Connecticut. John was not happy at Avon, and he was also not at all happy with America's almost militant neutrality. He wanted to return to England, but was prevented by the US authorities.

Before he left England, John had seen the Errol Flynn film *The Dawn Patrol*, about the Royal Flying Corps during the First World War, and "subconsciously determined to be an airman." On his eighteenth birthday, June 9, 1940, he announced that he had decided to join the RAF.

It took four months, but he did manage to get to Canada and join the RCAF. Eight months later, he received his pilot's wings. During the late summer of 1941, he was posted to an operational Spitfire unit, 412 (Canadian) Squadron. Still, Pilot Officer Magee did not see his first Spitfire until he reached England. While he was completing his training in Spitfires, he wrote the poem "High Flight." "It started at 30,000 feet and was finished soon after I landed," he said in a letter.

Magee's first combat took place on November 10, 1941. It was a rough initiation—his squadron lost three pilots, including the commanding officer. Magee did get a "squirt" at a Messerschmitt 109, but made no claim. Number 412 Squadron continued to take its losses; "We have had three squadron leaders in the last month," Magee wrote.

During a practice flight on December 11, Magee's Spitfire collided with another fighter. Both machines crashed, and both pilots were killed. John Magee was buried in Scopwick Cemetery, near Digby Aerodrome, which is close to the city of Lincoln.

Since his death, a number of legends have emerged concerning John Magee. Many believe that he was a fighter ace—he was not; he is credited with no enemy aircraft destroyed. Some believe that he took part in the Battle of Britain, though he did not see combat until more than a year after the battle had ended. Still others think that he was killed in combat—he was killed in a flying accident.

This is John Gillespie Magee's celebrated and much quoted poem, "High Flight":

Oh! I have slipped the surly bonds of Earth
And danced the skies on laughter-silvered wings;
Sunward I've climbed, and joined the tumbling mirth
Of sun-split clouds, — and done a hundred things
You have not dreamed of — wheeled and soared and swung
High in the sunlit silence. Hov'ring there,
I've chased the shouting wind along, and flung
My eager craft through footless halls of air. . . .

Up, up the long, delirious burning blue
I've topped the wind-swept heights with easy grace
Where never lark, or ever eagle flew —
And, while with silent, lifting mind I've trod
The high untrespassed sanctity of space,
Put out my hand, and touched the face of God.

★ ★ ★

While John Magee was trying to get to Canada, the United States was still intent upon remaining neutral and staying out of the war. There is no record of anyone ever having been arrested for trying to get into the RAF by way of Canada, but several young men were turned back at the border. The FBI kept a close watch on any Americans crossing the Canadian border, especially young fellows in their twenties.

A couple of Americans who were on their way to the war via Montreal were interrogated when their train was stopped at the frontier.[2] The officials who boarded the train were full of questions, but the flyers had the right answers.

"Where are you two fellows going, and why?" the federal agents demanded.

The two fellows decided that, under the circumstances, their best defense was to play dumb. "Who, us? We're just going to Montreal to visit a relative who owns a fish hatchery."

"Are either of you two guys pilots?"

They never heard of anything so idiotic in their entire lives. "Pilots? You must be nuts! Do we look like pilots?"

The FBI men ignored the question, but they did decide to inspect the baggage of the two travelers. Luckily for the would-be fighter pilots, it was only a cursory inspection—only the top layer of clothing in each suitcase was examined. If the agents had bothered to search underneath, they would have found the evidence they were looking for: flying helmets, goggles, and logbooks.

Satisfied with their luggage and their answers, the two federal agents passed the two Americans and wished them good luck.

The two visitors to Canada would need all the luck they could get in the coming months—they were Red Tobin and Andy Mamedoff. They met Shorty Keough in Montreal. The three of them arrived in France in June 1940 and eventually became the first three members of the new Eagle Squadron.

The border between the United States and Canada is very long, and the FBI could not be everywhere at once. Many, many more Americans slipped past federal agents than were apprehended. Not everyone who made it into the RAF wound up in the cockpit of a Spitfire or a Hurricane, however. The glamour boys of Fighter Command got most of the publicity, but others served with distinction in other commands.

John H. Stickell, from a small town in western Illinois, is one such pilot.[3] Stickell flew with RAF Bomber Command and was awarded the Distinguished Flying Cross. He became interested in flying when he was a teenager, but his parents would not let him take flying lessons, even though a flying school had just opened in Peoria. He was too young, they told him, and flying was too dangerous.

Stickell did not do anything about becoming a flyer until August 1940. Then, when he was twenty-six years old, he decided to join the Army Air Corps. He passed the medical examination, but was told that he needed at least two years of university education to become a pilot. The Air Corps also gave him a mental exam in November—they told him that he flunked.

It was too late for him to go to school, he explained, so he went to Windsor, Canada, and joined the Canadian Air Force instead. He started his training course in the early part of 1941.

By October 1941, Stickell had been commissioned as a pilot officer in the RCAF and received his wings. Shortly afterwards, he sailed to England and began training in twin-engine Wellington bombers.

For the next phase of his training he was scheduled to begin instruction on four-engine bombers. But on May 30, 1942, Stickell and his crew were ordered to do an operational sortie—they were going to bomb Cologne. Bomber Command were sending over one thousand aircraft to Cologne that night and wanted every airplane that could fly to participate. Stickell flew the same Wellington he had flown during his final training.

Pilot Officer Stickell returned from Cologne with only eight gallons of gasoline left in his Wellington's tanks—enough for only two minutes' flying. A bursting antiaircraft shell had torn open one of the bomber's fuel tanks. Luckily, the plane did not catch fire.

24480 A.C

A gathering of Eagles. Former Eagle Squadron pilots pose for the photographer after returning to England following a brief visit to the United States. All of the pilots wear miniatures of their RAF wings on the right side of their uniform, opposite their silver USAAF wings. Pictured here, left to right, are Major Carroll W. McColpin, Lt. John I. Brown, Capt. Reade Tilley, Maj. William J. Daley, Capt. John J. McClosey, Lt. Dale Taylor, Lt. A. L. Haynes, Capt. Harold Strickland, Lt. Bradford, Capt. Sam A. Mauriello , Lt. George L. Strauss, and Lt. Fred Cullen Smith. (Courtesy of the National Museum of the United States Air Force®.)

Two nights later, Stickell took his Wellington to Essen. This time, the bomber nearly became a victim of a German night fighter—bullets from the fighter shattered the Wellington's instrument panel, and one of the bullets grazed Stickell's sleeve.

Stickell eventually completed his four-engine training, as originally planned, and was assigned to 214 Squadron as pilot of a Short Stirling bomber, *B-Beer*.

His first trip over Germany at the controls of *B-Beer* came on July 3, 1942, his twenty-eighth birthday. His last operational sortie was in October of the same year. In between, he had gone on twenty-seven bombing missions: Nuremberg, Bremen Frankfurt, Düsseldorf, and Kassel, among other places. His Stirling was damaged by antiaircraft fire on several occasions. Over Coblenz, his rear-turret gunner was nearly killed by a bursting antiaircraft shell.

By this time, American bomber units were arriving in the British Isles in a fairly steady stream. The Flying Fortress crews were making their presence known on the ground in Britain as much as they were in the sky over Germany. Resentment was beginning to build against the Americans: the cause was mostly money. The Americans were paid several times more than their British counterparts and did not mind showing off their wealth by buying whiskey, cigars, and fancy presents for their British girl-friends—gifts that the British could not afford. This high spending led to bitterness on the part of the British pilots and aircrews. They did not see why the bloody Yanks in the US forces should get so much more money than they were getting paid.

Stickell was annoyed by all the complaining about money and how bloody the Yanks were for having so much of it. "For the first time, there was a note of ill-feeling between himself and the British air force boys." Stickell tried to convince the RAF that the Americans were not overpaid; he insisted that the RAF—including himself—were being grossly underpaid.

Nobody listened to him at first—it was easier, and more fun, for Britons to knock the Americans than to criticize their own country. But Stickell kept up his line of argument and eventually persuaded them that he was right. The Yanks should not be paid less; *they* should be paid *more*.

This was only a small diplomatic triumph in the stormy course of Anglo-American relations. But winning the argument did not get Stickell, or anybody else, an increase in pay. In October, Stickell and his crew were given custody of a new Stirling, *K-King*, and assigned to a Pathfinder unit. The Pathfinders went in to the target ahead of the main bomber force and lit up the area by dropping flares and firebombs.

Life as a Pathfinder was not any easier than it had been with 214 Squadron. *K-King* always managed to get back to base, but Stickell saw other Stirlings limp back to the field all shot up, with dead and wounded aboard. It did not take long for him to come to the conclusion that there was absolutely no future in being a Pathfinder pilot. Of the sixty men who completed their training with him, only three were still alive.

Future or not, Stickell flew eighteen trips as a Pathfinder, including two to Berlin. This gave him a total of forty-eight operational missions, which was three more than the Air Ministry allowed. The absolute maximum was forty-five—thirty as an operational pilot and fifteen additional as a Pathfinder.

The RAF planned to ground Stickell and assign him to a training command. Stickell wanted to keep flying operations, but the RAF flatly refused. Stickell decided to transfer to the US forces.

The US Army Air Force offered him a commission as a major and his own Flying Fortress squadron, as soon as one became available. Now that Stickell had the Distinguished Flying Cross and forty-eight combat sorties to his credit, the American authorities were willing to overlook the fact that he did not have a university background. But Stickell had the feeling that the air force planned to keep him on the ground. The US Navy, on the other hand, promised that he could continue flying. So Stickell joined the Navy.

The Navy gave Stickell exactly what he wanted—assignment to an operational bomber unit. After a visit to his home in Illinois, he was posted to an aircraft carrier in the southern Pacific.

On December 12, 1943, Lieutenant Stickell took part in a bombing raid against a Japanese installation in the Gilbert Islands. During the raid, his aircraft was hit by enemy antiaircraft fire. Stickell managed to bring his plane home in spite of being badly wounded. Six days later, he died from his injuries.

Not many people know about John Stickell, either in the United States or in Britain. He made no attempt to conceal his real nationality—when King George presented Stickell with the DFC, he mentioned that he knew Stickell was an American.

There are several reasons why Stickell remains obscure, while many others, with lesser war records, became widely known to the American public. For one thing, he was a bomber pilot. Bomber crews rarely received the publicity accorded fighter pilots—"knights of the air dueling the foe in single combat" makes for more exciting copy than a six-hour round-trip flight to Germany in a Stirling.

Also, Stickell did not begin flying operations until May 1942. By that time, the United States had become involved in the fighting and was mainly interested in hearing about "our boys" in the US forces.

Stickell's motives for joining the RAF were fairly straightforward—he wanted to fly, and the USAAF would not take him. John Magee's reasons are a bit hazier—he felt compelled to defend the land of his heart (as he probably would have put it) and had recently seen Errol Flynn and David Niven battle the beastly Hun in *The Dawn Patrol*. Magee's reasons are a vague mix of duty and romanticism. The vast majority of the Americans who volunteered for the RAF did not really know why they did it, or at least have not put their motives into words.

Frank A. Roper, who joined the RCAF in November 1940, was one such volunteer. As a pilot officer and a flying officer, Roper completed thirty bombing missions between October 1941 and July 1942, flying four-engine Manchester and Lancaster bombers, and was awarded the Distinguished Flying Cross.

Roper was either the first, or one of the first, Yanks to complete a tour of bomber operations with the RAF.[4] But Roper gave no indication of why he decided to go to Canada in the autumn of 1940 when it would have been much easier to stay at home and wait for what the fates, and his local draft board, had in store for him.

Even over a half-century later, the inarticulate boys having turned into old men, the reasons were still difficult to put into words.[5] One former Hurricane and Spitfire pilot, who lived in semi-retirement in New Jersey for many years, was embarrassed when he was asked his motives. He did not know why and said that it all had happened fifty years before anyway— he supposed that he was just too young and stupid to know any better.

Another volunteer probably came closer to reflecting the motives of his fellow volunteers with his reply. He said that he did not really know why any of them went. Part of it was for romantic reasons—going off to the wars and joining a foreign air force. There were mercenary reasons, as well—he had always paid for flying lessons, and now someone was going to pay *him* to fly.

The old former pilot explained, very quietly, that he was very young at the time and not very bright, and he might have joined the British air force for any number of reasons. But whatever his reasons, he was glad that he went. By the time he left the RAF in 1943, he hoped that he had made a difference.

ACKNOWLEDGMENTS

"**W**hy did you join the RAF?" This question was put to many ex-"Yank in the RAF" types countless times. It is a straightforward question, but I never once received a straightforward answer.

I would like to thank all the former pilots who put up with me and my persistent questions, including all the people who insisted upon remaining anonymous. (I never realized that fighter pilots were such a bashful lot.)

Most of the document research was done in the relative peace and serenity of the Imperial War Museum's reading room. The Museum staff was, once again, extremely patient with me as I rummaged through just about every book, periodical, and document I could find concerning the RAF between 1939 and 1942.

Mr. Terry Charmin was especially patient. He looked up several bits of information that I was not able to find myself and made a number of helpful suggestions concerning books and documents. His help is much appreciated.

George Clout, down in sunny Worthing, gave me several excellent ideas, which were incorporated into this book, and pointed me in the right direction concerning any number of reference sources. George talked, and I listened. His time and interest are also appreciated, and his knowledge of the RAF during the time in question proved invaluable.

Peter and Carolyn Hammond of Chiswick, London, also bore a hand with my research. They collected a good deal of information that was written during the fiftieth anniversary of the Battle of Britain, while many RAF veterans were still living. Most of this was useful as reference material. They also checked a few facts, read some of the chapters, and offered some very useful suggestions.

In the US, the staff at Maxwell Air Force Base, Alabama, were also extremely courteous and helpful. They supplied many declassified documents relevant to my subject.

In the area of photos and photo research, I would like to express my gratitude to the staff at the Smithsonian Institution's National Air and Space Museum for their indispensable help. They found all the photos that I asked for and managed to find a few things that I had never seen. They also produced a stack of newspaper and magazine cuttings related to the Yanks in the RAF, which also proved highly useful.

My apologies to anyone whose name I left out of my notes to each chapter—it was an error of oversight. Also, the attached bibliography is less than complete; I am certain that I left out several items that ought to have been included. These oversights are solely the fault of the author, such as they are and such as he is.

The photos appear courtesy of the following institutions, with credits as indicated: United States National Archives; Smithsonian National Air and Space Museum; Courtesy of the National Museum of the United States Air Force; and the *Bernardsville News*, Bernardsville, NJ.

I would like to offer a special "thank you" to Brett Stolle of the National Museum of the United States Air Force. The images of the Eagle Squadrons and the US 4th Fighter Group provided proved to be invaluable.

The ladies of the Union, NJ Public Library—Susan, Laura, Kathleen, and all of their colleagues—also deserve a vote of thanks for their kind, and professional, assistance.

A special acknowledgement goes out to my agent, Alison Picard. Without Alison's effort, this book never would have seen the light of day.

And last, but certainly not least, I would like to offer a very special and affectionate "thank you" to Laura Libby. Thank you, Laura, for putting up with me and for all your help and understanding.

D. A. Johnson

★★★ APPENDIX A ★★★

EQUIVALENT RANKS

Royal Air Force	U.S. Army Air Force
Air Chief Marshal	General
Air Marshal	Lieutenant General
Air Vice-Marshal	Major General
Air Commodore	Brigadier General
Group Captain	Colonel
Wing Commander	Lieutenant Colonel
Squadron Leader	Major
Flight Lieutenant	Captain
Flying Officer	First Lieutenant
Pilot Officer	Second Lieutenant

★★★ APPENDIX B ★★★

PILOTS WHO SERVED WITH THE THREE EAGLE SQUADRONS

KIA: Killed in Action

KOAS: Killed on Active Service

71 Squadron

James K. Alexander	
Charles F. Ambrose	
Luke E. Allen	
Newton Anderson	
Paul R. Anderson	KOAS, London, Mar. 8, 1941
Stanley M. Anderson	
Thomas J. Andrews	
Rodger H. Atkinson	KOAS, North Weald, Oct. 15, 1941
John Butler Ayer	KIA, English Channel, April 17, 1942
Charles E. Bateman	
Wayne A. Becker	
Duane W. Beeson	
Ernest R. Bitmead	

Vernon A. Boehle	
Victor R. Bono	
Robert A. Boock	
William O. Brite	
Raymond C. Care	
Lawrence A. Chatterton	KOAS, North Weald, Oct. 22, 1941
Walter M. Churchill	
James A. Clark	
Oscar H. Coen	
Gilmore C. Daniel	POW (escort), Bethune, Oct. 13, 1941
Gregory A. Daymond	
Arthur G. Donahue	KIA, English Channel, Sept. 11, 1942
Forrest P. Dowling	
William R. Driver	KOAS, North Weald, Aug. 5, 1941
John DuFour	
William R. Dunn	
Jack E. Evans	KIA (circus), St. Omer, Aug. 27, 1942
Hillard S. Fenlaw	KIA (sweep), Boulogne, Sept. 7, 1941
Morris W. Fessler	POW (rhubarb), Boulogne, Oct. 28, 1941
John F. Flynn	KIA (bomber escort), St. Omer, Apr. 27, 1942
Victor J. France	
C. O. Galbraith	
Don Geffene	
William D. Geiger	POW, Sept. 17, 1941
Humphrey T. Gilbert	KOAS, England, May 1, 1942
James A. Gray	
William I. Hall	POW, July 2, 1941
James C. Harrington	
Joseph F. Helgason	KOAS, Debden, Aug. 6, 1942
Howard D. Hively	
Walter J. Hollander	
Alfred H. Hopson	

William T. Humphrey	
William B. Inabinet	KOAS, Martlesham Heath, Jan. 9, 1942
Joseph M. Kelly	
Byron F. Kennerly	
Vernon C. Keough	KOAS, Kirton-in-Lindsey (North Sea), Feb. 15, 1941
Stanley M. Kolendorski	KIA (sweep), Holland, May 17, 1941
Phillip H. Leckrone	KOAS, Kirton-in-Lindsey, Jan. 5, 1941
John F. Lutz	
John J. Lynch	
Nat Maranz	POW, June 1941 (not in E.S. at the time)
Robert L. Mannix	
Harold F. Marting	
Sam Mauriello	
George S. Maxwell	
Ben F. Mays	KIA (circus), Hazebrouck, Apr. 12, 1942
Carroll W. McColpin	
Thomas P. McGerty	KIA (bomber escort), North Sea, Sept. 17, 1941
James L. McGinnis	KOAS, Martlesham Heath, Apr. 26, 1941
Richard D. McMinn	
Michael G. McPharlin	
Stanley T. Meares	KOAS, North Weald, Nov. 15, 1941
Henry L. Mills	
Edward T. Miluck	
Richard A. Moore	POW
W. Brewster Morgan	
William H. Nichols	POW, Boulogne, Sept. 7, 1941
Leo S. Nomis	
Virgil W. Olson	KIA (bomber escort), North Sea, Aug. 19, 1941
Edwin E. Orbison	KOAS, Kirton-in-Lindsey, Feb. 9, 1941
William T. O'Regen	
Wendell Pendleton	
Chesley G. Peterson	

Steve N. Pisanos	
Eugene M. Potter	
Robert L. Prizer	
Peter Provenzano	
Arthur F. Roscoe	
Gilert C. Ross	
Dean H. Satterlee	
Ross O. Scarborough	KOAS, North Weald, Nov. 15, 1941
Anthony J. Seaman	
Robert S. Sprague	
Hubert L. Stewart	
Harold H. Strickland	
R. H. Tann	
Kenneth S. Taylor	KOAS, North Weald, Aug. 9, 1941
William D. Taylor	KIA (rhubarb), Flushing, Aug. 31, 1942
William E. G. Taylor	
George Teicheira	KIA (circus), Bruges, Belgium, June 1, 1942
Eugene Q. Tobin	KIA (sweep), Boulogne, Sept. 7, 1941
Reginald Tongue	
Charles W. Tribken	
Murray S. Vosburg	
Thomas C. Wallace	
Rufus C. Ward	
Jack W. Weir	KOAS, North Weald, Aug. 28, 1941
Gordon H. Whitlow	
Henry Woodhouse	
Frank G. Zavakos	

121 Squadron

Thomas W. Allen	KIA (sweep), North Sea, May 31, 1942
Fred E. Almos	
Frederick C. Austin	KIA (sweep), Boulogne, Apr. 17, 1942
Ernest D. Beatie	
Leon M. Blanding	
Carl O. Bodding	KIA (sweep), Dunkirk, Apr. 28, 1942
Douglas E. Booth	
Frank R. Boyles	
Robert V. Brossmer	KIA (sweep), English Channel, May 4, 1942
John I. Brown	
John A. Campbell	
George C. Carpenter	
Norman R. Chap	
Howard M. Coffin	
Forrest M. Cox	
William J. Daley	
Bruce C. Downs	
Joseph E. Durham	
Selden R. Edner	
Paul M. Ellington	
Roy M. Evans	
Gene B. Fetrow	
Frank M. Fink	
Phillip J. Fox	
Ralph W. Freiberg	KIA (sweep), English Channel, May 4, 1942
Frederick A. Gamble	KOAS, North Weald, May 3, 1942
Jack D. Gilliland	KOAS, Ipswich, Jan. 8, 1942

James E. Griffin	
Chester P. Grimm	
Gilbert O. Halsey	
James R. Happel	
Charles A. Hardin	
Kenneth R. Holder	KIA (patrol), English Channel, Dec. 12, 1941
William L. Jones	
Jack L. Kearney	
William P. Kelly	
Hugh C. Kennard	
Loran L. Laughlin	KIA, Kirton-in-Lindsey, Jun 21, 1941
Jackson B. Mahon	POW, Dieppe, Aug. 19, 1942
Clifford H. Marcus	
Clarence L. Martin	
Earl W. Mason	KOAS, Kirton-in Lindsey, Sep 15, 1941
Joseph G. Matthews	
Richard E. McHan	
Donald W. McLeod	
Collier C. Mize	
John. J. Mooney	KIA (rhubarb), Ostend, June 16, 1942
Herbert T. Nash	
Lyman D. O'Brien	
Julian M. Osborne	
Cadman V. Padgett	
Vernon A. Parker	
Richard F. Patterson	KIA (rhubarb), Belgium, Dec. 7, 1941
James E. Peck	
Peter R. Powell	
Lawson F. Reed	

Donald H. Ross	
James M. Sanders	
Warren V. Shenk	
Nicholas D. Sinetos	
Leroy A. Skinner	POW, Apr. 28, 1942
John T. Slater	KIA (recon), North Sea, Sep 21, 1942
Bradley Smith	
Fred C. Smith	
Fonzo D. Smith	
Kenneth G. Smith	
Frank J. Smolinsky	
Aubrey C. Stanhope	
Malta L. Stepp	
Benjamin A. Taylor	
James L. Taylor	KIA, Dieppe, Aug. 19, 1942
Clifford R. Thorpe	
Reade F. Tilley	
Thaddeus H. Tucker	
Fred R. Vance	
Vivian E. Watkins	
Royce C. Wilkinson	
W. Dudley Williams	
Donald K. Willis	
Donald A. Young	
Norman D. Young	KIA (circus), Berck-sur-Mer, Jul 31, 1942

133 Squadron

Richard L. Alexander	
William A. Arends	KIA (sweep), St. Omer, June 20, 1942
Henry J. Ayres	
William H. Baker	KIA (escort B-17s), Morlaix, Sept. 26, 1942
Charles S. Barrell	KOAS, Duxford, Sept. 27, 1941
Richard N. Beaty	
Joe L. Bennent	
Edwin H. Bicksler	
Donald J. Blakeslee	
Richard G. Braley	
Edward G. Brittell	POW (escort B-17s), Morlaix, Sept. 26, 1942
Hugh C. Brown	KIA (weather test), North Sea, March 16, 1942
George R. Bruce	KOAS, Eglinton, Oct. 27, 1941
Charles A. Cook	POW (escort B-17s), Morlaix, Sept. 26, 1942
James G. Coxetter	KOAS, Eglinton, Oct. 27, 1941
Stephen H. Crowe	
Ben P. DeHaven	
Eric Doorly	
Wilson V. Edwards	
Grant E. Eichar	
David R. Florance	KIA (sweep), Fécamp, May 19, 1942
William K. Ford	KIA (sweep), Fécamp, May 31, 1942
Tony A. Gallo	
Donald S. Gentile	
James A. Goodson	
Leroy Gover	
Dick D. Gudmundsen	KIA (escort B-17s), Rouen, Sept. 6, 1942

Harry C. Hain	
Fletcher Hancock	KIA (sweep), Abbeville, June 5, 1942
Carter W. Harp	
Robert D. Hobert	
Marian E. Jackson	POW (escort B-17s), Morlaix, Sept. 26, 1942
H. A. Johnston	
Karl K. Kimbro	
Coburn C. King	KIA (escort Bostons), Abbeville, Jul 31, 1942
Donald E. Lambert	
Lyman S. Loomis	
Andrew Mamedoff	KOAS, Isle of Man, Oct. 8, 1941
Joseph G. Matthews	
Hugh H. McCall	KOAS, Isle of Man, Oct. 8, 1941
Carrol W. McColpin	
Cecil E. Meierhoff	
George H. Middleton	POW (escort B-17s), Morlaix, Sept. 26, 1942
Carl H. Miley	
Ervin L. Miller	
Denver E. Miner	
George E. Mirsch	
John Mitchellweis	
Moran S. Morris	KIA (sweep), Fécamp, May 31, 1942
Robert S. Mueller	
Don D. Nee	
James C. Nelson	
Gene P. Neville	KIA (escort B-17s), Morlaix, Sept. 26, 1942
Gilbert I. Omens	KOAS, Biggin Hill, Jul 26, 1942
Kenneth D. Peterson	
Robert L. Pewitt	KIA (sweep), Fécamp, May 19, 1942

Hiram A. Putnam	
Chesley H. Robertson	
Leonard T. Ryerson	KIA (escort B-17s), Morlaix, Sept. 26, 1942
Seymour M. Schatzberg	KOAS, Biggin Hill, July 19, 1942
Fred R. Scudday	
William C. Slade	
Glen J. Smart	
Dennis D. Smith	KIA (escort B-17s), Morlaix, Sept. 26, 1942
Robert E. Smith	
Walter G. Soares	KOAS, Duxford, Sept. 27, 1941
George B. Sperry	POW (escort B-17s), Morlaix, Sept. 26, 1942
Andrew J. Stephenson	
Roy N. Stout	KOA, Isle of Man, Oct. 8, 1941
Edwin D. Taylor	
Eric H. Thomas	
William R. Wallace	
John W. Warner	
Vivian E. Watkins	KIA, Holland, Apr. 24, 1942
Samuel F. Whedon	KOAS, Kirton-in-Lindsey, Apr. 3, 1942
William J. White	KOA, Isle of Man, Oct. 8, 1941
Walter C. Wicker	KIA (sweep), Ostend, Apr. 27, 1942
Roland L. Wolfe	
Gilbert G. Wright	POW (escort B-17s), Morlaix, Sept. 26, 1942

NOTES

ORB: Operations Record Books. Squadron log books are located in the Public Record Office/National Archives (UK), Kew, Richmond, Surrey.

CHAPTER ONE: NONE OF AMERICA'S BUSINESS

1. *Time*, June 24, 1940.

2. James Goodson, *Tumult in the Clouds* (New York: St. Martin's, 1983), p. 29.

3. *Herald Tribune* article and Oath of Allegiance from *Flight* magazine, October 1940.

4. One of the six travelers to Canada was Chesley Peterson, who will be mentioned later.

5. There were actually three Neutrality Acts that were passed by Congress between 1935 and 1937. Among other things, they banned the export of weapons to any belligerent nation and the use of any American vessels to trans-

port them, made it illegal for US citizens to travel on ships of any belligerent nation, and prohibited any loans or any form of credit to any belligerent nation. The United States was determined to stay out of any and all foreign wars. The act that banned the export of weapons and the use of American vessels to transport them was repealed in 1939.

6. James A. Goodson thought that some Americans who joined the RAF early in the war did lose their citizenship temporarily but soon had it restored for practical reasons. When the US entered the war, the Army Air Force desperately needed experienced pilots and air crews. American authorities did everything possible to expedite the transfer to the US forces of the pilots who had violated the Neutrality Acts, including restoring US citizenship if it had been lost.

7. Norman Longmate, *The G.I.'s: The Americans in Britain, 1942–1945* (New York: Charles Scribner's Sons, 1975), p. 15.

8. The seven "official" Americans in RAF Fighter Command during the summer of 1940 were W. M. L. Fiske (609 Squadron, died August 17, 1940), Arthur Donahue (64 Squadron), J. K. Haviland (151 Squadron), Phil Leckrone (616 Squadron), and Andrew Mamedoff, Vernon Keough, and Eugene Tobin (609 Squadron).

9. Norman Gelb, *Scramble!* (Orlando, FL: Harcourt Brace Jovanovich, 1985), p. 98.

10. Biographical information regarding Jimmy Davies is from his article in *Air Log*, June 1940.

11. John R. McCrary and David E. Scherman, *First of the Many: A Journal of Action with the Men of the Eighth Air Force* (New York: Simon & Schuster, 1944), p. 210.

12. Gelb, *Scramble!* p. 172.

13. Ibid.

14. *Times* (London), August 19, 1940. Note that this does not take into account Jimmy Davies of Bernardsville, New Jersey, who became the first American ace of the war. (F/Lt. Davies technically did not take part in the Battle of Britain. He was killed on June 25, 1940. The Air Ministry's "official" dates for the battle are July 10 to October 31, 1940, which means that Davies was shot down two weeks before the battle officially began.) No one can say for certain how many "Canadian" pilots who were killed in the battle were actually from the United States—I have tried to find out, but to no avail.

15. Arthur Donahue, *Tally Ho! Yankee in a Spitfire* (New York: Macmillan, 1941), p. 1.

16. Ibid., p. 57.

17. Information about Tobin, Mamedoff, and Keough is derived from many sources. The best is Eugene Tobin's article (with Robert Low), "Yankee Eagle over London," *Liberty*, March–April 1941.

18. David Crook, *Spitfire Pilot* (London: Greenhill Books, 1988), p. 129.

19. Ibid., p. 130.

20. Francis Mason, *Battle over Britain* (London: McWhirter Twins, 1969), p. 176.

21. Information on Tobin's combat experience was taken from multiple sources, the best being Tobin and Low, "Yankee Eagle over London."

22. Robert S. Raymond, *A Yank in Bomber Command* (Pacifica, CA: Pacifica Press, 1998), p. 8.

23. Damage to Andy Mamedoff's Spitfire as noted in 609 Squadron's ORB.

24. Red Tobin's story from Tobin and Low, "Yankee Eagle over London."

25. Crook, *Spitfire Pilot*, p. 130.

26. Longmate, *G.I.'s*, p. 13.

CHAPTER TWO: HISTORICAL PREJUDICES

1. Statistics on Fighter Command losses in Derek Wood and Derek Dempster, *The Narrow Margin* (London: Hutchinson, 1961), p. 261.

2. Opinion poll findings in William Manchester, *The Glory and the Dream* (Boston: Little, Brown, 1973), p. 276.

3. Vern Haugland, *The Eagle Squadrons* (New York: Ziff Davis, 1979), p. 33.

4. Norman Gelb, *Scramble!* (Orlando, FL: Harcourt Brace Jovanovich, 1985), p. 186.

5. Clive Barnes, editorial, *Evening Standard* (London), December 27, 1988.

6. Manchester, *Glory and the Dream*, p. 270.

7. Charles Sweeny, introduction to *The Eagles Roar!* by Byron Kennerly (New York: Harper & Brothers, 1942), p. viii.

8. Manchester, *Glory and the Dream*, p. 277.

9. The account of the early days of 71 (Eagle) Squadron was taken from many sources, especially 71 Squadron's ORB, but also including: Earl Boebert, "The Eagle Squadrons," *AAHS Journal* (Spring 1964); James Saxon Childers, *War Eagles* (New York: D. Appleton-Century, 1943); Haugland, *Eagle Squadrons*; Kennerly, *Eagles Roar!*; and many, many magazine articles from 1940 and 1941.

10. 71 Squadron's ORB.

11. Haugland, *Eagle Squadrons*, p. 120.

12. Clifton F. Berry, "Battle of Britain 1940," *Air Force Magazine*, September 1980.

13. Kennerly, *Eagles Roar!* p. 129.

14. *News Chronicle*, March 3, 1940.

CHAPTER THREE: A VERY ODD ASSORTMENT

1. Norman Longmate, *The G.I.'s: The Americans in Britain, 1942–1945* (New York: Charles Scribner's Sons, 1975), p. 91.

2. J. E. Johnson, *Wing Leader* (New York: Ballantine, 1957), p. 51.

3. James Saxon Childers, *War Eagles* (New York: D. Appleton-Century, 1943), p. 111.

4. Ibid., p. 329.

5. 71 Squadron's ORB.

6. Vern Haugland, *The Eagle Squadrons* (New York: Ziff Davis, 1979), p. 36.

7. Ibid.

8. Childers, *War Eagles*, p. 330.

9. Earl Boebert, "The Eagle Squadrons," *AAHS Journal* (Spring 1964).

10. Haugland, *Eagle Squadrons*, p. 39.

11. Leo Nomis, "Fighting under Three Flags," *Defence Update International*, nos. 47 and 48.

12. Haugland, *Eagle Squadrons*, p. 16.

13. William R. Dunn's experiences with joining the RAF, including his early days with 71 Squadron, from William Dunn, *Fighter Pilot* (Lexington: University Press of Kentucky, 1982), p. 43.

14. Ibid., p. 48.

15. Boebert, "Eagle Squadrons."

16. 71 Squadron's ORB.

17. The advice for fledgling fighter pilots is from "Tips from an Eagle Pilot," *Air Forces General Information Bulletin*, bulletin no. 8 (Washington, DC: Intelligence Service, US Army Air Force, January 1943).

18. Dunn, *Fighter Pilot*, p. 110.

19. 71 Squadron's ORB.

CHAPTER FOUR: FAILURES TO COMMUNICATE

1. Wallace Stegner, "Who Are the Westerners?" *American Heritage* (December 1987).

2. Earl Boebert, "The Eagle Squadrons," *AAHS Journal* (Spring 1964).

3. Ibid.

4. Ibid.

5. James Saxon Childers, *War Eagles* (New York: D. Appleton-Century, 1943), p. 30.

6. Boebert, "Eagle Squadrons."

7. *Flight*, August 15, 1941.

8. Childers, *War Eagles*, p. 114.

9. Peter Townsend, *Duel of Eagles* (New York: Pocket Books, 1972), p. 340.

10. Boebert, "Eagle Squadrons."

11. Norman W. Schur, *British Self-Taught: With Comments in American* (New York: Macmillan, 1973), p. xii.

12. *Herald Tribune* quote is from David Alan Johnson's "Divided by a Common Language," *Heritage*, December 1989.

13. Byron Kennerly, *The Eagles Roar!* (New York: Harper & Brothers, 1942), p. 44.

14. Robert S. Raymond, *A Yank in Bomber Command* (Pacifica, CA: Pacifica Press, 1998), p. 12.

15. Clifton F. Berry, "Battle of Britain 1940," *Air Force Magazine*, September 1980.

16. Norman Franks, *The Greatest Air Battle* (London: Grub Street, 1992), p. 140.

17. Berry, "Battle of Britain 1940."

18. Arthur Donahue, *Tally-Ho! Yankee in a Spitfire* (New York: Macmillan, 1941), p. 21.

19. William Manchester, *The Glory and the Dream* (Boston: Little Brown, 1973), p. 244.

20. Ibid., pp. 278–79.

21. Ibid., p. 246.

22. Sir Archibald Sinclair remarks from Assistant Chief of Air Staff, "Origins of the Eighth Air Force: Plans Organization, Doctrines," *US Air Force Historical Study No. 102* (October 1944).

23. Norman Longmate, *How We Lived Then* (London: Hutchinson, 1971), p. 485.

CHAPTER FIVE: CONFLICTS AND RIVALRIES

1. Information on 121 Squadron's early days, including personnel, was taken from 121 Squadron's ORB and from Vern Haugland, *The Eagle Squadrons* (New York: Ziff Davis, 1979), pp. 43–55.

2. Clayton Knight statistics from Earl Boebert, "The Eagle Squadrons," *AAHS Journal* (Spring 1964).

3. James Saxon Childers, *War Eagles* (New York: D. Appleton-Century, 1943), p. 238.

4. Ibid., p. 213.

5. Ibid., p. 238.

6. 121 Squadron's ORB.

7. *News Chronicle* (London), May 19, 1941.

8. 121 Squadron's ORB.

9. The St. Valentine's Day Massacre, as well as the doings of Al Capone and other gangsters of the 1920s, were reported in most London newspapers, including the *Times*. The British were (and are) more interested in American affairs than most Americans imagine.

10. George Orwell, "George Orwell's America," *American Heritage*, February–March 1984.

11. Information on Bill Dunn's August 27, 1941, combat experience from his autobiography, *Fighter Pilot* (Lexington: University Press of Kentucky, 1982), pp. 77–88.

12. Information on S/L Taylor, as well as biographical details of his successors, from Boebert, "Eagle Squadrons," and from Childers, *War Eagles*, pp. 59–67.

13. Details of 133 Squadron's early days from 133 Squadron's ORB, as well as from Boebert, "Eagle Squadrons," and Haugland, *Eagle Squadrons*, pp. 55–57.

14. Haugland, *Eagle Squadrons*, p. 56.

15. Details of the Spitfire Mark V from J. E. Johnson, *Wing Leader* (New York: Ballantine, 1957), pp. 75–76.

16. Duke-Wooley's account of a Spitfire pilot's discomfort from Norman Franks, *The Greatest Air Battle* (London: Grub Street, 1992), p. 140.

CHAPTER SIX: COLORFUL CHARACTERS AND "OLD SCHOOL TIE BOYS"

1. Biographical information on Leo Nomis from his own article, "Fighting under Three Flags," and from James Saxon Childers, *War Eagles* (New York: D. Appleton-Century, 1943), pp. 217–19. Biographical information on Sam Mauriello from Childers, *War Eagles*, pp. 149–50. Biographical information on Newton Anderson from Childers, *War Eagles*, pp. 212–14.

2. Information on the death of Red Tobin from 71 Squadron's ORB.

3. Richard Collier, *Eagle Day* (London: JM Dent, 1980), p. 145.

4. Information on the death of Andy Mamedoff from 133 Squadron's ORB.

5. David Crook's remarks regarding Keough, Mamedoff, and Tobin in Norman Gelb, *Scramble!* (Orlando, FL: Harcourt Brace Jovanovich, 1985), p. 187.

6. Earl Boebert, "The Eagle Squadrons," *AAHS Journal* (Spring 1964).

7. William Dunn, *Fighter Pilot* (Lexington: University Press of Kentucky, 1982), p. 65.

8. Boebert, "Eagle Squadrons."

9. Michael J. F. Bowyer, *Action Stations 1: Wartime Military Airfields of East Anglia 1939–1945* (Cambridge: PLS, 1979), p. 73.

10. 121 Squadron's ORB.

11. 71 Squadron's ORB.

12. Boebert, "Eagle Squadrons."

13. Childers, *War Eagles*, p. 15.

14. Leo Nomis's comments are from his article "Fighting under Three Flags."

15. Robert S. Raymond, *A Yank in Bomber Command* (Pacifica, CA: Pacifica Press, 1998), pp. 69–70.

16. George Orwell, "George Orwell's America," *American Heritage*, February–March 1984.

17. Raymond, *Yank in Bomber Command*, p. 198.

18. Norman Longmate, *The G.I.'s: The Americans in Britain, 1942–1945* (New York: Charles Scribner's Sons, 1975), p. 96.

19. Alistair Cooke, *Alistair Cooke's America* (New York: Alfred A. Knopf, 1977), p. 8.

20. Boebert, "Eagle Squadrons."

21. Childers, *War Eagles*, p. 238.

CHAPTER SEVEN: NO MORE BLOODY YANKS!

1. Vern Haugland, *The Eagle Squadrons* (New York: Ziff Davis, 1979), p. 87.

2. Comments on Chesley Peterson from Earl Boebert's article, "The Eagle Squadrons," *AAHS Journal* (Spring 1964).

3. James Saxon Childers, *War Eagles* (New York: D. Appleton-Century, 1943), p. 288.

4. 121 Squadron's ORB.

5. John R. McCrary and David E. Scherman, *The First of the Many* (New York: Simon & Schuster, 1944), p. 24.

6. Haugland, *Eagle Squadrons*, p. 108.

7. Editorial from *Times* (London), August 19, 1941.

8. Childers, *War Eagles*, pp. 239–40.

9. Norman Longmate, *The G.I.'s: The Americans in Britain, 1942–1945* (New York: Charles Scribner's Sons, 1975), p. 271.

10. Ibid., p. 258.

11. William Dunn, *Fighter Pilot* (Lexington: University Press of Kentucky, 1982), p. 63.

12. Information on the Eagles' losses from 121 and 133 Squadron's ORB.

CHAPTER EIGHT: BELLIGERENT ALLIES

1. Byron Kennerly, *The Eagles Roar!* (New York: Harper & Brothers, 1942), p. 35.

2. Information about the German propaganda scheme involving US POWs from declassified interviews with Eagle Squadron pilots, Public Records Office, Kew, Richmond, Surrey.

3. William Manchester, *The Glory and the Dream* (Boston: Little, Brown, 1973), p. 316.

4. Ibid., pp. 316–17.

5. Leo Nomis, "Fighting under Three Flags," *Defence Update International*, nos. 47 and 48.

6. Ibid.

7. Vern Haugland, *The Eagle Squadrons* (New York: Ziff Davis, 1979), p. 92.

8. Information about John Lynch's and Leo Nomis's attack on a Ju 88 from 71 Squadron's ORB.

9. Observations on the conduct of fighter pilots are from Earl Boebert, "The Eagle Squadrons," *AAHS Journal* (Spring 1964).

10. "Ten Commandments for Fighter Pilots" in William Dunn, *Fighter Pilot* (Lexington: University Press of Kentucky, 1982), p. 47.

11. Boebert, "Eagle Squadrons."

12. Norman Longmate, *The G.I.'s: The Americans in Britain, 1942–1945* (New York: Charles Scribner's Sons, 1975), pp. 86, 220.

13. Information regarding "Operation Thunderbolt," the Channel dash by three German warships, from 71 and 121 Squadron's ORB.

14. 133 Squadron's ORB.

15. Ibid.

16. Ibid.

17. 121 Squadron's ORB.

CHAPTER NINE: YANKEE DOODLE GOES TO TOWN

1. Information regarding P/O Mahon's combat from 121 Squadron's ORB.

2. Information regarding 71 Squadron's April 27 attack from 71 Squadron's ORB.

3. Len Deighton, *Fighter: The True Story of the Battle of Britain* (New York: Ballantine Books, 1977), p. 249.

4. Information about the promotion of "Weak Eyes Anderson" from 71 Squadron's ORB.

5. Graham Wallace, *RAF Biggin Hill* (London: Putnam, 1957), p. 251.

6. Quotes regarding early June 1942 fighter sweep in 71 Squadron's ORB.

7. Wallace, *RAF Biggin Hill*, p. 252.

8. Grover Hall, *1,000 Destroyed* (Fallbrook, CA: Aero Publishing, 1978), p. 75.

9. Information on the early days of the Eighth Air Force from Roger Freeman, *The Mighty Eighth* (Garden City, NY: Doubleday, 1970), pp. 1–15.

10. Wallace, *RAF Biggin Hill*, p. 257.

11. Assistant Chief of Air Staff, "Origins of the Eighth Air Force: Plans Organization, Doctrines," *US Air Force Historical Study No. 102* (October 1944).

12. Information on the first combat sorties of Eighth Air Force from Freeman, *Mighty Eighth*, pp. 6–8.

13. Robert S. Raymond, *A Yank in Bomber Command* (Pacifica, CA: Pacifica Press, 1998), p. 79.

14. 121 Squadron's ORB.

15. Freeman, *Mighty Eighth*, p. 12.

CHAPTER TEN: LIKE A GREAT SUSTAINED ROAR

1. Norman Franks, *The Greatest Air Battle* (London: Grub Street, 1992), p. 14.

2. Operational data—take-off time, time of arrival over Dieppe—from the ORBs of all three Eagle Squadrons.

3. Information about Strickland's encounter with the Focke-Wulfs from Brian James, "I Gather It Was You Who Shot Me Down," *Times Saturday Review*, July 14, 1990.

4. 121 Squadron's ORB.

5. Ibid.

6. 71 Squadron's ORB.

7. Franks, *Greatest Air Battle*, p. 172.

8. James Saxon Childers, *War Eagles* (New York: D. Appleton-Century, 1943), p. 162.

9. Information about Peterson's bail-out incident from Childers, *War Eagles*, pp. 176–77; Vern Haugland, *The Eagle Squadrons* (New York: Ziff Davis, 1979), p. 153; and Franks, *Greatest Air Battle*, p. 127. All three accounts are substantially the same.

10. Information about McPharlin's encounter with a Ju 88 from Childers, *War Eagles*, pp. 177–81; and Franks, *Greatest Air Battle*, pp. 128, 187.

11. 133 Squadron's ORB.

12. Franks, *Greatest Air Battle*, p. 170.

13. Ibid., p. 173.

14. German claims on August 19 from ibid., p. 236.

15. Eagle Squadron losses and official claims and 31st FG losses from ibid., pp. 239–45.

16. Ibid., p. 181.

17. Ibid., p. 182.

CHAPTER ELEVEN: A MOST DEMOCRATIC ARMY

1. Results of enemy action on August 27 and "Now No. 334. Sq. USAAF" in 71 Squadron's ORB.

2. Comments on Flying Fortress gunners are from a declassified interview with Carroll McColpin in 1942.

3. Graham Wallace, *RAF Biggin Hill* (London: Putnam, 1957), p. 254.

4. 133 Squadron's ORB.

5. Remarks on the rivalry between the three Eagle Squadrons are from Earl Boebert's article, "The Eagle Squadrons," *AAHS Journal* (Spring 1964).

6. Vern Haugland, *The Eagle Squadrons* (New York: Ziff Davis, 1979), p. 161.

7. James A. Goodson, *Tumult in the Clouds* (New York: St. Martin's Press, 1983), p. 66.

8. W. W. G. Duncan Smith, *Spitfire into Battle* (London: John Murray, 1981), p. 65.

9. Leo Nomis, "Fighting under Three Flags," *Defence Update International*, nos. 47 and 48.

10. Robert Raymond's impressions of his first days in the US forces are from his memoirs, *A Yank in Bomber Command* (Pacifica, CA: Pacifica Press, 1998), pp. 209–13.

11. Bill Dunn's remarks on his transfer from the RAF to the US Army Air Force are from his memoirs, *Fighter Pilot* (Lexington: University Press of Kentucky, 1982), pp. 111–12.

12. Information on J. K. Haviland from "J. Kenneth Haviland Is Alive and Well . . . ," *Air Force Magazine*, December 1980. Several books and periodicals mention Lance C. Wade, John J. Lynch, James H. Little, and David C. Fairbanks, including Raymond Tolliver and Trevor Constable's *Fighter Aces of the USA* and E. C. Baker's *Fighter Aces of the RAF*. Information on Alger Jenkins of Montclair, New Jersey, and Alan Reed, who graduated from Princeton University in 1940, is from the author's interview with the late Jack Areson of Montclair, New Jersey, also a graduate of Princeton.

CHAPTER TWELVE: MORE ENGLISH THAN THE ENGLISH

1. D. A. Young's encounter with the Ju 88 in 121 Squadron's ORB.

2. Most details of the Morlaix raid are from 133 Squadron's ORB. Infor-

mation about the raid itself, as well as the impact on 133 Squadron, also provided in Earl Boebert, "The Eagle Squadrons," *AAHS Journal* (Spring 1964), and Vern Haugland, *The Eagle Squadrons* (New York: Ziff Davis, 1979).

3. Don Gentile's account of the Morlaix raid is from James A. Goodson, *Tumult in the Clouds* (New York: St. Martin's, 1983), p. 61.

4. Account of the Peterson press conference is in Grover C. Hall, *1,000 Destroyed* (Fallbrook, CA: Aero Publishing, 1978), pp. 49–50.

5. Details of Goodson's and Alexander's fighter sweep from James Goodson, *Tumult in the Clouds* (New York: St. Martin's, 1983), pp. 67–68.

6. Roger Freeman, *The Mighty Eighth* (Garden City, NY: Doubleday, 1970), p. 40.

7. Ibid., p. 236.

8. "Terrible Twins," *RAF Flying Review*, August 1958.

9. Hall, *1,000 Destroyed*, p. 24.

10. The 4th FG's total for March–April 1944 and final total from Freeman, *Mighty Eighth*, pp. 230–31.

11. Bierne Lay Jr., letter to the author.

12. Sholto Douglas's speech was found in several newspapers and magazines. Here, the quotes are from the *Times* (London), September 30, 1942.

13. 121 Squadron's ORB.

14. Ibid.

15. Norman Longmate, *The G.I.'s: The Americans in Britain, 1942–1945* (New York: Charles Scribner's Sons, 1975), p. xiii.

16. Ibid., p. 14.

CHAPTER THIRTEEN: YOU'RE AN AMERICAN, I BELIEVE

1. Biographical information on John G. Magee Jr. from Hermann Hagedorn, *Sunward I've Climbed* (New York: Macmillan, 1942), and from Dr. A. H. Lankester, "A Tribute to John Magee, the Pilot Poet," *This England* (Winter 1982). Text of "High Flight" also from Hagedorn, *Sunward I've Climbed*.

2. The account of the two Americans and their crossing into Canada from Red Tobin, "Yankee Eagle over London," *Liberty*, March–April 1941.

3. John H. Stickell biographical information supplied by Marvin S. Bloomer of Maquon, Illinois.

4. Frank A. Roper, interview with the author.

5. Information from anonymous RAF volunteers via correspondence with the author.

SELECT BIBLIOGRAPHY

"America's Spitfires." *Air Enthusiast*. August–November 1981.

Anonymous. *A Short History of No. 151 Squadron*. St. Andrews, Scotland, 1954.

Ashworth, Chris. *Action Stations 5: Military Airfields of the South-West*. Cambridge, UK: PLS, 1982.

————. *Action Stations 9: Military Airfields of the Central South and South East*. Cambridge, UK: PLS, 1985.

Athin, Ronald. *Dieppe 1942*. London: Macmillan, 1942.

Baker, E. C. *Fighter Aces of the RAF, 1939–1945*. London: William Kimber, 1962.

Bekker, Cajus. *The Luftwaffe War Diaries*. New York: Doubleday, 1968.

Berry, F. Clifton, Jr. "Battle of Britain 1940." *Air Force Magazine*. September 1980.

Billingham, Mrs. Anthony. *America's First Two Years*. London: John Murray, 1942.

Boebert, Earl. "The Eagle Squadrons." *AAHS Journal*. Spring 1964.

Bowyer, Michael J. F. *Action Stations 1: Wartime Military Airfields of East Anglia 1939–1945*. Cambridge, UK: PLS, 1979.

————. *Action Stations 6: Military Airfields of the Cotswolds and the Central Midlands*. Cambridge, UK: PLS, 1983.

Braybrooke, Keith. *Wingspan (RAF Debden)*. Saffron Walden, Essex: WH Hunt & Son, 1956.

Brogan, D. W. *The American Character*. New York: Alfred A. Knopf, 1944.

Calder, Angus. *The People's War*. London: Hutchinson, 1972.

Chennault, Claire Lee. *Way of a Fighter*. New York: Putnam, 1949.

Cherry, Alex. *Yankee RN*. London: Jarrolds, 1951.

Childers, James Saxon. *War Eagles*. New York: D. Appleton-Century, 1943.

Collier, Basil. *The Defence of the United Kingdom*. London: HMSO, 1957.

Collier, Richard. *Eagle Day*. London: J. M. Dent, 1980.

———. *1941*. London: Hamish Hamilton, 1981.

Cooke, Alistair. *Alistair Cooke's America*. New York: Alfred A. Knopf, 1977.

Crook, David. *Spitfire Pilot*. London: Greenhill Books, 1988.

Davies, Jimmy. "The Story of an American Fighter Pilot in the R.A.F." *Air Log*. June 1940.

Davis, Burke. *War Bird*. Chapel Hill: University of North Carolina Press, 1987.

Deighton, Len. *The Battle of Britain*. London: Jonathan Cape, 1980.

———. *Fighter*. London: Jonathan Cape, 1977.

Donahue, Arthur. *Tally Ho! Yankee in a Spitfire*. New York: Macmillan, 1941.

Douglas, Sholto. *Years of Command*. London: Collins, 1966.

Dunn, William. *Fighter Pilot*. Lexington: University of Kentucky Press, 1982.

"Eagles Switch to US Army." *Life*. November 2, 1942.

"The Famous Fourth." *Air Britain Digest*. November 1952.

Franks, Norman. *The Greatest Air Battle*. London: William Kimber, 1979.

Freeman, Roger. *The Mighty Eighth*. New York: Doubleday, 1970.

———. *The Mighty Eighth War Diaries*. London: Jane's, 1981.

Fry, Gary, and Jeffrey Ethell. *Escort to Berlin*. New York: Arco, 1980.

Galland, Adolf. *The First and the Last*. London: Eyre Methuen, 1955.

Gallico, Paul. *The Hurricane Story*. New York: Doubleday, 1960.

Gelb, Norman. *Scramble!* Orlando, FL: Harcourt Brace Jovanovich, 1985.

Goodson, James A. *Tumult in the Clouds*. New York: St. Martin's, 1983.

Hagedorn, Hermann. *Sunward I've Climbed*. New York: Macmillan, 1942.

Hall, Grover C. *1,000 Destroyed*. Fallbrook, CA: Aero, 1978.

Halpenny, Bruce. *Action Stations 8: Military Airfields of Greater London*. Cambridge, UK: PLS, 1982.

————. *Action Stations 2: Military Airfields of Lincolnshire and the East Midlands*. Cambridge, UK: PLS, 1982.

————. *Action Stations 4: Military Airfields of Yorkshire*. Cambridge, UK: PLS, 1982.

Haugland, Vern. *The Eagle Squadrons*. New York: Ziff Davis, 1979.

Hough, Richard, and Denis Richards. *The Battle of Britain*. London: Hodder & Stoughton, 1989.

"J. Kenneth Haviland Is Alive and Well . . ." *Air Force Magazine*. December 1980.

Jablonski, Edward. *Airwar*. Garden City, NY: Doubleday, 1979.

James, Brian. "I Gather It Was You Who Shot Me Down." *Times Saturday Review*. July 14, 1990.

Johnson, David. *The London Blitz*. New York: Scarborough House, 1990.

Johnson, David Alan. *The Battle of Britain*. Conshohocken, PA: Combined Books, 1998.

————. "Divided by a Common Language." *Heritage*. December 1989.

Johnson, J. E. *Wing Leader*. New York: Ballantine, 1957.

Kennerly, Byron. *The Eagles Roar!* New York: Harper & Brothers, 1942.

Lankester, A. H. "A Tribute to John Magee, the Pilot Poet." *This England*. Winter 1982.

Lee, Raymond E. *The London Observer*. London: Hutchinson, 1972.

Longmate, Norman. *How We Lived Then*. London: Hutchinson, 1971.

————. *The G.I.'s: The Americans in Britain, 1942–1945*. New York: Charles Scribner's Sons, 1975.

Maguire, Eric. *Dieppe: August 19*. London: Cape, 1963.

Manchester, William. *The Glory and the Dream*. Boston: Little Brown, 1973.

Mason, Francis. *Battle over Britain*. London: McWhirter Twins, 1969.

McCrary, John R., and David E. Scherman. *The First of the Many*. New York: Simon & Schuster, 1944.

Mencken, H. L. *The American Scene*. New York: Alfred A. Knopf, 1965.

————. *The American Language*. New York: Alfred A. Knopf, 1937.

Miller, Alice Duer. *The White Cliffs*. New York: Coward-McCann, 1940.

Moulton, Tom. *The Flying Sword*. London: Macdonald, 1964.

Nomis, Leo. "Fighting under Three Flags." *Defence Update International*, nos. 47, 48.

"No. 601 (County of London) Squadron." *Air Reserve Gazette*, no. 9 (1947).

Orwell, George. *The English People*. London: Collins, 1947.

—————. "George Orwell's America." *American Heritage*. February–March 1984.

Panter-Downes, Mollie. *London War Notes*. London: Longmans, 1972.

Parrish, Thomas, ed. *The Encyclopedia of World War Two*. London: Secker & Warburg, 1978.

Ramsey, Winston G. *The Battle of Britain Then and Now*. London: Battle of Britain Prints, 1980.

Rawlings, John. *Fighter Squadrons of the RAF*. London: Macdonald and Jane's, 1969.

Raymond, Robert S. *A Yank in Bomber Command*. Pacifica, CA: Pacifica Press, 1998.

"Return of the Eagles." *Air Clues*. November 1976.

"Return of the Eagles." *RAF News*. September 11, 1976.

Schur, Norman. *British Self-Taught: With Comments in American*. New York: Macmillan, 1973.

Settle, Mary Lee. *All the Brave Promises*. New York: Delacorte, 1966.

Sims, Edward. *American Aces of World War Two*. London: Macdonald, 1958.

"605 Squadron." *Air Reserve Gazette*. January 1949.

"605 Squadron." *Wing*, victory edition. 1946.

Smith, David J. *Action Stations 7: Military Airfields of Scotland, the North-East and Northern Ireland*. Cambridge, UK: PLS, 1981.

—————. *Action Stations 3: Military Airfields of Wales and the North West*. Cambridge, UK: PLS, 1981.

Smith, W. W. G. Duncan. *Spitfire into Battle*. London: John Murray, 1981.

Springs, Elliot White. *War Birds*. London: Temple Press Books, 1966.

Stegner, Wallace. "Who Are the Westerners?" *American Heritage*. December 1987.

"Terrible Twins." *RAF Flying Review*. August 1958.

"Tips from an Eagle Pilot." USAAF. Pamphlet. No author. No date.

Tobin, Eugene, and Robert Low. "Yankee Eagle over London." *Liberty*. March–April 1941.

Toland, John. *The Flying Tigers*. New York: Random House, 1963.

Tolliver, Raymond, and Hans Schraft. *The Interrogator*. Fallbrook, CA: Aero, 1979.

Tolliver, Raymond, and Trevor Constable. *Fighter Aces of the USA*. Fallbrook, CA: Aero, 1979.

Townsend, Peter. *Duel of Eagles*. New York: Pocket Books, 1972.

"US Eagle Feature Section." *UK Eagle*. July 22, 1960.

"US Eagle Squadrons." *Air Pictorial*. September 1979.

Wallace, Graham. *RAF Biggin Hill*. London: Putnam, 1957.

Wehlen, Russell. *The Flying Tigers*. London: Macdonald, 1943.

Willis, John. *Churchill's Few*. London: Michael Joseph, 1985.

Wood, Derek, and Derek Dempster. *The Narrow Margin*. London: Hutchinson, 1961.

"The Yanks of the Eagle Squadron." *Airman*. October 1965.

Ziegler, Frank H. *Under the White Rose*. London: Macdonald, 1971.

UNPUBLISHED SOURCES

Air Forces General Information Bulletin, January 1943.

Assistant Chief of Air Staff. "Origins of the Eighth Air Force: Plans Organization, Doctrines." *US Air Force Historical Study No. 102*. October 1944.

Constance Miles, war journal.

Declassified documents, dated between August 1942 and August 1943, from the Air Ministry in London.

Declassified documents from the US Army Air Force, concerning the transfer of US nationals from the RAF to the USAAF.

Declassified interviews with Eagle Squadron pilots.

Mass Observation Archive: Eighteen opinion poll reports on various subjects, ranging from attitudes toward other nationalities to war jokes, between December 1940 and February 1942.

Operations Record Books (logbooks) for 71 Squadron, 121 Squadron, 133 Squadron, 601 Squadron, 609 Squadron, and several other RAF fighter squadrons. Public Record Office/National Archives (UK), Kew, Richmond, Surrey.

Robert S. Raymond, war diary and letters.

Someone Else's War (television script). Courtesy Television South.

USAAF. *History of the 336th Fighter Squadron, 4th Fighter Group*.

INDEX